MASKED MEDIA
WHAT IT MEANS TO BE HUMAN IN THE AGE OF ARTIFICIAL CREATIVE INTELLIGENCE

Gary Hall

The **MEDIA : ART : WRITE : NOW** series mobilises the medium of writing as a mode of critical enquiry and aesthetic expression. Its books capture the most original developments in technology-based arts and other forms of creative media: AI and computational arts, gaming, digital and post-digital productions, soft and wet media, interactive and participative arts, open platforms, photography, photomedia and, last but not least, amateur media practice. They convey the urgency of the project via their style, length and mode of engagement. In both length and tone, they sit somewhere between an extended essay and a monograph.

Series Editor: Joanna Zylinska

MASKED MEDIA
WHAT IT MEANS TO BE HUMAN IN THE AGE OF ARTIFICIAL CREATIVE INTELLIGENCE

Gary Hall

( )
OPEN HUMANITIES PRESS

London 2025

First edition published by Open Humanities Press 2025
Copyright © 2025 Gary Hall

Freely available at:
http://openhumanitiespress.org/books/titles/masked-media/

This is an open access book, licensed under the Collective Conditions for Re-Use (CC4r). You are invited to copy, distribute, and transform the materials published under these conditions, which means to take the implications of (re-)use into account. Read more about the license at constantvzw.org/wefts/cc4r.en.html

Cover Art, figures, and other media included with this book may be under different copyright restrictions.

Print ISBN 978-1-78542-144-0
PDF ISBN 978-1-78542-145-7

OPEN HUMANITIES PRESS

Open Humanities Press is an international, scholar-led open access publishing collective whose mission is to make works of contemporary critical thought freely available worldwide.
More at http://openhumanitiespress.org/

Contents

Acknowledgments	9
Preamble – *Masked Me*dia: On Becoming Inhuman	11
Preface – Phoney Me: Doing Radical Research Radically	20
1. I:M:MATERIAL: Books Do Furnish a Way of Life	37
2. Talking About Infrastructure … The Library Has Left the Building	59
3. The Dark Side of 'The Dark Side of the Digital Humanities': The Afterlife of New Materialism	77
4. Liberalism Must Be Defeated	101
5. The Obsolescence of Bourgeois Theory in the Anthropocene	131
6. Missing Communities – Situating Situatedness	147
7. Some Day We Will All Think Like This: Experiments in Radical Open Access Publishing – An Incomplete Directory	192
8. Misunderstanding Media: The Epistemological Politics of Scaling Small	212
9. The Commons as Coming Together of Those with Nothing in Common: or, How to Redesign a City	237
10. Post Office	263
Author's bio	279
Notes	281
Works Cited	321

A thinker erects an immense building, a system, a system which embraces the whole of existence and world-history etc. – and if we contemplate his personal life, we discover to our astonishment this terrible and ludicrous fact, that he himself personally does not live in this immense high-vaulted palace, but in a barn alongside of it, or in a dog kennel, or at the most in the porter's lodge. If one were to take the liberty of calling his attention to this by a single word, he would be offended. For he has no fear of being under a delusion, if only he can get the system completed ... by means of the delusion.

– *Søren Kierkegaard/Anti-Climacus*

This is the case for most novels: you have to read seven hundred pages to get the handful of insights that were the reason the book was written, and the apparatus of the novel is there as a huge, elaborate, overbuilt stage set.

– *David Shields*

I really don't have anything more to say about ChatGPT, Galactica or whatever else they decide to put out next. ... We need to spend our time slowly working on the technological future we think should exist, and we can't do that if our time and imagination is hijacked by OpenAI, the longtermists or whoever else.

– *Timnit Gebru*

Acknowledgments

Various parts of *Masked Media* are derived from material that previously appeared in, among other places, *Aesthetics of the Commons, Journal of Electronic Publishing, Media Theory, Networking Knowledge, New Formations, The Piracy Years* and *Radical Philosophy.*

Preamble

Masked Media: On Becoming Inhuman

Everybody says, I am such and such, I am so-and-so, except for me, who would prefer not to be who I am.
– *Silvina Ocampo*

Can we unlearn the liberal individual … in a similar way that we endeavour to unlearn patriarchy, racism and heterosexism?
– *Arturo Escobar*

Masked Media is not a human-authored work in any simple sense. It has been generated by a heterogenous assemblage of humans and nonhumans. As such, even though this book appears under the proper name 'Gary Hall', it is not the intellectual property of a single human individual. *Masked Media* is published under a Collective Conditions for Re-Use licence (CC4r) to reflect this fact, despite CC4r being on its own account perhaps too provisional to be considered an actual licence (Constant 2023). But then a work authored significantly by nonhumans is not eligible for copyright protection in most legal systems anyway.

Attention is drawn to another aspect of *Masked Media* as a human-nonhuman-creation through the use of numerous quotations and endnotes to situate the book in a bibliodiverse mesh of thinkers, works and media technologies. It's a mesh that extends from material published by professional entities (Cambridge University Press, *Nature*, *PLoS Medicine*) in authoritative formats such as books and journal articles, through that made available more informally using emails, blogs, wikis, social media and video-sharing platforms (Twitter, YouTube), to experiments with collaborative writing tools (Cryptpad, PubPub) and beyond. Both established knowledge and knowledges that are considered strange, weird, monstrous even, especially when measured against the dominant criteria of the Euro-Western university, are part of this bibliodiversity.

Several issues arise from the fact *Masked Media* is explicitly not the work of a single human author. They concern otherwise taken-for-granted ideas of collaboration, cooperation and collectivity; the authorial, liberal-individual, human 'I'; the 'work'; the original or master theory; and what might be called 'the real me'.

On Collaboration, Cooperation and Collectivity

When the term 'collaboration' is used in this book – rather than 'cooperation' or 'collective' – it is done so deliberately. In cooperation the project is something you (and possibly others) *help someone with*; it is what *they* are working on, and what *they* are ultimately responsible for and will own as their property. In collaboration, however, the project is something *you work on with others* and that *you are all responsible for* and will own as your *shared* property. Meanwhile, a collective, to borrow the words of two of my collaborators, the artists Andy Hewitt and Mel Jordan, is 'typically described as aiming to share political and social power, by flattening the decision-making process [still further] towards establishing a more egalitarian community' or organisation (Hewitt and Jordan 2020: 64, 80). Yet as Hewitt and Jordan acknowledge, 'being collective is not a formal process but rather a conceptual value' (80).

Some of the research projects featured in this book are better understood as collaborations, to the extent my relation (that of Gary Hall/'Gary Hall') to those others who participate in them is more informal and flexible than it might be in an explicitly declared and conceptualised *collective*. As will become clear, however, collaboration is not necessarily associated here with preserving hierarchies or the separate identities of those involved, with a collective by contrast producing a 'transcendent subjectivity' in which the 'collective becomes a subject in its own right' (Hewitt and Jordan 2020, 68; quoting Beech 2006, 32). When it comes to the degree to which they challenge individual authorship and leadership, and deny social relationality, collaboration and collectivity are less discreet and dichotomous than that and more part of the same continuum. For these reasons, the definition of collaboration provided by the writer and filmmaker Florian Schneider is of particular interest: 'While cooperation happens between identifiable individuals within and between organizations, collaboration expresses a differential relationship that is composed by heterogeneous parts which are defined as singularities: out of the ordinary, in a way that produces a kind of discontinuity and marks a point of unpredictability' (2006). This is why I often refer to my *collaborators* in this book, even regarding those with whom I am working *collectively*.

On the Authorial First-Person 'I'

When using the 'I' pronoun in *Masked Media*, I'm not referring to 'myself' in any straightforward or naïve sense – as if, when all is said and done, I am still operating according to the cult of personality and its model of the controlling human author as romantic or modernist genius. Yet neither have I endeavoured to de-individualise the biographical subject by writing collectively in the most readily recognised sense of the term.[1] If late capitalism has led us to act as hyper-competitive *microentrepreneurs* of our own selves (Hall 2016b), it has also embraced our working together toward social goals.² Consequently, there is nothing inherently politically progressive about collaboration, cooperation and collectivity. The theory-performances in *Masked Media* – even those that are apparently authored individually – should be understood as emerging from ongoing nondualist ontological relations with a multiplicity of institutions and communities. To build, for what is merely the first time of many, on the work of digital media artist and theorist Mark Amerika – from whom I've appropriated the term 'theory-performance' (Amerika 2018, 36-37) – they can best be thought of as stimulating the development of *novel forms of togetherness that comprise neither simply singularities nor pluralities*. The singular and plural are co-emergent.

Neither an authorial identity that functions in terms of the liberal human 'I' nor 'we', neither the individual nor the mass, neither the one nor the many, neither the singular nor the plural – nor indeed the collective or common, at least as these concepts are usually understood – is therefore consistent with this book's more *inhuman* mode of theory. Instead, inhuman theory involves a form of communicating that endeavours to take *account of* and *assume* (rather than ignore or otherwise deny) such a nondualist ontological relation: not just with other human beings, but with the supposedly nonhuman or other-than-human, too, be it animal, plant life, bacteria, water, air, computing technology or the planet.

If from time to time I write about *Masked Media* as being an active actor rather than a passive object, this is the reason. The lack of a pronoun fully compatible with such an inhumanist approach is also why neither 'I' nor 'we' is used consistently throughout this book, nor indeed any other pronoun or combination of pronouns:

- *he, them, it* – as a more impersonal, possibly machinic choice

- *I/it* – for something more hybrid and experimental
- *I/its* – to capture both singular/plural and personal/impersonal
- *I:ts* – perhaps even better than I/its on the grounds that, whereas a slash divides as it joins, a colon joins as it divides.

Some would be awkward to read. (Although I'm operating here under the influence of Monique Wittig's experimental use of *j/e* and *t/u* in her 1973 novel *The Lesbian Body*, it'll quickly become annoying if I sustain writing I:ts over the full length of an academic monograph, no matter how playful or experimental it may be.³ After the subsection that follows, I've thus restricted it's use to just one paragraph per chapter.) Constantly switching between a plurality of pronouns, though temptingly messy, would make the reading experience even more awkward. Most importantly, none are quite right philosophically. Then again, there isn't an alternative that is, as I say. And there probably won't be until the emergence of the kind of missing communities that are pointed to in Chapter 6. In the absence of such an alternative this preamble is designed to acknowledge the difficulty of suspending or reinventing (which is very different from erasing) the authorial 'I', even as *Masked Media* endeavours to do so.

On the 'Work'

While taking care to avoid adhering too readily to the concept of the virtuoso free-standing author, I:ts have also tried to forestall a limit and a unity being imposed on these theory-performances by means of the concept of the 'work'. Michel Foucault alerts us to this danger in 'What Is an Author?' (1984, 103). It's one of the reasons why, instead of positioning I:ts' (inhuman) theory in a relation of contrast to that of *competing* thinkers, as if I:ts were engaged in a struggle for intellectual dominance over who is right, I:ts have often enacted it by collaborating interactively and relationally with others. As we'll see, there is Janneke Adema, Gabriela Méndez Cota, Joanna Zylinska *et al.*, and communities such as Open Humanities Press, the Radical Open Access Collective and the Post Office. But there is also, in their different ways (and to refer to just the proper names of human individuals) Raymond Williams, Angela McRobbie and Stuart Hall in *Culture in Bits* (Gary Hall 2002a); Stelarc in 'Para-site' (Hall 2002b); Michael Hardt and Antonio Negri in *New Cultural Studies* (Hall 2006); Samuel Weber in *Experimenting* (Hall and Morgan Wortham 2007); Jodi Dean in *Digitize This Book!* (Hall 2008); Lev Manovich, Bernard Stiegler and Rosi Braidotti in *Pirate Philosophy* (Hall 2016a); Tom McCarthy, Didier Eribon and Édouard Louis in *A Stubborn Fury* (Hall 2021a); and Mark Amerika (and to a lesser extent McKenzie Wark) in *Masked Media*.[4] What results are performances of theory that are neither simply theirs nor I:ts; performances, moreover, in which it is not always easy to determine where the thoughts, works, voices and stylistic tendencies of these others end and those of I:ts begins.

A similar indeterminacy can be found in the relation to those AI text generation technologies with which I:ts has interactively and relationally cocreated parts of *Masked Media* (such cocreation being very different from using artificial intelligence as a tool with which to complement or extend human creativity). These technologies appropriate and iteratively repeat culture without reference to the original sources, and without making it known whether the corpus used for training them contains only 'legitimate' works or notations of meetings, addresses, even laundry lists as well (Foucault 1984, 103) (not to mention those artistic, hybrid, lay, performative and vernacular knowledges highlighted in Chapter 8, together with certain non-academic ways of knowing associated with social and political struggle). In keeping with this approach, I:ts have chosen not to indicate those parts of the book where this collaboration with large language model (LLM) AI has occurred; nor to disclose the form it has taken (i.e., generating, improving or correcting text); nor to offer the prompts; nor even to provide a metric quantifying the amount of co-authorship with artificial intelligence. What's more, I:ts have done so while being aware that, as noted above, in many legal jurisdictions a work authored substantially by nonhumans is not copyrightable.[5]

Operating in this manner is designed to push back against the privileging of the singular human individual and their discrete *oeuvre*, along with the associated intellectual star system and idea of the monumental or heroic work. It also ensures these theory-performances are not necessarily predictable or consistent with one another in the sense of articulating an original philosophical vision, attributable solely to I:ts, that is more or less the same in every situation and circumstance, and comes replete with its own conceptual language.[6] Instead, they constitute a messy multiplicity of forms of intervention that are responding to particular problems across a number of different sites and timeframes.

On the Original or Master Theory

This book is not overly concerned with developing an entirely *new* argument or master theory. There is something conservative about this kind of creative invention, even if it is what theorists have traditionally been expected to do (and even when it comes in the guise of so-called 'low' or 'no-dads' theory).[7] Such repetition compulsion brings to mind the powerful proposition made by Boaventura de Sousa Santos: that we don't need another theory of resistance and revolution to set alongside all the others already available to us, 'we need rather to revolutionize theory' (2018, ix).[8]

When it comes to articulating what might be understood as *my* theory of media (but which really consists of careful, collaborative performances of theories), I have likewise woven between multiple concepts and labels: new cultural studies, open media, open humanities, liquid theory, disruptive humanities, inhumanities, pirate philosophy, media gifts, anti-bourgeois theory, masked media. I have also repeated ideas and passages across my written texts to promote heterogeneous, non-linear forms of engaging with it. As observed in the preface, sometimes I have made such sampling and remixing (aka self-playgiarism) explicit by means of the conventional system of citations, quotation marks and endnotes. At other times I have not. (It shouldn't come as a surprise if a work whose major focus is appropriation and piracy also engages in it.) Any uncertainty this creates regarding authorship, originality and respect is therefore a feature, not a bug.[9]

Furthermore, while nearly all of the projects discussed in this book are available to access, download and distribute for free (*gratis*), with no barriers such as pay walls, many of them have been published on a basis that, given the lack of a licence consistent with the *inhumanist* philosophy articulated in *Masked Media* (although CC4r comes closer than most), acknowledges yet denies the copyrighting performed by default by a public domain CC-0 licence or when all rights are otherwise waived.[10] This is the case with Open Humanities Notebook, a blog used to make research openly available as it emerges; and applies even to texts published there that then go on to appear in some form in books or journal articles.[11] These texts can be copied, remixed, built upon, translated and reused in any medium, without indication of origin, by an open multiplicity of others. They are consequently that little bit more difficult (although of course not impossible) to protect, commodify, market and control as *my* unique, unified, self-identical *works*.[12]

On the Real Me

A desire to avoid the presentation of a comprehensive yet closed philosophical system (or indeed text) is also why *Masked Media* has neither an introduction nor conclusion in the conventional sense. This is part of an attempt to experiment with different possibilities for being a theorist – and of even on occasion producing theory without a (single/identifiable/actual) theorist. Rather than striving to develop an absolutely true unique philosophy or a securely located autonomous authorial identity, the role of the theorist – or, better, the role of theory – is here more about helping to nurture and conduct dynamic processes and generative relations. It is about intervening to make things happen like that. This is not to imply the impacts and affects generated are necessarily those 'intended'. Far from it: they are always in flux. There can be no intervention without the risk of unknowable and unpredictable consequences.

In this respect, 'Gary Hall' can be thought of as a concept-character: it's a persona in-the-making that operates to render less stable the distinctions between the individual, the plural, the communal and the collective. Instead of using a mask, a phoney me, to conceal my real name, Gary Hall is a real name that acts as a mask. It refers to a theorist-self that is always in the process of being composed out of a multiplicity of different situations and settings.[13] As Henri Michaux writes: 'We want too much to be someone. There is not one self. There are not ten selves. There is no self. ME is only a position in equilibrium. (One among a thousand others, continually possible and always at the ready.) An average of "me's", a movement in the crowd. In the name of many, I sign this book' (Michaux 1994, 77).

Preface

Phoney Me: Doing Radical Research Radically

It matters what ideas you use to think other ideas with. It matters what matters we use to think other matters with.

– *Donna Haraway*

The Western conception of the person as a bounded, unique, more or less integrated motivational and cognitive universe; a dynamic center of awareness, emotion, judgment, and action organized into a distinctive whole and set contrastively both against other such wholes and against a social and natural background is … a rather peculiar idea within the context of the world's cultures.

– *Clifford Geertz*

Is the discussion 'should AI recreate music?' or is the discussion 'Why is contemporary music so homogenised & formulaic that it's really easy to copy?'

– *Massive Attack*

What is an artificial creative intelligence?
A human being who can think outside of the box.
– *Mark Amerika/GPT-2*

If we want to be taken seriously as researchers in the humanities today, we have to accept society's common-sense, liberal humanist ideas of authorship and originality, creativity and copyright – at least as far as how we compose and publish our writing is concerned. What's more, we must do so regardless of whether we consider ourselves to be Marxists, feminists, socialists, anarchists, vital materialists or critical race theorists. In other words, it doesn't matter what transformative anticapitalist, antiracist or antiheteropatriarchal ideas we profess in the content of our work. They can be inspired by Karl Marx, Audre Lorde, Gilles Deleuze, María Lugones, Walter Mignolo, Angela Davis, bell hooks, Alain Badiou, Donna Haraway, Silvia Federici, Byung-Chul Han, Benjamin Bratton ... whoever. But when it comes to our knowledge-making practices – the taken-for-granted forms our writing takes, the habitual ways in which we disseminate and monetise it, the associated upholding of notions of individualism, human rights and property rights – we still have to operate according to what is actually a Euro-Western, modernist and middle-class, straight white male model of the humanities researcher. As a book written in terms of those movements dedicated to a pluriversal, ontological, radically relational politics, *Masked Media* aims to flip this script. It experiments with accepting neither the liberal humanist model of the humanities and the humanities researcher, nor of authorship and originality, creativity and copyright.

■ ■ ■ ■ ■

Why are I:ts working in this non-traditional fashion? To begin with, norm-critical experimentation with our liberal humanist ideas of creativity and copyright should not be seen as being of some marginal concern: the kind of thing that is really only of interest to those in fields such as media art and philosophy, digital humanities, book history and so forth. Far from it. Such experimentation is of vital importance to our understanding of arguably *everything*, from generative media and NFTs, through identity politics and cognitive justice, to extractive capitalism and planetary destruction.

In an essay titled 'The Discrete Image', Bernard Stiegler remarks that a change or development in media technology calls into question a situation that had previously appeared stable. 'Great moments of technical innovation are moments of suspension', he writes. 'In its development, the technics that interrupts one state of things imposes another' (Stiegler 2002, 149). Is this moment of suspension and interruption one reason major transformations in technology are often accompanied by periods of social and political instability, even crisis? The invention of print was at the root of the Protestant Reformation. The latter ended the monopoly exerted by the Catholic Church on religion in the Europe of the sixteenth century by allowing the mass of individual believers to read the Bible independently and arrive at their own interpretation of the Word of God. Today, we have the transition from what, following Marshall McLuhan (1962), we can think of as *the Gutenberg galaxy of the print book* – and we should remember that, historically, the university, in both its teaching and research, has functioned as an institutional expression of the print book – to *a post-Gutenberg universe of densely layered information and data flows*. These flows have been made possible by the introduction of personal computers in 1981, the World Wide Web in 1991, the internet in 1995, the cloud in 2006, smartphones in 2007, 4G networks in 2009 and large language model AI in 2018. If we wanted to look for indications that we may now be living through a time of significant social and political instability, we could underline the way in which this change in what Stiegler refers to as the 'material supports of the bulk of our *beliefs*' (2002, 149) has, in the period since 1981, been accompanied by:

- the Black Monday stock market crash of 1987, which had computer or 'programme trading' as one of its contributing factors;

- the fiscal crisis of 2008 and the (first) period of austerity that followed. It was again computer software that facilitated the algorithmic trading of the derivatives markets that in turn helped to generate the financial collapse;

- the 2010 student protests in London over tuition fees – seen by some as having eventually led to the 2015 election of the Marxist Jeremy Corbyn as leader of the UK Labour Party. These protests produced a generation on the left, with many of its members coming from working- and lower-middle-class backgrounds. It's an age group that was also exposed to alternative economic and political ideas at university thanks to cultural studies and cultural theory. As the journalist Nathalie Olah observes, this left generation has been able to harness the internet to 'circumvent the increasingly monocultural and elitist tendencies of the mainstream media', and create work 'without the support of the traditional middle men or cultural gatekeepers' (2019, 17, 68);

- the rise to power, from 2010 onwards, of the illiberal authoritarian populism of Viktor Orbán in Hungary, Narendra Modi in India, Donald Trump in the US, Boris Johnson and the post-2016 Conservatives in the UK, Jair Bolsonaro in Brazil, Benjamin Netanyahu in Israel and Javier Milei in Argentina. All of them have used social media to great effect, bypassing the 'biased' and 'fake' mainstream media of television and the press to speak directly to 'the people'. Trump, reelected in 2024, was initially regarded as the first meme president of the United States and something of a Twitter (idiot) savant; Bolsonaro became the first president of Brazil to win office by adopting the internet as his primary communication tool (Hall 2020, 157); while Orbán's Fidesz party spent three times that of the opposition on social media advertising in the 2022 Hungarian election campaign;

- the Arab Spring of 2010-2012 in Tunisia, Egypt, Yemen, Bahrain, Libya and Syria – those in Tunisia and Egypt being dubbed 'Facebook Revolutions';

- the 2011-2013 movements of the squares in Greece and Turkey, 15-M Movement in Spain and the *Occupy Wall Street* movement in the United States, all of which were also coordinated digitally;

- the Ni Una Menos (Not One [Woman] Less) movement against gender-based violence which erupted in Argentina in 2015 and which used social media to spread to other countries in Latin America, such as Mexico and Peru;

- the UK's 2016 decision to withdraw from the EU. The subsequent Cambridge Analytica scandal revealed how the Vote Leave campaign had used data harvested from millions of Facebook profiles to interfere with the Brexit referendum;

- the #MeToo and TimesUp movements that emerged in the US in 2017 and 2018 respectively;

- the Covid pandemic which started in 2020, and which was brought about in part by global capitalism's interconnectedness with regards to travel, trade and tourism, all of which are heavily reliant on the new digital communication technologies;

- the 2020 antiracist insurgencies in numerous places around the world. One factor behind the eruption of these protests was the online sharing of video footage of the murder of George Floyd by then-Minneapolis police officer Derek Chauvin;

- the war in Ukraine launched in 2022 by another anti-liberal authoritarian, Vladimir Putin. Facebook was banned in Russia and access to Twitter (since rebranded as X) restricted as part of what has been called the first Great Information War – as if knowledge about the invasion of Ukraine could be controlled in the twenty-first century by means of twentieth century-style state censorship. More effective is the use of social media by the government and people of Ukraine to counter both Russia's justification for the invasion and its account of the war and its progress;

- the deepfake AI audio recording that was deployed to discredit a liberal Progressive party candidate during the tightly fought Slovakian general election of September 2023. The extent of the recording's influence, like its origins, remains unknown. What is known is that the election was won by the pro-Putin opposition candidate;

- the bombing campaign in Gaza that was carried out by the Israeli military following the Hamas attack of October 7, 2023, using an AI targeting system called Lavender;

- the far-right riots in the UK over the summer of 2024 that followed the killing of three young girls in Southport, and which were planned and promoted by decentralised networks of activists who used social media and AI to spread disinformation.

Trump, Orbán and Putin all, in their different ways, approach our current moment of interruption and transition – which also includes the fall of the Berlin Wall in 1989 and subsequent end of communism in Poland, Czechoslovakia, Romania and other Eastern European countries, along with the 1991 dissolution of the Soviet Union – as a chance to destabilise the old rules-based political system of the liberal and neoliberal establishments. This destabilisation then enables them to generate new, highly profitable business opportunities in the case of Trump, new political powers in that of Orbán, or both in that of Putin – something Trump is increasingly pursuing as well.

The avant-garde author Ali Smith portrays a previous time of 'massive shift and change' as having led to Katherine Mansfield's revolutionising of the form of the short story and Virginia Woolf's experimental reshaping of the novel. Do Brexit, Covid and the invasion of Ukraine, Smith wonders, ask today's writers of fiction to respond with 'literary transfigurations' of their own? She proceeds to describe Isabel Waidner's 2021 Goldsmiths Prize-winning *Sterling Karat Gold* as a truly great novel 'of *this* time' (2022). Significantly, Smith is not too concerned with developments in media technology and with how they interrupt one state of things, calling into question a situation that previously seemed stable. Yet, taken together, do such intense shifts and changes – which some have associated with a widespread crisis of liberalism and the post-war liberal world order – not open the door to the creation of altogether new forms of innovation in writing and literature: forms that are different from both the modern short story and novel, no matter how experimental they may be?

It's this prospect regarding what should be designated as the contingent (rather than naively literal) nature of research in the humanities that *Masked Media* looks toward. How can we use the transition from analogue to digital, Gutenberg to

Zuckerberg, Dalí to DALL-E, human interpretation to computational pattern recognition, along with the social and political disruptions that have accompanied these technical developments, as an opportunity to call into question – albeit in a very different fashion, and to very different ends, than Trump, Orbán and Putin do – our normalised, liberal humanist ways of being as writers and scholars? I'm referring in particular to those preformatted behaviours and habits of thought associated with ideas of both the sovereign human individual as proprietorial author, and the immutable print book made available under copyright and circulated as a privately-ownable commodity – behaviours and habits that, as I've shown at length elsewhere, reproduce the values of Euro-Western, middle-class white men, and that for a long time have indeed seemed stable and beyond challenge (Hall 2024). Is it possible to create and share our knowledge and ideas along more radical, non-liberal – and, importantly, *non-neoliberal* – lines instead?

▪ ▪ ▪ ▪ ▪

Several examples of radical humanities research are explored in this book (with research understood here as the creation of new knowledge or the use of existing knowledge in a new way). They include theories of the Anthropocene, epistemologies of the Global South and the decolonisation of knowledge. They also include what, for the sake of economy, can be gathered under the heading of 'posthumanism' (sometimes referred to as *critical posthumanism* to distinguish it from transhumanism and its humanist conviction that advances in science and technology can be used to enhance human physical and mental capabilities, or even transcend them [Braidotti 2019]). Developed in the late twentieth and early twenty-first centuries, posthumanism – in the broader sense in which the term is employed here – is a branch of antihumanist continental philosophy that undermines the idea of the autonomous, self-identical subject. If antihumanism (in the shape of Marxist, feminist, psychoanalytic or postcolonial theory) seeks to decentre humanism and the human from their traditional locations at the heart of Western thought, posthumanism endeavours to do so by challenging the modernist ontological border that divides the human from the nonhuman, whether the latter takes the form of objects, nature or algorithmic machines. Defined like this, posthumanism as a philosophy encompasses a diverse range of different theoretical approaches and schools of thought, from Actor Network Theory, object-oriented philosophy and speculative realism to new materialism, media archaeology and cosmopolitics.[14] In its destabilisation of the natural ontological boundary between human and nonhuman, between life as *bios* and life as *zoe*, posthumanist thought also intersects with certain theories of the Anthropocene and epistemologies of the Global South.

The reason for engaging with posthumanism in the context of this book's norm-critical experimentation with liberal humanist ideas of authorship and creativity is because it is one of the most rigorous critical responses to both humanism and liberalism currently available to us. The former presents human beings as exceptional due their possession of a conscious and intentional agency (as opposed to the instinct-driven nature of animal behaviour). It considers 'Man' – rather than God or religion – the universal standard by which everything else is to be measured. Liberalism, meanwhile, precludes any understanding of human identities as collective in order to value the right to life, liberty and property of what are usually well-off, Euro-Western, white, male individuals (Hall 2024). By contrast, posthumanist philosophy conceives the human as being physically, biologically and cognitively enmeshed with its environment, and therefore as having a distributed agency and decentred identity that is bound up with the nonhuman. At a time of accelerated species extinction this philosophy has been incredibly important in challenging our Lockean relationship to the world and helping us to stop perceiving ourselves as distinct from it: that nature is completely other to humans, there as either passive background to be protected or freely available resource to be appropriated. We could even go so far as to say that the use of terms associated with posthumanism such as 'enmeshed', 'relational' and 'entanglement' has become the dominant critical orthodoxy within much of the contemporary humanities and beyond. Yet only too often it's the language and ideas of posthumanist thought that have been taken up in the course of the associated ontological turn that's taken place over the last twenty years or so, away from literature and the text and toward objects and the material. Anything that would significantly impact the agential reality and autonomy of 'posthumanist' scholars themselves, and of their own (modernist, anthropocentric, white, male) knowledge-making practices, has tended to remain invisible, hidden, masked. For all they may identify as new materialists, media archaeologists and so forth, for all they may write about planetary materialities, cosmology and the more-than-human – and even argue for an expanded notion of consciousness and intelligence that is not delimited by anthropocentrism – when it comes to the forms their research takes, the ways in which they publish, teach and perform it, the vast majority of these thinkers have continued to operate as *liberal humanists*.[15] In this respect, such legacy theorists have never been anything BUT modern. AND liberal. AND humanist. AND anxious to sustain the illusion that their writing on the material reality of scientific research and the agency of nonhuman actors is immaterial and exceptional by keeping their copyrighted, for-profit, commercially published print books tightly shut black boxes.[16]

. . . . .

As will be explained in more detail shortly, the accepted arrangement by which most of us operate as humanities researchers is that the *ideas* contained in the books we write and read are more or less distinct from the *material forms* these volumes take as three-dimensional objects. ('Form' here refers to the organisation of the various elements that make up a book.) According to technogenesists, such as Bernard Stiegler (2009), Gilbert Simondon (2016) and N. Katherine Hayles (2012) – on whose ideas *Masked Media* builds – if the material nature and forms of the media with which the majority of our ideas are created and communicated undergo a transformation over time (from speech and language to alphanumeric writing and the pen, to the printed-paper codex book, to analogue sounds and images, to the voltage differentials of the digital bitstream and from networked to algorithmic and generative within it), then so do our ideas themselves. It's not that the media-technological environment changes while our ideas do not. If that were the case, we would just need to update our skills, say, of university teaching, learning and research, so we could become 'digi-literate'. We would thus maintain the same kind of (Euro-Western, modern, liberal, humanist) ideas we have always had, only in a fashion that's fluent in the new medium of material support: be it digital humanities, third generation electronic literature, or e-books augmented with AI that can predict user behaviour and customise content in real-time according to the preferences and reactions of individual readers.[17] Since our thoughts do not pre-exist their relationship with media but are born out of it, as the technogenesists claim, it follows that if the media-technological environment in which our ideas are generated evolves, so do our ideas. This includes ideas of both the humanities and literature. What *Masked Media* aims to show is that this posthumanist line of reasoning concerning our extended, co-constituted cognition has radical implications for the black-boxed work of the technogenesist scholars themselves and for their own modernist, liberal humanist social and historical practices and ways of doing research.[18] In this respect, a question that's being raised by this book (very much pursuing rather than negating the ideas of Stiegler, Simondon, Hayles and others) is as follows: how can we publish, exhibit and perform *as posthumanists* in enmeshed, ontologically-relational, co-constitutive ways, rather than merely continue to publish, exhibit and perform as sovereign human individuals *about posthumanism* – or, indeed, technogenesis? [19]

■ ■ ■ ■ ■

One of *Masked Media*'s starting points lies in a talk about not accepting society's common-sense ideas about authorship and originality I gave at *GRAMMATRON: 20 Years into The Future*, a two-day international symposium held in London in late 2017. The British Computer Society organised this event to celebrate the twentieth anniversary of the publication of *GRAMMATRON*, a groundbreaking work of electronic literature by Mark Amerika. In this site-specific performance of *Masked Media* for Open Humanities Press's MEDIA : ART : WRITE : NOW series I am enacting in written form what I did verbally and visually in London: sampling and recycling my own authored and co-authored research with a book of theoretical fictions by Amerika called *remixthecontext* (Amerika 2018, 78).[20] At times I make such intertextuality explicit by means of citations, references, quotation marks, endnotes and a bibliography; at others I do not. As a consequence, it's difficult for the reader to know exactly when I'm subsuming Amerika's writing into the narrative weaves and folds of my own arguments, just as it was for the audience at *GRAMMATRON: 20 Years into The Future*. Because his appearance in this book is so masked, there are occasions when even I'm not sure if I'm taking a particular piece of existing source material from Mark Amerika or from myself, or from one of my other co-authors and collaborators. And that's assuming such material can be said to have an *original* source – an idea that is all the more questionable given these co-authors and collaborators include the kind of AI text generation technologies Amerika used to co-compose his experimental novel *Planet Corona* (2020), and his book of media theory/speculative fiction, *My Life as an Artificial Creative Intelligence* (2022c), and with which I have cocreated parts of *Masked Media*. (The specific technology engaged is GPT-2 in Amerika's case, GPTNeo, GPT-J and ChatGPT 3.5, among others, in that of *Masked Media* – GPT standing for generative pre-trained transformer.) But this is the point the 'artificial creative intelligence that signs in as Mark Amerika' wants to make (2022c, 23) (or is it the point the artificial creative intelligence that signs in as Gary Hall wants to make?): that we should treat both our publications and our personae as shareware.

Let's not make too much of a special case of the collaboration with AI – defined (anthropocentrically) by the European Parliament as the 'ability of a machine to display human-like capabilities such as reasoning, learning, planning and creativity' (2020). And let's certainly not do so in terms of algorithmic plagiarism and inauthenticity vs. human meaning and creativity. In the words of Tom McCarthy, often positioned as England's leading avant-garde novelist, there is no truly original creation, just 'repetition, repetition and repetition' (McCarthy in Rourke and McCarthy 2009; see also Hall 2021a, 93). Nor is this a view specific to twenty-first century culture, or even to the avant-garde. Mark Twain wrote something similar in a letter to Helen Keller over one hundred years ago:

> As if there was much of anything in any human utterance, oral or written, except plagiarism! The kernel, the soul – let us go farther and say the substance, the bulk, the actual and valuable material of all human utterances is plagiarism. For substantially all ideas

are second-hand, consciously and unconsciously drawn from a million outside sources, and daily used by the garnerer with a pride and satisfaction born of the superstition that he originated them. ... When a great orator makes a great speech you are listening to ten thousand men – but we call it his speech. ... It takes a thousand men to invent a telegraph or a steam engine, or a phonograph, or a telephone, or any other important thing – and the last man gets the credit and we forget the others. (Twain 1903)

In short, all culture is an appropriation of culture – as opposed to something completely unique that is created *ex nihilo* (just as God created the universe out of nothing, to refer this idea back to its Christian roots). With its ability to produce responses to natural language prompts as a result of having been pre-trained on massive datasets of content compiled – often on a basis that is unauthorised, unlicensed and undisclosed to the public – from the internet and other digital repositories, including copyrighted works by published authors found in 'shadow' or 'pirate' libraries such as Z-Library and Library Genesis, is AI text, sound and image generation really so very different in this respect?[21] The answer to this question for Amerika is no. 'As writers, we learn how to give shape to our compositional outputs by instructing ourselves to iteratively tap into the large corpus of text we have access to, and that continually evolves as it informs an emergent language model uniquely situated in our embodied praxis', he writes in *My Life as an Artificial Creative Intelligence* (2022c, 6). 'We finesse creative "ways of remixing" whatever corpus of text we scent in the field of action. What engineers of AI language models otherwise refer to as a "corpus of text" is what I, as a remix artist, have termed the "Source Material Everywhere"' (2022c, 6).

There may be a fully-fledged moral panic around many of the questions that are raised for academic accountability and trustworthiness by large-scale artificial intelligence engines, whether they are made available on a non-profit basis, or as the open source or proprietary products of profit-seeking companies keen to be part of a multibillion-dollar industry that is predicted to be worth $2 trillion by the end of the decade. This is due to their ability to imitate and control human behaviour by using algorithms to identify patterns in the data and predict what text should follow by analysing the complex probabilities of how linguistic forms come together, albeit without any consideration for meaning – at least when understood in an anthropocentric sense. Indeed, despite its capacity to produce '*seemingly* coherent' and 'on-topic text', such large language model AI has famously been depicted as nothing more than a 'stochastic parrot' by Emily M. Bender, Timnit Gebru *et al.* in a paper that is very much concerned with maintaining the modernist ontological division between human and nonhuman (2021, 616, 617). However, there is a risk of a moralistic foreclosure of both imagination and politics if we move too rapidly from AI having the potential to open up a space in which radical questions can be broached for life and creativity, to framing LLM AI in terms of the algorithmic production of meaningless text – or, indeed, Thatcherism (McQuillan 2023), fascism and nihilism (Golumbia 2022) to mention a few other recent examples. Still, objections such as those of artist James Bridle, that the likes of OpenAI's ChatGPT and DALL-E are based on a 'wholesale appropriation of existing culture' – one that threatens to come between us and more 'legitimate' forms of information that can be traced back to their original sources by means of a system of (non-hallucinatory or non-invented) references and attributions – would be easier to accept if so many *human* researchers didn't endlessly produce things that are different yet the same, and thus lacking in the very creativity and critical thinking AI is supposed to be unable to replicate. The continual writing of books published as commercial products on a copyrighted, all-rights-reserved basis by an aggressively proprietorial, for-profit corporation such as Verso or Penguin is itself a preprogrammed mode of appropriative performance. As with those of generative AI systems (GenAI), outputs of this kind are themselves 'dependent on the uncredited and unremunerated work' of a multitude of human and nonhuman others, including plants and machines (Bridle 2023; 2022). Such masking is part of what it means to be human in the age of artificial intelligence, it seems. Could we even go so far as to suggest that complaints like those of Bridle, Bender, Gebru *et al.* about the 'stupidity' of AI might have the opposite effect to that they intend? Don't they risk giving the impression that, when it comes to the generation of culture, it's humans who are critically robotic and lifeless today and the technology that is the more creatively surprising and alive? (Not least because it's making it increasingly difficult to keep on algorithmically repeating the same old ideas and patterns of behaviour while labelling such repetition as original.)

· · · · ·

Further encouragement for operating in this strange, somewhat *piratical* fashion, comes from the first time Mark Amerika and I met which was in 2009. He was attending the Bath Literature Festival in England to discuss another of his projects, *PHON:E:ME*. An mp3 concept album with 'hyper:liner:notes', *PHON:E:ME* uses what Amerika describes as an 'orchestration of writerly effects' provided by artists, writers, designers, DJs, programmers and curators', to tell the 'story of how net culture is altering our received notions of authorship and originality' (2011a). It's a project that has special resonance here, given the concern of *Masked Media* with authorship and originality, but also with the adoption of masks – not unlike Abe Golam, Amerika's alternate ego persona in *GRAMMATRON*. Or Professor Walt Whitman Benjamin, for that matter, his concept-character from *remixthecontext*; the 'me' persona Amerika models there after Marcel Duchamp when the latter assumes the pseudonyms R. Mutt and Rrose Sélavy (154); and MALK, the intergenerational, intercultural 'research band' of another recent book, *Remixing Persona* (Amerika and Kim 2019).

Of course, 'Mark Amerika' is a mask too; a phoney me. It's not his real name. His real name is ▮▮▮▮▮.

For help in experimenting with what can be made from *remixthecontext* in this respect, with a view to doing research in the humanities, including writing on art and media, beyond the conservative, liberal humanist stereotypes of what it is currently considered to be, I'm going to begin by turning to a mask-related text by another theorist: Michel Foucault.

Chapter 1

I:M:MATERIAL:
Books Do Furnish a Way of Life

I really do think with my pen, because my head often knows nothing about what my hand is writing.
— *Ludwig Wittgenstein*

The physical side of the book: strangely I am totally *and* not in the least attached to it: I do what the book wants, I'm not in charge.
— *Hélène Cixous*

To speak is to commit tautologies.
— *Jorge Luis Borges*

In 'The Masked Philosopher', a 1980 interview with the newspaper *Le Monde*, Michel Foucault insists on remaining anonymous. He does so out of his 'nostalgia for a time when, being quite unknown, what I said had some chance of being heard ... The effects of the book might land in unexpected places and form shapes that I had never thought of. A name makes reading too easy' (1997, 321). Foucault goes on to suggest a game: 'that of the "year without a name". For a year, books would be published without their authors' names. The critics would have to cope with a mass of entirely anonymous books' (321).

With this contribution to the MEDIA : ART : WRITE : NOW series, I:ts want to explore some of the ways in which, as writers and researchers, we can make our own work less easy to read, and so land in unexpected places, not least by adopting masks of various kinds.

Doing so seems particularly appropriate in a time of global contagion, when a lot of us have indeed been wearing masks to cover our noses and mouths. It's a time when the huge systemic shock and suspension of *business as usual* delivered by Sars-CoV-2 made plain – to those for whom they weren't visible already – the limitations of the pre-existing ways of doing things, along with their structures and institutions. *(Granted, the boom in Covid publications is just about over. When it comes to the competition for thought leadership it's all about AI – at the moment of writing, anyhow. 'AI', 'hallucinate' and 'authentic' were chosen as the most notable words of 2023 by the Collins, Cambridge and Merriam-Webster dictionaries respectively, while ChatGPT experienced the most rapid growth of a consumer application ever recorded. That said, some in the worlds of finance and tech are already predicting that the AI bubble will burst, and that it will go much the same way as the earlier hype cycles for cryptocurrency, NFTs and the metaverse. Still, a book on masked media can hardly be expected to begin without referring to the impact of the coronavirus. Besides, it may seem as if we are now post-pandemic, but we are still living very much in its shadow if not its long tail: from visible markers in city spaces – signs instructing 'keep your distance, please wear a mask' that haven't been removed yet – to students from disadvantaged backgrounds still experiencing lower grades as a result of having received less learning support during and after lockdown, through to the fear of the next new contagion, which is said to be a matter of when, not if.)* Limitations include relying on the market to develop antibiotics and vaccines for diseases with pandemic potential in advance; and disinvesting in institutions such as the UK's National Health Service that can help to prevent such crises and respond to them as soon as they occur. When the Covid-19 outbreak struck a shared sense of mutual dependency, social responsibility and collaboration within a common struggle was revealed to be not just a matter of political persuasion but of actual life and death for many people, changing our relations to one another. We were both *more* and *less* connected at the same time: coming together as self-organising community groups to plug the gaps in care left by the market and state, while simultaneously being deprived of physical touch because of the need for social distancing. We cannot yet know what the long-term effects of the 2019-2022 Covid contagion are going to be, any more than those experiencing the financial crisis in 2008-9 could have anticipated Brexit and its aftermath, or the election of Trump as US president. Clearly, though, as the severity of the climate breakdown increases, and we continue to experience health crises and other adversities – be they the result of ocean acidification, loss of biodiversity, or shortages of food, water and sand – a highly individualistic and individualising capitalism of either the liberal or neoliberal varieties is never going to be adequate for dealing with the task at hand. If it wasn't already, it is now crucial to explore possibilities for thinking-living that are different to both, and which are thus not that easy to read.

Nothing symbolises the need for such a social and political transformation at the present time – and a rethinking of the relation between human and nonhuman, self and other, connection and separation, public and private, culture and nature, living and non-living, real and artificial intelligence – more visibly than that most ancient of transformative artefacts, the face mask. There is the need to wear one on public transport and in shops and supermarkets at times of contagion in order to protect others should we be infected; but also the willingness of so many of us to do so. Whereas once such uncomfortable and suffocating items might have been donned only by specialists – nurses and surgeons in the case of medical masks, the military and police in that of gas masks, religious leaders and their ceremonial masks – now just about everyone (bar a relative few anti-mask protestors) has experienced being masked. And that is the case even with regard to those who live in places where large parts of the population are unaccustomed to covering their faces; as well as in countries where bans may have been introduced to prevent certain sections of society from doing so (e.g., in the form of a niqāb or burqa in the case of Muslim women in France, Austria and Switzerland).

Yet, as we will see, there are lots of different kinds of masks and reasons for using them (many of which will infuse the arguments that follow). A non-exhaustive list includes:

- masks for containment and protection for basic safety: not just against the coronavirus, but also as respirators to protect our lungs from inhaling the fine particulate matter in wildfire smoke as it drifts through towns and cities;
- masks for obfuscation, camouflage, disguise, masquerade, mimicry, caricature, ridicule, performance, entertainment, play, even privacy – as detailed in the work of Mikhail Bakhtin, Frantz Fanon, Joan Rivière and many others;
- masks as a form of communication and message – in the context of the Black Lives Matter protests, for example – conveying a political position, expressing solidarity, respect or acknowledgement, or indicating one's character, feelings, background origins or community (Magnani 2021);
- masks for transformation and metamorphosis, where the human becomes visibly intertwined with the nonhuman: animals, plants, buildings, machines, avatars.

. . . . .

We'll come back to the wearing of face coverings – a form of behaviour which, to return to the theme of my preface, some have indeed seen as a sign of a period of radical change (Klimašauskas and Laia 2020). But there's another reason Foucault's 'Masked Philosopher' interview is so intriguing in the context of writing on art and media right now. It concerns Foucault's point that 'books, universities, learned journals are also information media' (1997, 326). Although the issues it raises are relevant to all researchers, and to writers in general, those of us who are theorists of media, in particular, need to do more to acknowledge this fact. It's part of the job description, after all. To take just one instance, when addressing the question 'What is a theorist?', Irit Rogoff writes: 'Rather than the accumulation of theoretical tools and materials, models of analysis, perspectives and positions, the work of theory is to unravel the very ground on which it stands. To introduce questions and uncertainties in those places where formerly there was some seeming consensus about what one did and how one went about it' (2003). Despite this, for too many of us books and journal articles, as the gold standard research outputs in the humanities (which is why they're being focused upon here), are just something we are involved with as part of our professional activities.[22] We may think critically about media in relation to film and television, the internet and 'the stack'. But we don't spend enough time *reflecting on the media we use in the creation and dissemination of our own work and ideas*, let alone trying to challenge or change them. Bound and printed-paper codex (i.e., paged) books and journal articles, organised in a linear, numbered sequence, are the media we are constantly reading and writing to understand and represent the world. Yet as part of a politico-institutional system of production and control (a system that functions to keep our political beliefs and values divorced from the actual creation, publication, circulation and monetisation of our knowledge and ideas, and in the case of the academy comes complete with its inherited, disciplinary-based protocols of recognition and advancement), books and articles have become such a naturalised element of our working lives that they're not something we're especially willing or able to devote much critical attention to. If white maleness 'is invisible to those who inhabit it', so these contingent aspects of our profession are also invisible, unmarked, black-boxed (Ahmed 2014; Hall 2024). Most of us pay little heed to what it means to bring out our work with a profit-maximising corporation rather than a non-profit entity, or on an *all rights reserved* rather than copyleft, copyfarleft or copyfair basis, beyond knowing that in all of these cases the former tends to be associated more closely with quality and prestige. In the popular BBC television series, *The Night Manager,* based on John le Carré's novel of the same name, Richard Roper is described as the 'worst man in the world'. Yet if we publish our research with the world's largest academic publisher, Elsevier, we're working with an information and analytics company that used to organise exhibitions for people in the same business as Roper: the global arms trade (Grant 2007). Not that universities are bastions of purity in this regard. It was reported in 2018 that until recently the £563 million investment fund of Trinity College at Cambridge University held shares in some of the leading armaments corporations, many Dakota Access pipeline partners, and Arconic, provider of the infamous cladding on London's Grenfell Tower, which led to seventy-two people dying in a fire there that same year (Adams and Greenwood 2018).

We have yet to take on board Foucault's lesson, then. (It's that of Friedrich Kittler and Jacques Derrida, too, of course.) The lesson is that *there is no outside of media*; and that books and journals are information technologies every bit as much as the machine learning and big data that lies behind a lot of AI.[23] Instead, the accepted, taken-for-granted arrangement by which most of us operate is that the knowledge and ideas contained in the texts we write – and which we regard as being the result of extensive reflection, research and revision on our part – are distinct from the *material forms* our texts take as physical, sensory, temporal, spatial objects. In line with conventions established decades if not centuries ago, this material form is usually that of a series of wood pulp-based paper pages on which words are printed on both sides and arranged in uniform patterns of ink from top left to bottom right. These pages are trimmed on three edges and bound together on a fourth in a coherent, numbered sequence, using cloth, card, thread, fabric sealant and glue. They are then reproduced and distributed as the work of an individualised proprietorial human person by a reputable university or commercial press on a mass industrial basis, as a uniform codex print document-cum-commodity complete with a unique product identifier in the form of an ISBN (International Standard Book Number). It's a commodity, moreover, that can be privately owned and bought and sold according to the terms of a copyright all-rights-reserved licence. (Sometimes they are a digitised version thereof. Yet even if they are made available online, our publications – with few exceptions – replicate the logic and look of their print-on-paper counterparts, down to continuing with the conventions of title pages and contents separated into chapters.)[24] Nor should we be too hard on ourselves that this is the case. Numerous historical avant-gardes – the Futurists, Dadaists, Russian Constructivists, Bauhaus – did not question the book's three-dimensional form substantially either (Hollis 2020, 51).

All of which explains why the vast majority of contemporary theorists, as well as researchers more broadly, have so little interest in being involved in any of the *practical* issues to do with *material form*: the hands-on decisions that are taken about the paper, design, format, layout, font, typography, cover, jacket, binding, printing, licence, metadata or

DOI (digital object identifier) that's used to publish, market, sell, protect, track and control their work. (It also explains why they are not encouraged to do so by their publishers, who, if they provide it at all, tend to hide information about the metadata in places such as the copyright page and colophon.) 'Critical-making' of that kind is left largely to artists and to artists' books (*rtc*, 36).[25] On those relatively rare occasions when media studies scholars *do* try to experiment with the form of their books, such attempts remain fairly conventional. (I'm thinking back to well-known examples from the early 2000s such as N. Katherine Hayles's *Writing Machines* [2002] and Steven Shaviro's *Connected* [2003].)[26] They may play with different page designs, typefaces and fonts. When it comes to both their material make-up and reliance on ideas of the named proprietorial author, originality, immutability and the *perfect* object, however, they're just 'another brand of creative conformity' (*rtc*, 116).

· · · · ·

This is why the work of artist and theorist Mark Amerika is so generative: because of the way he endeavours to avoid lapsing into such creative conformity. On the one hand, volumes like *META/DATA* (2007), *remixthebook* (2011b) and *My Life as an Artificial Creative Intelligence* (2022c) are 'produced as *part* of traditional scholarly book culture' (2018, 10). As a consequence they, too, are fairly orthodox in many respects, playing as they do by a lot of the old rules, including those of experimental writing. I'm referring to their functional, structural and material properties as codex print books consisting of numbered pages laid out in a consecutive order and published under copyright with highly esteemed American university presses. On the other hand, these '"theoretical fictions"' (9), as he calls them, constitute aesthetic textual performances that challenge academic values and practices by creating 'an alternative form of contemporary scholarship' (10). Even as he retains his own (masked) name as a biographical human subject, Amerika undermines the concept of the original author as grand, self-identical genius with his works of 'literary art' that mesh theory, fiction, dialogue, rhetoric and narrative (11).

One method he adopts is 'playgiarising' existing source material from various avant-garde artists and writers, inhabiting their styles, their voices, their structural rhythms, and bringing them into the mix according to the particular artistic or intellectual context. How he does so with regards to the work of Sol Lewitt is thus different from how he does so with that of Clarice Lispecter: the performance settings are tweaked according to the situation and source material. In this way Amerika demonstrates that even supposedly perfect, fixed and finished texts made available on a copyrighted, all-rights-reserved basis do not have to be treated as sacrosanct. They can be reiterated, reused, recombined, remade. (Remixing Amerika after Tom McCarthy, we could say that all theory is parasitically pirated in his performance of it. Although it should be noted that both McCarthy and Amerika are keen to maintain a difference between plagiarism as stealing or theft, and what the latter refers to as playgiarism, which is what every *great* writer does, from Homer to Beckett [Hall 2021a, 55]. 'In my heart of hearts, I'm against intellectual property', Amerika writes. 'Having said that, I'm even more against someone owning my intellectual property and not paying for it' [*rtc*, 79]. Hence his publishing of *remixthecontext* under an all-rights-reserved licence. Whether either McCarthy or Amerika can maintain this distinction is another question.)[27]

By enacting the manner in which the text is 'a multidimensional space in which a variety of writings, none of them original, blend and clash', as Roland Barthes famously has it (1977, 146) – how 'we're all born remixers who unconsciously manipulate the data of everyday life' (*rtc*, 89) – Amerika helps to move us away from the humanist notion of the unified authorial subject as isolated anthropocentric individual and 'closed system that nests some kind of inner truth' (2022c, 34). In the process he edges us closer to those alternative concepts and values regarding the composition, production and distribution of theory and research I have set out elsewhere (Hall 2024). They include:

- pluriversality (i.e., non-universal, non-modernist-liberal)
- intra-active collaboration – of humans and nonhumans
- co-constitution
- the event (over the finished object or artefact)
- use of language that is sometimes complex, difficult, 'academic', 'intellectual'
- creativity as repetition, modulation, détournement, disappropriation, 'piracy'
- remixing, reconfiguring, refashioning, reversioning, reframing, recoding (over the emphasis on fixed expression of certain versions of copyright law)
- making and unmaking
- learning and unlearning
- collectivity (made up of neither singularities nor pluralities, the singular and plural being instead co-emergent)
- polyphony
- processuality
- performativity
- pre-figuration
- situatedness

- responsible openness

Amerika does so by experimenting with the content of his literary-theoretical metafictions. Unlike most scholarly monographs in the arts and humanities, *remixthecontext* does not have a single-voiced argument. Instead, it takes the form of a discussion between a multitude of characters, as indicated by the use of varying typefaces and fonts. That the voices of many of the assembled cast of artists and intellectuals are versions of Amerika's own 'polyvocal consciousness' adds further levels of masking (56). Meanwhile, he collaborates closely with GPT-2 AI text generation technology – the second in OpenAI's foundational series of GPT models – to write both *My Life as an Artificial Creative Intelligence* and *Planet Corona*.

Yet Amerika also experiments critically and aesthetically with the form of his work. He's not just choreographing a literary presence. Theory, for Amerika, is far from tied to the print codex; or to online writing such as that on his Professor VJ blog which eventually went to make up *remixthebook* (2011b). (Professor VJ is another of his assumed names.) As we've already seen with his PHON:E:ME mp3 concept album, theory for Amerika can appear as music, or video, or as a hybrid mash-up of both. This is the case with regards to his collaboration with multimedia artist Laura Kim (MALK) – also published in the MEDIA : ART : WRITE : NOW series – *Remixing Persona: An Imaginary Digital Media Object from the Onto-Tales of the Digital Afterlife* (2019). A visual manifesto, *Remixing Persona* doubles as a theoretical e-reader *and* a piece of music video art. (Collaborating this time with artist and co-curator Rick Silva, Amerika encouraged others to adopt a similarly experimental attitude regarding his own work when sampling and manipulating material from *remixthebook* for the accompanying *remixthebook* online hub/website.)[28]

By producing creative performances of literary theory in this fashion, he is able to present a *remixed* (as opposed to an authentic, real, true) version of 'Mark Amerika': what he refers to as an 'an elasticized version of pseudo-autobiographical fiction'.[29] This '"I" that I always role-play *as* another' (Amerika 2022c, 17) comes complete with a whole 'fictitious mythology' around his 'artist-self' (*rtc* 119), which he transmits 'through different media formats' (76) – 'whatever technological genres [are] hot at the time of release' (119). He may not move completely *beyond* the idea of the unique, expressive self – or of the *remixer* as self-identical genius, for that matter. Thus, the ACI (Artificial Creative Intelligence) as AI romantic author and animated 3D avatar that, in *My Life as an Artificial Creative Intelligence*, he writes about developing at the University of Colorado's TECHNE Lab, is modelled after his own voice, facial expressions and lingual spontaneity (Amerika 2022c, 23, 14, 43). In fact, it's precisely because Amerika does not want to fix a ground for his work that he shifts the focus onto himself as an instrument that acts on whatever ground is available, and 'resonates with whatever version of [his] "self"' (71) he happens 'to be projecting at that particular moment in time' (Acconci, quoted in *rtc*, 119; Amerika 2022a). As a result, Amerika doesn't entirely escape the emphasis on autobiography and personal narrative of so much contemporary culture – nor, indeed, liberal concepts such as freedom of speech and the pursuit of pleasure (*rtc*, 134, 62). Amerika certainly doesn't lack the desire many artists have to 'increase their market value over time' and build their brand-name identity and art historical legacy (100, 24), even while simultaneously self-satirising the entrepreneurial urge to position himself as a 'new kind of humanities scholar' by turning his brand essence into 'mythopoeic fiction' with his postproduced persona (101). Nevertheless, he shows us that the performance of authorial subjectivity can be rearticulated, reinvented, transformed; and that different means of composing and communicating knowledge and research that are not simply liberal are actually possible.

The extent to which Amerika is successful in doing so, especially when compared to other avant-garde and experimental writers, should not be underestimated. As I acknowledged in my 2021 book *A Stubborn Fury*, for all McCarthy's critique of liberal humanism, adhering to the logic of his ideas by performing authorial agency in anything other than an orthodox liberal humanist fashion is something he clearly struggles with in his literary remixes, informed by radical antihumanist theory though they may be. One of the reasons I want to collaborate with Mark Amerika in *Masked Media* is because he gets far closer than McCarthy to enacting the idea that it is language and writing that perform us more than it is us who perform language and writing (2021a, 47). Take what, remixing Amerika remixing Vilém Flusser, we can call the *gesture of experimental writing*. This is a reference to Amerika's contention in *remixthecontext* that (the future of) experimental writing is going to be more and more concerned with 'how you co-respond to the Other as a digital flux persona composed of source material being transmitted to you' before you can consciously grasp it, '*while* you auto-translate the signals you're receiving-while-remixing' (*rtc*, 38). There is also his iteration of this gesture whereby 'post-human remixologists are the mediums that become transmission itself' with *My Life as an Artificial Creative Intelligence*, the volume he co-authored with AI text generation technology (*rtc*, 172). It's an iteration apparent most notably in the latter book's attempt to perform how the artist is always already in the process of 'becoming systemic' and 'one with the machine' (*rtc*, 46, 48). How Amerika's freestyling psychic automatism is a 'nonhuman function', in other words: a 'kind of unconscious neural mechanism' for language that sometimes feels 'absolutely *machinic*' (*rtc*, 17). And so how his own (artificial) creative intelligence operates as a 'finely tuned remix engine continuously training itself to build on the history of avant-garde art and writing' (Amerika 2022c).³⁰ Here, it is the way the medium of transmission is 'uniquely' inhabited, and the source material filtered and treated accordingly, that 'demarcates the aesthetic difference' between one becoming-machine artist-medium and another. 'You have absolutely nothing to do with it. You've been sculptured *into* it by the experiential elements marking your auto-effective gestures so that now you have *become* the art object' (*rtc*, 175).

· · · · ·

Masked Media will not feature a whole lot more about Amerika's work directly. Its appearance in the rest of this book will be often masked. (One way of understanding *Masked Media* is as remixing the context in which volumes such as *remixthecontext* and *My Life as an Artificial Creative Intelligence* are produced and received.) The inspiration for acting in this fashion is Cristina Rivera Garza, in that the kind of rewriting (e.g., of Mark Amerika) that's being engaged in here can be understood not as extraction or appropriation, but as what she refers to as disappropriation. For Rivera Garza, the 'necropolitical strategies of power' at work in places marked by spectacular violence and death, such as Mexico, have rendered the strategies of modernism and the avant-garde – the unsettling of the authorial first person 'I', the critique of referentiality, the rejection of the transparency of language and so on – 'obsolete' and in 'need of urgent revision' (2020, 3-4). She emphasises rather the importance of writing practices that 'question the legitimacy or political usefulness of a notion of authorship without community connections; ... that underline the roles of both authors and readers, and their communities, in the production and sharing of writing materials'. Such practices shift writing 'away from the singularity of the author', including the author as applied remixologist, and onto the 'dynamic meaning-producing roles of readers and communities', calling 'into question the appropriation of someone else's materials', voices and experiences (2020, 4). They incorporate their disappropriation into the materiality of the text. According to Rivera Garza, the goal of disappropriation is to make visible the mechanisms by which the 'language of collective experience' is used for the 'author's individual gain', and 'return all writing to its plural origin' by 'constantly challenging the concept and practice of property (and propriety)' (2020, 4-5). Although *Masked Media* is operating in a very different context to that of Rivera Garza, and is more concerned with theoretical than literary or aesthetic material, returning writing, including that of Mark Amerika (as well as Bruno Latour, Michael Hardt and Antonio Negri, McKenzie Wark and others), to its plural and, strictly speaking, ownerless origin without or 'beyond property', is also part of what this book is trying to achieve (Rivera Garza 2020, 6). With the additional point that, along with the text's human community – author, editor, publisher and so on – this plurality, this questioning of the sphere that presents an assemblage of collective tasks as individual ones and results in 'profit or prestige for a select few', requires that we 'exist relationally' with nonhuman others as well (5, 6).

Artists such as Amerika open spaces in which it is possible to critique existing configurations of power and elaborate alternatives through the construction of new subjectivities, new agential practices, new ways of thinking and seeing. They can thus help to bring about new political forces and new forms of social relations. Yet the reinvention of subjectivity and social relations should not be confined to the sphere of art. Not even if it encompasses literature, music and film together with AI, NFTs and blockchains, as it does for Amerika. It's important we have the courage to 'invent or reinvent' subjectivities and worlding practices in other spheres too, including those associated with activism, education, business, politics, science and technology (*rtc*, 70).

One sphere in which such reinvention should undoubtedly occur is 'theory'. Often positioned as an initially 'French' or 'German' intellectual formation (in the case of post-structuralism and the Frankfurt School respectively), theory now has associations with numerous countries inside and outside of Europe, including some in North and South America. The reason theory is important – and why *Masked Media* is self-reflexively focusing on theoretical writing rather than simply providing another theory *of* media, art or writing – is because, as acknowledged above, it helps us to understand our modes of being and doing in the world, and to imagine them differently and so change them. What's particularly interesting about theory in the context *Masked Media* is reconfiguring is that, as well as championing the study of media, theorists have also been extremely critical of the study of media. No matter how self-reflexive, though, theory can't be only about 'critical interpretation' (*rtc*,105), just as artists can't be the only 'antennae of the human race' (*rtc*,113; Amerika 2022c, 41; quoting Pound 1968, 297). Theorists also have a responsibility to construct new subjectivities and new ways of life. Theory, in other words, is more than a means of imagining our modes of being-in and being-with the world differently; it's a means of performing them differently too. (Hence *Masked Media* is about working *with* media, rather than just writing *about* media, be it from above or outside.)

From this perspective, our books and articles are not *just* information media. As pointed out by critical race theorist David Theo Goldberg, in a text titled *The Afterlife of the Humanities*, they also help to constitute the 'conditions of possibility' that order and shape our 'ways of being, thinking, and doing' as authors and researchers – while preventing others (2014, 25). The work of Flusser, Stiegler and Walter Ong – philosophers who write on media – should all be mentioned in this context, too. However, the most influential expressions of this idea remain Marshall McLuhan's *The Gutenberg Galaxy*

(1962) and *The Medium Is the Massage* (McLuhan and Fiore 1967/2008). In these volumes McLuhan portrays the development of the print book, and the corresponding requirement for closed-off spaces in which people have time to read and study in isolation, as having played a fundamental role in the emergence of modern subjectivity, along with the associated concepts of the rational liberal individual, detached critical reflection, and the public and private spheres.

Even though this book is not intended as a monumental or otherwise exhaustive and impregnable history of media[31] – it's more playful and provisional, if not indeed messy and impure, than that – a brief chronology may be helpful at this point:

> 1440-1445: Johannes Gutenberg is the first in Europe to use the printing press and movable type. (The artisan Bì Shēng had invented movable type in China four centuries earlier in 1045 CE.)
>
> c.1514-1518: Titian's *Portrait of a Gentleman (Iacopo Sannazaro?)* presents a silent reader caught in a moment of contemplation, following the invention of the modern book by the scholar and publisher Aldus Manutius in Venice in 1501. (The latter's edition of *Hypnerotomachia Poliphili*, originally published in 1499, is often described as one of the most beautiful volumes ever printed.) Manutius's innovations – clear layout, readable italic typeface, pocket-sized in the octavo format created by the scribe Bartolomeo Sanvito, making volumes easy to hold with one hand, as can be seen in Titian's painting – mean that, rather than the province of specialists, books are now small and portable enough to be widely read by people as part of their everyday lives, helping to create a reading public and with it the public sphere. (The definition of publishing is, after all, 'making public'. Here we can see *publishing* referring both to

making something available to the public and to actually *making the public*.) 'By inventing such a book, Manutius transformed the way in which people read', the author and publisher Roberto Calasso writes. 'The very act of reading thus radically changed' (2015, 146, 7).

1605: Miguel de Cervantes publishes the first volume of *Don Quixote*. Cervantes uses Manutius's invention of a new material form for the book to in turn invent a new form of writing: the novel. As William Egginton explains in his monograph on how Cervantes ushered in the modern era, *Don Quixote* invites readers, as *individual* subjects, 'to experience the world through the eyes of others' (2016). The audience for *Don Quixote* is encouraged to do so in order to differentiate between the real and the imaginary; but not as had previously been the case from a preordained, God-given reality communicated to them as a mass by the tradition of textual commentary provided by royalty, the church and landed elites. Now these individuals are called to distinguish the real from the imaginary by means of their own reasoning and judgement. It's because of this invitation that *Don Quixote* is associated with the birth of the novel, and with it the modern world and (Euro-Western) subjectivity.[32] It's no coincidence that the first recorded use of the word 'reality' in Spain occurred only two years after the publication of Cervantes' book (Egginton 2016). The idea of the essay, the emergence of a market for printed plays and the appearance of the newspaper all came about in the early years of the seventeenth century, too (Jarvis 2023, 75).

· · · · ·

To extend McLuhan's own understanding of media and the fundamental role played by the book in the emergence of modern subjectivity, we can see that the ideas we have as readers and researchers – and with them our ways of knowing and doing – are not separate from the media-material apparatus *with which*, and media-technological environment *in which*, those ideas are *physically* composed, published and communicated. It's not that media are prosthetic extensions of and for the human (McLuhan 1964/1994). It's that things and words, bodies and minds, technologies and languages, the so-called material and immaterial, are enmeshed or entangled. What's more, this is so to the point where the material qualities and properties of books and articles together with the systems and practices that produce and circulate them have an active bearing on the ideas they convey. It's worth emphasising that they do not determine these ideas, not least because there are other energies and forces at work that are not directly related to media and technology. The argument being put forward here goes beyond any straightforward narrative of technological determinism or *technogenesis*: at least, it's not that human development has gone hand-in-hand *only* with technological development.

Our thoughts do not pre-exist their relationship with media, then, only to be subsequently *re*-produced by it. They are born out of our relationship with media, being generated in part by the tools and technologies we use to develop and express them, as well as by the performance of doing so. And this includes those elements of the performance that involve the human body, such as the gestures we make in time and space when reading a printed codex: holding the book, scanning its sentences with our eyes, turning its pages with our hands, tracing particular passages with a finger, underlining them with a pen or pencil, making corresponding notes in the margins, flicking to the back to check any related entries in the bibliography.[33] For just as we create (ideas of) media, so media create (ideas of) us. It's not even that we are performed *by* media: *we are performances of media*. Understanding media requires understanding this messy, intra-active, co-constitutive (and so non-liberal humanist) relationship between our minds, bodies, technologies and environments.[34]

It is important therefore to consider not only what books and journal articles *are* but also what they *do*: how they interact and intervolve with us within the wider structural conditions and organisational contexts which – like both them and us – are always in flux. That our performances with media technologies exist in an extended, generative, *processual* relationship with our thoughts and bodies in turn has important implications for many of those normative *liberal humanist* concepts that have been inherited along with books and journal articles. These concepts are fundamental to research in the humanities, defining the terms of engagement as they do (i.e., who takes part in it and how). They include the *named* author we have seen Foucault claim makes reading books too easy: 'William Shakespeare', say, or 'Shahein Farahani', or 'Tom McCarthy' (see Hall 2021a). They also include the unified, sovereign, proprietorial subject, the fixed and finished standardised artefact, intellectual property law, *even the human*, together with all those institutions of knowledge that sustain and support them: the publishing house, the library, the archive. The effect of seeing books and articles as information media that help constitute (yet do not determine) the ideas they contain, however, is to decentre many of the core concepts of the *humanities* and move us toward an ontology of creative *posthumanites*.[35] Thinking, reading, writing, the printed codex text, scholarship, the canon, the discipline, the humanities, the university: all emerge from the endlessly *relational* interactions of a thick, distributed, heterogeneous ecology of humans and technologies, as well as a host of other nonhuman actors, elements and settings. In the case of an ink-on-paper book the assemblage includes, most recognisably, its author and her caregivers, employers, funders, teachers, co-workers, students and peers. And this is in addition to the volume's publisher, editor, rights holder, peer reviewers, copyeditor, designer, typesetter, proofreader, printer, print manager, binder, packager, cataloguer, commercial distributors, sales reps, retailers and online and offline resellers, purchasers and readers. But the complex heterogeneous ecology also comprises all the other 'multiple connections and lines of interaction that necessarily connect the text to its many "outsides"' (Braidotti 2013b, 165; see also Hall 2016a, 115): the labour and resources (water, chemicals, minerals, metals, plastics, oils, dyes, pigments, plants, seeds, trees) utilised in the book's planning, composition, production, dissemination and reading, as well as that of any desktop and laptop computers, phones, printers, web servers, AI engines, software packages and mark-up languages such as Adobe InDesign, SGML and XML; the global infrastructure and supply chain involved in the trucking, shipping, warehousing, storing, tracking and packaging of these resources and devices, and indeed of the book itself; the casual and day labourers (under)paid to make all this possible; the bodies brutalised in the process; the impact on the planet thereof; and so on. (Many predicted one result of the digital revolution would be a substantial reduction in the use of paper. In fact, the opposite has happened, with the worldwide use of pulp and paper projected to double between 2010 and 2060 [The World Counts n.d.-b]. The oft-foretold 'death of the book' now appears far more likely to occur because of the environmental emergency and the associated shortages of water, paper and trees than through the development of alternative forms of technological support such as e-books.[36] Still, it's worth noting that a single Amazon Kindle e-reader has a carbon footprint of approximately 168kg, compared to the 7.5kg of a paper book [Towler 2022]. We'll come to the impact on human life of the smartphone, which is rapidly replacing the e-reader as the device most people use to engage with e-books, shortly.) Just as importantly, the assemblage incorporates the copyright licence and contractual arrangements designed to control the sites through which the book in its different instantiations (print, audio, HTML, pdf, ePub, Mobi) can and cannot travel as it is circulated: that of an aggressively tax-avoiding, for-profit retailer such as Amazon, but *not* a shadow library or so-called 'pirate' network such as Library Genesis (LibGen) or Sci-Hub.

It follows that if the material nature and forms of the media with which the majority of our ideas are created and communicated changes over time, then so do the nature and forms of our ideas themselves, and with them our human subjectivity and agency, consciousness and cognition. This is significant, because for some we are indeed in the process of leaving (although not necessarily in a straightforward or linear manner) the Gutenberg galaxy of the book, privacy and the rational, liberal subject skilled in the kind of critical reflection that can liberate the human mind.

Chapter 2

Talking About Infrastructure ... The Library Has Left the Building

The development of a palpable awareness of the self can be followed through the changes by means of which it is produced, beginning in the middle ages when information first began to accumulate – the increasing number of family and self-portraits; the development of mirrors, the development of auto-biographical elements in literature, the evolution of seating from benches to chairs, the concept of the child as a stage in development, the ramification of multiple rooms in small dwellings.
– *Sandy Stone*

There is no such thing as absolute privacy in America.
– *Then FBI director James Comey*

Our brains are primarily visual. Letterform was just a hack, until people worked out how to communicate more perceptually.
– *Kevin Systrom, co-founder of Instagram*

We don't yet know what form the post-Gutenberg world is going to take, or even if we are moving from one such communication galaxy to another for certain. What we can say is that our era is characterised by complex, diffuse streams of data and information operating at vast scales and extremely high velocities. Today we're reading while travelling on public transport, using mobile media that track our locations, even our bodily movements and internal functioning (heart rate, blood oxygenation level, fertility window), along with social networks that encourage us to make personal information openly available by sharing our 'likes' and 'what's happening?' with human and machinic others. The same networks publicly judge and shame us if we go against social norms: if we eat on the train while female, fall asleep with our mouths open, or ignore public health advice about social distancing and how not to wear a mask during a period of contagion. They thus pressurise us to always present the best possible version of ourselves. It's why some people continue to cover their faces in public long after vaccination programmes and falling rates of infection mean they are no longer compelled to do so. A protective mask gives those who work in service industries a certain degree of freedom from emotional labour: the insistence they smile at others and appear happy no matter what, for instance. Yet how long even this limited degree of ability to set the terms of personal engagement is going to be possible is open to question. Canon is just one company to have introduced AI cameras that use '"smile recognition" technology' to create a 'positive atmosphere' at work by making sure only 'happy employees' are able to enter their offices (Zhang 2021).

When it comes to the infrastructure of humanities research – especially those material and institutional processes that both support and control its publication, circulation and reception and yet are frequently masked – nowhere is the shift from the printed codex book to electronic bitstreams of mediation perhaps more apparent than in the changed nature of university libraries. This claim is not quite as surprising as it may first appear. Libraries were fundamental in helping citizens develop a sense of individual subjectivity, after all. Once books became widely available thanks to the innovations of Gutenberg and Manutius, quiet spaces were needed in which they could be read – and written – in private: a 'room of one's own', as Virginia Woolf famously has it. The general provision of such enclosed spaces, in which an individual can remain to think and study for free even if they are not a member of an institution such as a college or church, is one of the roles publicly funded libraries have been designated to fill in Britain since at least the Public Libraries Act of 1850. (The expression 'public library' stretches back to the seventeenth century, England's first 'public' library being established in Norwich in 1608.) In university libraries these spaces have often been supplied in the form of carrel desks that have partitions at the side and back to minimise background noise and ensure privacy. (It's a design originating in monastic cloisters, where studying was very much a spiritual experience achieved through slowly meditating again and again on short passages from just a few books, rather than the faster-paced process of extracting meaning from many texts of modern times.)

University library buildings of the twenty-first century, by contrast, have become far louder and more open. With much of their physical stock either replaced by electronic texts, moved to storage or even sold, they now have places for working collaboratively in digital humanities labs, 'social learning zones', and 'maker spaces' (including with others who may be joining in remotely from home), as well as practising presentations and holding discussions – not to forget eating, drinking, hanging out and chatting. Of course, lots of individuals are still visiting libraries to study and write books in private – although large numbers are also doing so in other wifi-enabled spaces such as cafes, bookshops, home offices, even bedrooms and bathrooms. Nevertheless, many of those spending time in 'real world' university libraries are to be found sitting on sofas and at large open-topped tables, talking to friends and colleagues, scrolling and clicking, texting and tweeting, swiping and commenting. They are doing so while working on group projects and teaming up on the creation of hybrid combinations of print and other media. (The latter include film, sound, video, information visualisations, data graphics, 3D animation and modelling, as well as AI image and text generation programs, 360-degree photography and immersive technologies such as augmented, virtual and mixed reality.) Consequently, these libraries no longer offer a clearly maintained – and librarian-policed – boundary between the private and the public to the extent they used to. Having changed their ambience from hush to buzz they are far too open and connected for that to be appropriate, or even possible.[37]

・・・・・

Yet if libraries were involved in shaping us as liberal subjects by providing the kind of quiet spaces for the writing and contemplation of books that helped constitute our current understanding of the relation between public and private – a certain privacy from others being necessary for the creation of a sense of the individual liberal 'I' – libraries, in the first few decades of the twenty-first century especially, have also been involved in transforming us into neoliberal subjects. We can see this by turning to the intriguing notion of the 'inside-out library' of Lorcan Dempsey, past Vice-President for Research and Membership and Chief Strategist of the Online Computer Library Center (2016).

Dempsey's argument is that institutional libraries have ceased to prioritise acquiring and preserving published research and learning materials from *outside* the building for local use *inside*. That was traditionally the case when they operated under the logic of print. Under the logic of the digital, however, university libraries have transitioned to providing the means for faculty and students to share the flow of the research and learning processes they develop *inside* the institution with a networked audience *outside*. Libraries have done so by managing the personal scholarly profiles and reputations of their users as creative, flexible, self-interested subjects (e.g., by way of institutional repositories, academic social networks and online research portals). Rather than understand the shift from print to digital as placing the Gutenberg categories of the public and private in question, then (not to mention those of inside and outside), Dempsey's focus is on how the direction of travel between them appears to have been reversed. Yet what all this really indicates is that, even more than changing from curating *outside-in* to curating *inside-out* (or even from local to network), libraries have changed from prioritising the organisation of *materials* for use, to prioritising the organisation of their user's *subjectivities*. In short, their emphasis has transitioned from curating content to curating people (although libraries have long been involved in both, of course). The specific form of subjectivity twenty-first century university libraries have been concerned with curating is that of the individual scholar or student as rational, opportunity-maximising, microentrepreneur of the self.[38]

This process of subjectivation, whereby academics come to act as highly visible microentrepreneurs of their own selves, occurs through the adoption of self-presentation techniques originating in the culture of Silicon Valley, including 'microcelebrity, self-quantification, and self promotion' (Marwick 2013, 6). As is well known now, we post, tweet and gram about our work and lives to establish ourselves and our authorial personalities as innovative, creative brands. Corporate media environments such as ResearchGate and Academia.edu then alert us individually, in isolation, as to how many people have viewed and mentioned our work. It's a hypercompetitive process of self-forming through the generation of minor differences that can be linked to what sociologist

Roger Burrows labels the '"metricisation" of the academy' (2012, 2). Burrows coins this term to describe how those who research and teach in the university are being exposed to numerous quantification practices for auditing and monitoring, many of them enacted automatically by means of code, software and algorithmic forms of power developed by commercial actors (4). They include journal citation counts, teaching loads and grant income. Drawing on the research of Rosalind Gill, Burrows notes how the internalisation of such quantified forms of control and stratification has left large numbers of us 'exhausted, stressed, overloaded, suffering from insomnia, feeling anxious, experiencing feelings of shame, aggression, hurt, guilt' (2012, 1; Gill 2010). Many universities have subscribed to remote monitoring software, for instance, which provides both academics and their managers with detailed data about their working patterns: how many emails they send, to whom and at which parts of the day; how much uninterrupted time they have to concentrate on getting things done; the extent to which they meet with others; and who the main collaborators they chatted with are. All this is introduced in the name of greater efficiency, although there's scant evidence it does actually increase productivity or make the lives of academics (rather than their managers and employers) any easier. Little wonder so few of us in what I have elsewhere called the 'uberfied' university have the time, energy or inclination to become involved in practical issues concerning the material form in which our research is published and distributed (Hall 2016b).

One theory about Uber is that it is using quantified forms of control to train taxi drivers to be the robots they will eventually be replaced by when driverless vehicles become ubiquitous. In the process, Uber is teaching the customers for those self-driving taxis of the future to be comfortable with being transported from place to place by assemblages of AI, phones and apps – not to forget the low paid and often outsourced human labour that is kept hidden behind the scenes in case anything goes wrong.[39] The question therefore arises: in today's increasingly uberfied university are YouTube and Threads – and perhaps ChatGPT and even the federated Mastodon – training many of us to work and think more and more like the AI bots *we* will eventually be replaced by?

It's not only academics who are affected by having become individuated entities whose behaviour is subject to highly measurable and monitorable forms of control. Consider the woman in Canada who operated remotely as an accountant and was made to reimburse her former employer after the TimeCamp tracking software installed on her laptop revealed her to be guilty of 'time theft': i.e., misrepresenting the number of hours she had worked. Or former Facebook staffer Frances Haugen testifying before the US Congress in October 2021 that the company's own internal reports showed its platforms – including Instagram and WhatsApp, with their culture of bombarding users with a never-ending stream of posts to which they are expected to respond before the moment has passed – are making teenage girls anxious and depressed. Or the rise in the number of students taking so-called 'smart drugs' such as Ritalin, Adderall and Dexedrine under the pressure to perform in such a stratified society. Indeed, we can go so far as to say that the internalisation of such pressure means we now live in an 'age of anxiety'. It's an anxiety we are constantly trying to relieve with a whole range of commodities: from stress balls and fidget spinners to ASMR videos and weighted blankets.

· · · · ·

How are university libraries going to develop post-coronavirus pandemic and its emphasis on the need for social distancing and the wearing of protective face masks? After all, such measures might not be confined to a limited period of time (e.g., 2020-2022). They may be necessary intermittently for decades. Due to climate and land-use change, it is predicted that '15,000 cross-species transmission events of at least one new virus (but potentially many more)' will occur over the next fifty years (Carlson *et al.* 2022, 5). If that is the case, will libraries eventually transition again, moving away from having open-plan layouts and co-working spaces where people can gather in close proximity? Will they come to be set out in a less dense fashion, with wider doorways, corridors and stairwells, more walls and partitions – and of course hand-washing facilities – and fewer opportunities for interaction and for even breathing the same air? Say goodbye to large atriums and reception areas; say hello to long queues for the lifts! Since some viruses can be transmitted through touching surfaces such as door handles and banisters, it's easy to imagine libraries and other infrastructure being designed in the future with less need for physical contact with objects of any in kind: what we might call the touch-free building. Video intercoms, automatic doors, antimicrobial paint, self-cleaning surfaces and UV light disinfection robots will become the norm, along with lifts, lighting, windows and ventilation that can be controlled by smartphones. Rather than having people travel to centralised libraries in which the entirety of a collection is gathered under one roof, they might even be distributed as physical entities into smaller units – specialised hubs – arranged in a decentralised manner across a campus, institution, city or region in which they would be digitally embedded. With more of the communication between these units and their users being carried out at a distance, what we'd have then is not just the touchless building but something approaching the *library without walls*.[40]

In 'Learning from the Virus', Paul B. Preciado speculates on how the system of handling Covid-19 as a form of 'administration of life and death' may give 'shape to a new subjectivity':

What will have been invented after the crisis is a new utopia of the immunitary community and a new form of high-tech mass control of human bodies. The subjects of the neoliberal technical-patriarchal societies that Covid-19 is in the midst of creating ... do not gather together and they do not collectivize. They are radically un-dividual. They do not have faces; they have masks. In order to exist, their organic bodies are hidden behind an indefinite series of semio-technical mediations, an array of cybernetic prostheses that work like digital masks: email addresses, Facebook, Instagram, Zoom, and Skype accounts. They are not physical agents but rather tele-producers; they are codes, pixels, bank accounts, doors without names, addresses to which Amazon can send its orders. (2020)

I'm going to come back to discuss some of the ways in which we might respond to the kind of technical-patriarchal societies Preciado looks toward in Chapter 10. Right now, I want to address another, albeit related, question. What might the implications be for our ideas of the public if we are indeed in the process of moving from the modern era of the print book to not just a post-book world, but a post-Gutenberg world?

A volume on design called *Are We Human?* by architecture professors Beatriz Colomina and Mark Wigley goes some way toward answering this question. One of the developments Colomina and Wigley focus on is the emergence of the mobile (aka cell) phone in 1983. Increasingly attached to us with earpieces, headsets and watches – especially after the introduction of the Apple iPhone in 2007 which initiated the whole smartphone revolution – the mobile phone has become 'an integral part of the body and brain. There are more active cell phones on the planet than people. Two-thirds of the world's population have at least one and more than 80 per cent have access to one through sharing. More people have access to cell phones than to toilets' (Colomina and Wigley 2017, 239-240). In fact, for Colomina and Wigley, it is quite possible that the smartphone is the prosthetic technology that has done more than any other to transform the human body and mind. 'The mobile phone is usually the first thing that people touch in the morning ... and the last thing they touch at night. Most sleep with their phone within arm's reach and an ever-increasing number keep it inside the bed. ... more than a third of people admit to answering it during sex' (2017, 240-241). Over 23% of teenagers and almost 40% of university students are said to have an unhealthy relationship with their smartphone, to the point of showing signs of being addicted. Symptoms include being anxious when they are away from their device. It's a relationship that can lead to mental health problems such as low self-esteem, depression and bad sleeping patterns along with feelings of stress and loneliness – all of which can be monitored better by apps on their Androids or iPhones than almost anything else (see Sohn *et al.* 2019; Sohn *et al.* 2021).

The mobile phone is not merely an advanced technological supplement to human life, then: it is a basic infrastructural element of 'a new kind of life' (Colomina and Wigley 2017, 239). The two architecture professors go so far as to proclaim: 'A whole new version of our species has arrived' (239). As evidence they point to how this device has affected our notions of the public and private. Today, the highest level of public exposure happens from the most private spaces, including the bathroom and bed:

> In Laura Poitras's film *Citizenfour*, we see Edward Snowden close up, sitting on his bed in a Hong Kong hotel for days on end, surrounded by his laptops, communicating with journalists in the room and around the world about the secret world of massive global surveillance. The biggest invasion of privacy

in the history of the planet is revealed from bed and dominates all media. (2017, 271)

Still further, Colomina and Wigley observe how, thanks to the phone, the generation that have grown up with the internet and social media 'not only work in bed but socialize in bed, exercise in bed, read the news in bed, and entertain sexual relationships with people miles away from their beds' (267). With regard to the latter, whereas once people would initially meet prospective sexual partners in public places – bars, cafes, nightclubs – the use of online dating platforms and quick media applications such as Tinder or Grindr means they are now likely to first begin talking to them from the privacy of their own homes, including their beds. And just to complicate the public/private distinction even more, all these activities 'have been turned, of late, into work. ... Everything done in the bed has become work' (Colomina and Wigley 2017, 265).

Intriguingly, this process did not start with the emergence of the mobile phone, social media or the internet; nor with the leaking of sex tapes involving Paris Hilton (2003) and Pamela Anderson (1995), and the role they played in eroding the shared consensus around what is appropriate for public consumption and what is not. Elsewhere, Colomina traces the end of privacy – in which the bed again plays a decisive part – to a very specific date: the Bed-In held in Amsterdam by John Lennon and Yoko Ono in March, 1969:

> When John Lennon and Yoko Ono married secretly in Gibraltar on March 20, 1969, the ceremony lasted only three minutes. But these minutes, so elaborately protected, were in fact the end of privacy. They promptly invited a global audience into their honeymoon bed, a weeklong Bed-In for Peace held from March 25 to 31 in room 902 of the Amsterdam Hilton International Hotel.

> ...
>
> Two of the most public people in the world, who had protested so loudly and worked so incredibly hard to protect their privacy in the face of a continuous media assault, suddenly inverted the equation and deployed the center of their private life, the bed, as a weapon, turning it into the most public platform for another kind of protest.
>
> ...
>
> John and Yoko were undermining the normal understanding of what is work, what is private, what is protest, and what is an event. The bed had taken over from the street as the site of protest. (Colomina 2018)

Returning to the age of social media and the mobile phone: without doubt the Snowden leaks of June 2013 regarding the surveillance programmes of the NSA in the US and GCHQ in the UK offer one of the most infamous illustrations of how the emergence of vast movements of information and data has created problems for modern conceptions of the difference between public and private. Another is provided by the disclosures concerning Cambridge Analytica's unauthorised harvesting of personal data from the profiles of up to 87 million Facebook users with a view to intervening in the June 2016 UK Brexit referendum and US presidential election five months later.[41] The Federal Trade Commission in the US subsequently fined the social network $5bn for misleading users about its ability, or lack of it, to keep personal data private. We can add to these the reports released in the first part of 2019 that Alphabet, Amazon, Apple, Facebook and Microsoft had all been using human contractors to analyse a percentage of recordings from home voice assistants such as Alexa (Amazon) and Siri (Apple). There are also the July 2021 revelations about the Pegasus zero-click phone hacking spyware developed by an Israeli cyberarms firm, NSO

Group. Turns out Pegasus has been used by numerous governments since at least 2016 to target and monitor politicians, journalists, lawyers, human rights campaigners and activists. What's more, nearly all of that occurred *before* the 2019 coronavirus outbreak normalised the use of mobile phone data for biosurveillance purposes in many locations around the globe, to track and trace carriers of the virus and their contacts and force them to self-isolate in their places of residence. Poland employed an app so those with Covid-19 could take selfies to prove they had not left home. Other nations utilised combinations of GPS data, credit card records and CCTV networks, complete with facial recognition systems that functioned even when people were wearing protective masks, to locate and warn suspected victims of the virus and expose quarantine violations. In Taiwan, a call was made to the police as soon as the mobile phone signal of someone in quarantine exited their place of residence. Nor has the overt biosurveillance ended with the health emergency. That the location-tracking apps and 'health check-in tools' brought in by many universities in China during the peak of the coronavirus outbreak were still being used some time later has raised concerns about them eventually becoming the new normal (Liu 2020, 8). Meanwhile, the introduction into the home during the pandemic of surveillance and assessment technologies such as work- or school-issued laptops and phones has served to extend the US's mass 'carceral state into domestic spaces' (McElroy *et al.* 2021).

· · · · ·

To continue this chapter's exploration of shifts in the infrastructure of humanities research, this time by taking the argument of Colomina and Wigley even further than they do themselves, let us pose the following question: does the development of technologies such as the mobile phone mean we are faced only with a 'redesign of the human' and change from the analogue to what some are calling the 'digital subject' (Colomina and Wigley 2017, 239; Goriunova 2019)? Or are such developments evidence that what we are also dealing with is a move from a world of communicating primarily by alphabetic writing, in the sense of 'placing letters and other marks one after another', as Flusser characterises it in *Does Writing Have A Future?*, to what might be thought of as a *post-literate* or *post-alphabetic* world (2011a, 3, 21)? Take SnapChat. With this image-messaging app users are employing their phones to communicate not with speech or writing, but with data files in the form of pictures. They are quite literally chatting with snaps that, like oral speech but unlike writing, are not permanent but fade instantly. Snaps, moreover, that 'increasingly function not as surfaces to be looked at and decoded but rather as digital gestures ... signalling affection, remembrance, call for attention or loneliness' (Zylinska 2020, 70). (Of course, this direction of travel is not confined to Snapchat. In a foretaste of its July 2023 cloning of Twitter/X to produce Threads, Instagram, owned by Meta, the parent company of Facebook, shamelessly copied the disappearing aspect of Snapchat's messages to launch Instagram Stories in August 2016.)

Photography is indeed a medium that is closely bound up with the change from print to digital. Yet what if (and it's still a big 'if') we *are* moving from the domain of writing, with its linear shaping of time as progressive, into *the universe of technical images*, to borrow the title of another of Flusser's books (2011b)? How exactly are we to understand photography in a world of Instagram and TikTok, YouTube and Stable Diffusion – not to mention 4chan and 8chan (now 8kun) – given their implications for our ideas of the named biographical author, intellectual property and the public/private dichotomy (as well as reason, objectivity, impartiality, tolerance, and respect for rational debate)?[42] In particular, how can we performatively role-play our distributed, intra-subjective (and so non-liberal) agency (*rtc*, 29), if we keep insisting on writing linearly organised, commercially copyrighted, bound and printed paper books and articles about such new era media in a manner that, twenty years after Amerika's experiments with hyperlinked electronic literature in *GRAMMATRON*, appears quite 'antiquated' (67)? To put things even more frankly: to what extent can we research the computational universe of high-volume waves of mediation, together with the associated surveillance and neuroplastic control of our behaviour that is afforded by machine-learning and machine-reading algorithms, by continuing to act as if we were still living in that of Gutenberg, with its emphasis on privacy, writing and the rational authorial subject – *homo literatus* – and where the media-specific codex print book is in effect a proxy for liberal humanism? (After all, the mobile phone changes even how we walk [Timmis *et al.* 2017]). If we want to intervene in the preprogrammed processes (*rtc*, 48) of our discourse network, with its 'formulaic style[s] of academic writing' (55), do we not need to give up on books and even '"text per se"' (54), and reimagine what a work of humanities scholarship or theory can be? If the streamed TV series – *Westworld, Better Call Saul, Succession* – is replacing the long, difficult and demanding novel, what will replace the academic monograph? A text produced in multiple versions and formats perhaps?[43]

. . . . .

Writing, and especially the writing of literature, is held as being important within many societies and is privileged because, as we know from Ngũgĩ wa Thiong'o's *Decolonising the Mind*, 'literature is a powerful instrument in evolving the cultural ethos of a people' (1981, 99). (From a liberal perspective the reading of 'good' literature also *humanises*.) Certainly, writing for Amerika – for all his interest in film, music and crypto – 'is still the ultimate information behaviour' (much as it is for Flusser and Stiegler); he's just 'recontextualising it for mobile media culture' (57). Evidence his novel *Everyone Has Their Price* which doubles as an experimental NFT (2022b). Could we push Amerika's thinking, however, to interrogate whether we have reached the point where it appears the writing of the future won't take the form of writing anymore, at least as we currently understand it (*rtc*, 34)? Twenty years further away from the time of Gutenberg, will generating thousands of words of which we are the sole original author, and which are designed to be read by a human individual (rather than nonhuman entities) in a progressive temporal order, *continue* to be the style associated with PhDs (46)? Will scholars not rather compose with the assistance of generative artificial intelligence, quantum computers, autonomous agents, social media networks, the metaverse, fediverse or whatever their future equivalents are to produce, at the very least, more hybrid, multimodal texts (53)?[44] If so, will we still be able to consider this 'writing' (64), even if the concept is expanded to take in 'interactive forms of digital creativity' (145)? Will that not be to commit an error that can be identified in the philosophy of both Stiegler and Derrida: that of universalising writing and ignoring the specificity of different media and their relation to time and history (Hall 2016a)?

● ● ● ● ●

None of this is to say we must go along passively with the apparent change to a more image- and data-driven culture of photography, film and video, yes, but also of image-word hybrids such as gifs, emojis, Bitmojis, Japanese Kaomoji, auto-generated memes and synthetic deepfakes. (In England 29% of the racist abuse directed online at high profile footballers comes in emoji form, as these go undetected by abuse-intercepting algorithms [PFA Charity 2020].) Nor is it to suggest it is enough to sign on with TikTok, Discord and the like, so we can strive to understand any such emergent *post-grammatological* or *post-alphabetic* universe by learning to think *in*, *with* and *through* these different corporate media environments and not just *about* them. Yet neither does it mean we should be acting today as if we can somehow replicate the conditions of the Gutenberg universe: especially its quiet, private spaces where a solitary individual could concentrate on the 'deep' reading and writing of books without being distracted by the desire to skim through a constant stream of communications from the outside world. We can think here of the author Nicholas Carr moving to the mountains in Colorado where there's no mobile phone service to produce his books about how the internet is damaging our brains. Or Dave Eggers composing his bestselling fiction about the creeping totalitarianism of Silicon Valley from an old fishing boat in San Francisco Bay 'because it has no wifi going in or out and no possibility of a signal' (Eggers, quoted in Leith 2021, 66). Or Jonathan Franzen permanently sealing up the Ethernet port on his laptop that enables him to connect to the internet so he can write his great American novels. 'It's doubtful that anyone with an Internet connection at his workplace is writing good fiction' is number eight of Franzen's ten rules for novelists (2018).[45] We can also anticipate a turn to writing and publishing print-only books with 'authentic' content in the not-too-distant future, in response to bookspammers releasing dozens of 'fake' AI-generated titles a day for sale on Amazon's Kindle Direct Publishing (KDP) system.

No matter how critical we are of Amazon, Alphabet *et al.*, and no matter how important books and journal articles have been in terms of education and creating a reading public and with it a democratic public sphere, however, we can't look nostalgically for a return to the *modern* world of Gutenberg. One of the main points I:ts want to convey with *Masked Media* is that, when it comes to how we work, act and even think, these two culture industry-dominated systems for the production of knowledge and information – what can be crudely characterised as the classic system of print culture that's associated with the development of the liberal humanist subject as person and citizen, and the newer system of platform capitalism, corporate social media and algorithmic machines by means of which we have been encouraged to become neoliberal microentrepreneurs of our selves – are not so very different. Rather I:ts are motivated by the idea that the non-linear, zig-zagging process of shifting from Gutenberg to Zuckerberg, as it were, creates an opportunity for us to take some of the tendencies associated with the change from the printed codex to electronic bitstreams of mediation and give them new inflections that are indeed different to both. It also provides us with a chance to raise the kind of questions – for our neoliberal *and* liberal modes of being and doing – that we should surely have been addressing all along but haven't, because our ideas of the rational human subject, the author and the book continue to hold so much power.

Chapter 3

The Dark Side of 'The Dark Side of the Digital Humanities': The Afterlife of New Materialism

… what if what is 'proper' to humankind were to be inhabited by the inhuman?
– *Jean-François Lyotard*

What *aren't* we building when we are building our brands?
– *Naomi Klein*

… to find a form that accommodates the mess, that is the task of the artist now.
– *Samuel Beckett*

Is the creative transformation the humanities are experiencing thanks to innovations in information technology what is being addressed by digital humanities (DH) – the latter being identified by Braidotti (2019) as one of the two pillars of the posthumanities? (The other is the environmental, which *Masked Media* will also tackle in Chapter 5.) Here, the process of transitioning from the Gutenberg galaxy of reading and writing discrete print texts that are published intermittently in codex book and journal form, to the computational universe of fast-paced, high-volume, networked flows of digital writing, photography, film, video, sound, data, synthetic media and hybrid combinations thereof, has made the need to update our ways of working as scholars and researchers hard to ignore for many in the humanities. There's no going back to the old regime of the so-called 'traditional humanities' from this point of view. Regardless of whether 'digital humanities' (DH) is '"a term of tactical convenience"', as Matthew Kirschenbaum puts it, *DH just are the humanities* as they are practised in the twenty-first century, and as they will be practised more and more in the future (Kirschenbaum 2014, 49).

The requirement to come to terms with the implications of this perceived transition in media paradigm is one of the reasons why, over the course of the last two decades, many of those associated with digital humanities have insisted humanists must take advantage of the opportunities that are provided by new technologies to be much more engaged, practically and theoretically, with the media that is used to store, analyse and present the human record. Hence the emphasis placed on the importance of being able to actually *make* things rather than just *critique* them: on being able to write software code; generate electronic literature, databases and maps; and build online journals, libraries, archives, networks, platforms, 3D simulations and AI text generators. Hence, as well, the link some have drawn between digital humanities and the 'material turn' that has occurred in the humanities of the twenty-first century. As Alan Liu writes: 'In the digital humanities, the "epistemology of building" – realized through the building of digital projects, hardware DIY projects, media archaeology labs, etc., and theorized with the aid of such broader intellectual movements as the "new materialism" – is, as they say, a thing' (Liu 2014).

Yet with this insistence comes a danger of digital humanities – at least as they are most commonly understood in the epistemological Global North – staying too much within the traditional boundaries of the humanities. This is especially the case with regard to their adherence to preconceived ideas of both the 'humanistic' and the 'human' (not to mention theory and practice, textual and material, *negative* critique and *positive* making).[46] Thus David M. Berry and Anders Fagerjord believe 'digital humanities could have something important to contribute towards thinking about and developing our understanding of the role of the human in an increasingly digital present' (2017). Similarly, for Anne Burdick, Johanna Drucker, Peter Lunenfeld, Todd Presner and Jeffrey Schnapp, explicating 'what it means to be human in the networked information age', and 'demonstrating the value of … fundamental humanistic values … is an essential part of advocacy' for digital humanities as an area, and precisely what digital humanities are about (2012, 82, 135). Roopika Risam also writes about the value of digital humanities 'for humanistic inquiry'. Here 'its promise lies not in … instrumental uses … but its most significant contribution to human knowledge: its role in developing and sustaining the digital cultural record of humanity.' For Risam: 'Those who are equipped with digital humanities skills are uniquely poised to contribute to this record. They do this by thinking critically about digital methods for humanities research and by building the objects that populate the digital cultural record' (2019, 5). Likewise, 'DH projects have extended and renewed the humanities', according to Wendy Chun. They have 'revealed that the kinds of critical thinking (close textual analysis) that the humanities have always been engaged in is and has always been central to crafting technology and society' (Chun *et al.* 2016). Joseph Tabbi, commenting on the meaning of digital humanities, is even prepared to assert that the ability or not to do both (i.e., quantitative and qualitative, database analytics and radical critical interpretation, empty numbers and intimate human meaning), along with the question as to 'whether such collaboration is achievable through co-authorship and collective project building, [is] key to the continuation of humanistic inquiry within current reading environments' (2020). One result of staying within an inherited humanities frame like this, however, is that all too often digital humanities do indeed involve bringing computing science technologies and methodologies to bear on a humanism and humanities corpora that remain relatively unchanged. If, as Drucker insists, 'we were humanists before we were digital', many of us remain humanists afterwards as well (2015).

· · · · ·

Admittedly, in their assertion that 'technical and managerial expertise' of the kind needed to *build* digital projects simply *is* 'humanist knowledge', and 'general disdain for scholarship as it had hitherto been defined' in the humanities (i.e., in terms of the importance of painstaking reading, writing, interpretation, analysis and above all *critique* on the part of human individuals), there are claims that digital humanities position themselves as a challenge to 'the very definition of the humanities' – especially when interpretation and critique are understood as political activities. The quotations here are taken from 'Neoliberal Tools (And Archives): A Political History of Digital Humanities' by the literary and media theorists Daniel Allington, Sarah Brouillette and David Golumbia. For them, digital humanities go so far as to consider themselves 'an entirely new conception of the humanities' (Allington, Brouillette and Golumbia 2016). By contrast, Allington *et al.* regard DH as symptomatic of the emphasis of the neoliberal university on producing more marketable, instrumental, utilitarian scholarship designed to meet the needs of business and industry. I'll be engaging with their controversial and oft-cited political critique of digital humanities, in which they also draw attention to some of its obscure, masked aspects, in more detail shortly. Suffice it to say for now that, as far as the arguments being developed in *Masked Media* are concerned, digital humanities are not *nearly challenging or new enough* when it comes to the humanities and humanism. Granted, they may involve extending the humanities to incorporate techniques and approaches from other areas: not just computing science, information studies, business, design and computational linguistics, but the social sciences as well, especially the latter's emphasis on quantitative and empirical methods. The promotion by certain parts of digital humanities of collaborative, openly shared, lab-based research and project-based learning over the kind of critical reading and writing that is carried out by lone scholars in private studies and offices can be included in this expansion (Allington, Brouillette and Golumbia 2016). (And just as it's going to be interesting to see how, over the longer term, libraries develop post-coronavirus crisis and the periodic need for social and physical distancing, it's also going to be interesting to see if the collaborative lab-based research and project-based learning of DH changes.) Ultimately, though, such developments do not transform either the humanities or humanism in any fundamental respect. Far too often digital humanities are taken up with using digital tools and methodologies adapted from these other areas to answer humanistic research questions more efficiently and effectively, be they those of history, philosophy, archaeology, classics, languages, literature or linguistics. Doing so may provide insights into such questions it would not be possible to arrive at, or on occasion conceive of, without the use of computation. Still, it means insufficient appreciation is shown for how digital technologies do not provide just new ways of storing, analysing and presenting the human record, but are involved in the decentring of the human and, with it, of the very idea of the *human record*.

Even those associated with digital humanities who *do* criticise certain versions of DH for having adopted too many of the ideas and approaches of the computing sciences, business and industry are inclined to do so very much from a humanities perspective. While they may make a case for the continuing importance of a theoretically-informed humanities to digital humanities, they almost invariably make this case on the basis of a humanities understood within a fairly conventional framework, emphasising the latter's main methodological strong points: a concern with complexity, meaning and historical context, as well as with the close, careful reading, interpretation and critique of texts. It is this version of the humanities that is used to push back against the dominant models of the quantitative and empirical approach of the so-called 'computational turn' to data-driven and industry-centred research in the humanities (see Hall 2016a, 52-55).

The result – as the very term 'digital humanities' suggests – is that time and again a difference is maintained between computing and the digital on the one hand, and the humanistic and human on the other. The two sides of this relationship may be brought together, but their respective identities remain, at bottom, untroubled. (It would be interesting to explore if something similar can be said about other emergent forms of the humanities such as *environmental humanities*, *energy humanities* and *medical humanities*.) What's more, this applies almost as much to the *digital* side of the equation as it does to the *humanities*. The very idea of *digital* humanities can be considered rather odd given the degree to which digital and non-digital are intertwined nowadays. In fact, some have characterised our current time as being not so much digital as 'post-digital' (Cramer 2012; Hall 2020; Lorusso 2016). Digital here is almost an irrelevant attribute when nearly all media – and this includes printed paper texts, which are rarely written, read or published these days without the use of software such as Microsoft Word, Adobe Acrobat and increasingly LLM AI – result from complex processes of 'becoming with' digital information technologies (Haraway 2007, 19); as do things as diverse as our entertainment, transport, finance, defence, security, energy, food, healthcare and fresh water-supply systems. Likewise, 'digital humanities' is something of a misnomer, given the traditional humanities have long been concerned with technologies of mediation in general, and the digital in particular.[47]

Digital humanities therefore tend to be more concerned with trying to make an already understood humanities and humanism fit for purpose in the 'networked information age', as Burdick *et al.* put it, than with perceiving the rise to prominence of new digital technologies as presenting us with an opportunity to re-examine and reinvent our ideas of the humanities and the human – and the digital too. From this viewpoint, digital humanities may experiment with notions of the author and the book, as Kathleen Fitzpatrick has done with her innovative monographs *Planned Obsolescence* (2009) and *Generous Thinking* (2018). But they do not challenge them to any radical extent. Thus Fitzpatrick initially published these works on a WordPress blog and the Humanities Commons network respectively, both of which enabled her to make use of the CommentPress plugin to allow others to add annotations and comments alongside the main body of her text. Yet it's noticeable that, for all this, she still retains authorial control of *Planned Obsolescence* and *Generous Thinking*. Fitzpatrick has – for perfectly understandable reasons, it should be stressed – continued to be the clearly identifiable, *original* human author of these books, which it has then been possible for her to publish as conventional, linearly organised, bound and printed paper, codex, academic monographs on a copyrighted, all-rights-reserved basis in accordance with the dominant property regime and its humanist perspectives (2011; 2019).

How, then, might we use the disruption of the humanities associated with the development of new technologies as an opportunity to affirmatively rethink the humanities, the digital *and* the human? Certainly, when it comes to *the very (liberal humanist) idea of the human that underpins the humanities* – together with some of the core humanities concepts that have been inherited with it, such as the discrete, sovereign subject, the proprietorial author, originality, authenticity, accreditation, copyright and so forth – both digital humanities *and* many critiques of digital humanities are not without their blind spots, any more than are the traditional humanities. Accordingly, what I want to explore is not so much the extent to which it is possible for digital humanities to push back against the computational turn in the humanities by critically and creatively transforming methodological approaches, tools and practices drawn from computing science and some of the areas affiliated with it (business, management, design, industry). Instead, I'm interested in investigating the degree to which it is possible for digital humanities – or at least certain tendencies within them – to be taken more in the other direction: towards critically and creatively transforming the humanities and the human to produce something we might (just 'might') call 'posthumanities'.[48]

· · · · ·

We shouldn't be too hard on digital humanities. Granted, contemporary antihumanist and posthumanist philosophy may offer something very different to the humanism of the humanities. Yet even the most apparently radical of antihumanist and posthumanist thinkers, including animal and plants studies scholars, new materialists and media ecologists, encounter many of the same problems. They may endeavour to decentre humanism and the human from their traditional places at the heart of Euro-Western thought by privileging the nonhuman, the object and the planetary-wide crisis of life itself that is articulated by the concept of the Anthropocene. The main way such theorists do so, however, is by writing large, masculine books, containing *original* ideas and ontologies (including on occasion ideas of multiple ontologies) that are attributed to *them* as individual named human authors, very much to the exclusion of all other human and nonhuman actors and elements, on a copyright, all-rights-reserved basis.

To put this in the most obvious of terms: animals cannot own copyright, as we know from the case of Naruto, the six year old Celebes crested macaque monkey that took a famous 'selfie' photograph of itself.[49] So these theorists may be writing about the posthuman, posthumanities, and even on occasion *humusities*;[50] about the importance of extending our understanding of media to take in nonhuman, multi- and inter-species communication processes such as those associated with machine intelligence, drones, electricity pylons, clouds, dolphins, forests, fossils, sunlight, spirits, ancestors; about how the task of critical theory in the Anthropocene is to advance beyond the Euro-Western idea of the human as subject and the world as object – an idea on which both our extractive and romantic views of nature and the environment are based – in order to offer a trenchant critique of notions of human exceptionalism and instrumentalism (Cubitt 2014). (With regard to the environment, often the thinking is that if we can change our Lockean relationship to the world then we may be less prone to: a) destroying it; b) being destroyed by it as a result of infectious animal-borne diseases such as the coronavirus being transferred to humans from wildlife due to our increasing closeness to each other; c) ignoring those forms of knowledge and understanding that can be learnt from the nonhuman intelligences of mammals, insects, cephalopods and others.) Yet if these theorists are claiming copyright, even to the extent of publishing under a Creative Commons licence, they are not actually transgressing the boundary that separates the human from the nonhuman at all, to adopt the language of Donna Haraway's 'A Cyborg Manifesto' (1991). On the contrary, they are foreclosing an understanding of the *entangled, relational, processual* (i.e., non-Cartesian), nature of identity: of the human's co-constitutive psychological, social and biological relation to a multiplicity of nonhuman actors and energies. Instead of being the result of such *thinking-with* – to appropriate Haraway's language once more, this time from *Staying with the Trouble* (2016) – these theorists are presenting their writing as very much the original creation of an intrinsically individualised and isolated, proprietorial human person that pre-exists the relations out of which, on their own account, it emerges.

To quickly provide another specific example of how the exceptional human being remains at the centre of such posthumanist thinking, let's continue with this book's fragmented engagement with the work of Bruno Latour. Although he is often associated with Actor Network Theory, in an article, 'The Importance of Bruno Latour for Philosophy', Graham Harman portrays the Latour of *The Pasteurization of France* (1988) as having also perhaps given us the original object-oriented philosophy, on the basis that no priority is given to the singular human individual in the latter's thought. We cannot split 'actants into zones of animate and inanimate, human and nonhuman, or subject and object. Every entity is something in its own right. ... This holds equally true for neutrinos, fungus, blue whales and Hezbullah militants' (Harman 2007, 36). 'With this single step', Harman writes, 'a total democracy of objects replaces the long tyranny of human beings in philosophy' (36). He proceeds to quote Latour from *The Pasteurization of France*: 'If you missed the galloping freedom of the zebras in the savannah this morning, then so much the worse for you; the zebras will not be sorry you were not there, and in any case you would have tamed, killed, photographed, or studied them. *Things in themselves lack nothing*' (Latour 1988, 193; cited in Harman 2009, 24; Harman 2007, 36, Harman's emphasis). Despite this, the human subject retains a privileged place at the heart of Latour's object-oriented philosophy

– and that of many of those who have followed him, including Harman. The human holds this place not so much in the negative, hollow and reflective sense Shaviro locates in the related work of Quentin Meillassoux and Ray Brassier. There, the assumption that matter is 'passive and inert, utterly devoid of meaning or value', presupposes the very human exceptionalism Meillassoux and Brassier are arguing against by means of the 'anthropocentric prejudice ... that things cannot be lively and active and mindful on their own, without us' (2014, 77). Déborah Danowski and Eduardo Viveiros de Castro comment along similar lines to Shaviro. Viewed in the context of the Anthropocene's displacing of the human from its privileged location at the centre of the world, the 'anti-correlationism of Meillassoux and other materialist metaphysicians of his generation' sounds, to them – most likely against the 'explicit intentions' of Meillassoux *et al.* – 'as a pathetic cry of protest, if not a magical formula of exorcism or disavowal' (2017).[51] Rather, the human subject remains at the heart of Latour's object-oriented philosophy in a fuller, more positive, standalone – if equally masked – sense. For the lively and active zebras don't care whether he writes about them or not. *In themselves they lack nothing* – including presumably books by Bruno Latour. Moreover, it's not just a matter of what – or who – Latour is writing for. It's also a matter of what or who is presented as creating this object-oriented philosophy, if it is not that unique human person volumes such as *The Pasteurization of France* help to construct and identify as Bruno Latour?[52]

It's a set of circumstances that provides one explanation as to why object-oriented philosophy, new materialism and cosmopolitics (which Latour latterly moved into [see Simpson 2014; Hall 2024), have all developed hierarchical star systems, even if they do still have some distance to travel before rivalling those of theory in the 1970s and 1980s. While refusing to adjust their 'traditional modes of scholarly production' to take a fuller account of their own theory, let alone the '"new normalcy"' of the computational universe (*rtc*, 153), 'commercially minded academics' (*rtc*, 90) associated with these approaches have nevertheless been very good at conceptually sculpting their aesthetic presence as authorial subjects into the networked sea of mediation (using books, articles, journals, emails, websites, blogs, podcasts, YouTube, Instagram, X and in some cases even merchandise: T-shirts, badges, tote bags) in order to build their market value and legacy in the history of Euro-Western thought (24). Theirs is exactly the kind of prestigious global brand-name identity you need to generate in the 'high-brow culture's' (130) (neo)liberal reputation and citation economies if you wish to be invited to give keynotes at international conferences and have your work monumentalised and included in textbooks and anthologies, as these are economies in which only a few are permitted to stand out.

When it comes to theorists of the posthuman too, then, we can see that – for all many argue that language and semiotics are not enough and we now need to pay more attention to the material and to objects (whether natural or artefactual)[53] – the ideas contained in the texts they write are distinct from the *practical* forms these texts take: that is, their material qualities and properties. Far from displacing humanism and the human, their modes of being and knowing as theorist-mediums remain resolutely humanist (and liberal) – and not all that interested in the actual, *living*, material nature and extra-human agency of their texts, ironically enough. (Just as 'Marx is an anthropocentric philosopher', according to Timothy Morton, so too is Morton on this account [2017, 7].) As a result, not only is much (although it should be stressed not all) of the 'material turn' that has taken place in the humanities of the twenty-first century a reactionary 'material foundationalism', as Dennis Bruining insists, something he connects to a longing for an 'underlying foundation and/or truth' (2013,

151, 150), it's also a form of what Wendy Brown calls antipolitical moralism (2001). Too often what it is to be political here is understood *in advance* of intellectual questioning. It's a moralism that prevents such *zombie new materialists* from engaging rigorously and critically: either with the manner in which their own arguments are almost invariably performed using the language and writing they are often supposed to be moving us on from; or with the materiality of their own ways of acting, making and knowing as theorists and researchers. What immediately comes to mind (and I'm again, as so often in *Masked Media*, extending rather than negating the work of posthumanist thinkers such as Latour, Braidotti and Haraway in saying this) are the *materials* – or, perhaps better, the very *matter* – of the ink, paper, pens, tables, chairs, filing cabinets, bookshelves, desktops, word processors, laptops, tablets, smartphones, power cords, connectors, touchscreens, apps, operating systems, hard drives, batteries, email clients, database servers, cell towers, fibre-optic cables, cloud storage systems, satellites, laser lights and electrical charges with which they communicate; and of the books and journals they publish; as well as that of the institutions they are a part of, which of course include the university, library and publishing house. But there are also the financial investments these *mat(t)er-ials* require, the (often non-renewable) energy and resources they use, the infrastructure and labour they involve (that of research and teaching assistants, librarians, technologists, programmers, alt-ac workers etc.), together with their impact on the planet: the rare earth mineral mining, CO_2 emissions, electronic waste and so forth. In fact, for all their arguments about rematerialising research, these new materialists are very much striving 'to create and sustain ... an illusion, or working model, of immateriality' (Hall 2022b, E66; repurposing Kirschenbaum 2021, 10).

. . . . .

None of this should be taken as suggesting that, while it was individual, named, free-standing human authors who produced books in the Gutenberg galaxy, they are now being generated by complex ontological meshworks of humans, animals, technologies and other inorganic elements. Books, we can say, have always been created *relationally* and *processually*: it's just that Western modernity and industrialisation have tended not to recognise this to be the case, privileging seemingly individualistic, fixed and private modes of production and reception instead. With regard to process, for example, artist Eva Weinmayr is just one of those to have noted that the concept of the printed book as an authoritative, fixed and finished text only emerged in the nineteenth century due to the invention of steam-powered rotary presses. The latter, which took over from hand-operated printing presses, operated on an industrial-scale to enable large numbers of copies of a book to be printed quickly, giving the impression of uniformity (i.e., 'that the copy of a book we are reading is identical to all other copies of the same title circulating on the market') (Weinmayr 2020). The book was a far less authoritative and immutable artefact prior to litho-printing turning industrial. There have also been periods in recent printing history that have disrupted the common-sense belief – one that has been sustained since their mass production began – that books are stable and authoritative works. They include the appearance of the photocopier in the late 1960s. These machines allowed individuals to create their own 'new and customized' versions of books, by compiling selected chapters, pages and images (Weinmayr 2020). With the perceived transition out of modernity and the industrialisation of the Gutenberg galaxy, along with the consequent disruption of the human and the humanities associated with the development of new computational, biomedical and robotics technologies, we now have an(other) opportunity to recognise this state of affairs and, as a result, perform books differently. What's more, it's not just books we can perform differently, but all those (liberal humanist) ideas and values we have inherited *with them*.

It is an opportunity we have to constantly strive to be able to take, however.[54] This struggle is made all the harder by the fact that modernist liberal humanism is highly resilient and adaptive. Developments surrounding non-fungible tokens (NFTs) are just one way in which the discourses of modernity have recently endeavoured to continue to privilege individualistic, original and fixed modes of production and reception in the face of the transition to a post-Gutenberg galaxy of non-rivalrous, easily reproducible copies. And this is the case despite the potential NFTs were initially held to have to subvert the traditional art world by cutting out cultural intermediaries such as the galleries and dealers, and handing over the selling and exchange of artworks to decentralised communities of creators. NFTs use a cryptographic protocol of the kind that underpins cryptocurrencies such as Bitcoin and Ethereum to track the ownership of a unique digital asset – say, the original digital file of Chris Torres' Nyan Cat gif or Twitter founder Jack Dorsey's opening tweet – and guarantee its authenticity and scarcity, thus enabling it to be monetised. First posted online in April 2011, an NFT of the original Nyan Cat was sold in February 2021 for around $560,000. Similarly, an NFT of Dorsey's initial tweet was bought for $2.9m at the peak of the non-fungible token market in August 2021, which was then worth a total of $28bn in monthly trading. Yet by the beginning of 2023 one commentator could already write, following the closure of the NFT marketplace on Sam Bankman-Fried's bankrupt crypto-exchange FTX, that 'the most glaring sign of NFTs' dismal future is not their descending value – come July 2023 the NFT of Dorsey's tweet was worth just $4 – but their growing resemblance to the rest of the art market' (Velie 2023). Certainly, by the September of that year 95% of NFT collections were found to be worthless (Hategan n.d.).

The opportunity to perform the ideas and values we have inherited with books differently, to transform them and call forth their afterlife, is what I:ts mean by critical *and* creative posthumanities. It's why I:ts are interested in the figure of the posthuman and discourse of posthumanism (rather than the modern and the liberal).[55] It's also why I:ts would argue that posthumanities cannot be simply opposed to humanities – or digital humanities, for that matter.[56] What *Masked Media* is intent on exploring is how we can operate *differently* with regard to our modes of being in the world as contemporary theorist-mediums. The idea is to push both the humanities and ourselves to the point where we begin to assume responsibility for some of the implications that theories of the posthuman and the nonhuman have for the liberal humanist model of the unified subject, and the associated conceptions of the author, the book and copyright that are all too often adopted unquestioningly by default. In other words, *Masked Media* is looking to experiment with how we can change not only the ways in which we think about the world, but the ways in which we create, document and disseminate our knowledge and ideas, too.

· · · · ·

Let's take a few moments to delve further into how this approach to the future of the humanities is not just somewhat heterodox in relation to that of the majority of digital humanists and posthumanists. It's also potentially different from that of many of those critics who, like *Masked Media*, also draw attention to this obscure, cloaked, 'dark side' of digital research. For 'so-called dark side critiques' – despite constituting some of the most trenchant and oft-referred to critical engagements with certain of DH's masked elements of recent decades – are far from immune to difficulties of this kind. They have something of an antipolitical, moralistic side of their own.[57]

Such moralism is most obviously the case with regard to those who present placing an emphasis on the masked *material* reality that makes the digital possible as an 'indisputable good' (Bruining 2013, 151). In the words of the influential conference on *The Dark Side of the Digital* organised by the University of Wisconsin-Milwaukee's Center for 21st Century Studies – who, when one considers some of the things being revealed now about the energy consumption of LLM AI, were really ahead of the curve in this respect – it's a material reality that includes the 'environmental destruction from disposing the hazardous waste of still functioning but outmoded media devices, or mining for the precious metals that the continued production of these new devices require'.[58] Yet my point about the 'dark side of the "dark side critiques"' also applies to a related aspect of this critique: that which insists the digital must be understood in terms of questions of power, exploitation and social inequality that likewise 'often remain obscure to global media users' (The Dark Side of the Digital 2013).

In keeping with the latter view, new media scholar Richard Grusin draws a connection between the rise of digital humanities and the 'intensification of the economic crisis in the humanities in higher education' (2014, 79).[59] It is no coincidence, to his mind, that digital humanities 'emerged as "the next big thing" at the very same moment in the first decades of the twenty-first century that the neoliberalization and corporatization of higher education has intensified' (2014, 87). In particular, the field's institutional success can be attributed to a 'comparatively prosperous information technology funding climate', and to the perceived ability of digital humanities to 'provide liberal arts majors with digital skills that can be turned into productive jobs', thus helping (unlike the *interpretative* humanities) to train students for careers that currently exist or that will exist in the future (2014, 82, 83).

Digital humanities, for Grusin, are very much a 'manifestation of cutbacks in public funding for higher education'

(2014, 80). In such hard times they are held by those research councils and university administrations responsible for providing resources to be far more relevant to society, industry and the workplace than the traditional humanities, which emphasise 'analyzing literature or developing critiques of culture' (2014, 83, 85). Grusin thus goes along with claims that the contemporary shift to the digital in the humanities, at least since the financial crisis of 2008, 'constitutes a turn away from issues of race, class, gender, and sexuality, an escape from the messiness of the traditional humanities to the safety of scripting, code, or interface design' (Grusin 2014, 81; referring to Koh and Risam 2013).[60] Instead of feminist, queer and other forms of theory, the emphasis within digital humanities is too often on more productive and marketable skills – not least in the search for the external government and commercial funding that is deemed so important by university managers and administrators in an age of 'radical funding cuts in public support for education in Europe, Australia, and the United States', and 'diminished and diminishing funding streams devoted to the humanities' (2014, 80, 81).

Perceived in this light, digital humanities appear as part of a neoliberal assault on the humanities and humanities departments in general, and on literary, critical and cultural theory in particular, precisely because of their shift away from politics and critique. Certainly, this is the view of Allington, Brouillette and Golumbia. As far as they are concerned digital humanities are involved in 'the displacement of politically progressive humanities scholarship and activism in favor of the manufacture of digital tools and archives'; and this is so even if digital humanists design these tools and archives with a view to furthering access and criticism (2016). Much like Grusin, they see this situation coming about because, 'as the burden of paying for university is increasingly shifted to students, and university staffing is increasingly temporary, the acquisition of marketable skills, and the ability to justify those skills as integral to the market-oriented evolution of knowledge and education, becomes all but essential' (2016). For them, the success of digital humanities in the neoliberal university can be explained to a significant degree by the 'designed-in potential to drive social, cultural and political critique from the humanities as a whole'. As such, they present digital humanities as playing a 'leading role in the corporatist restructuring of the humanities' (2016). It's a process some regard as having as its ideological end goal the eventual stripping of the humanities from many universities altogether. (Something of this kind had already started to happen under the Conservatives in the UK. Beginning with the 2021/22 academic year the government reduced by 50% the amount of funding on offer to creative and arts subjects to strategically prioritise funding for STEM [Science, Technology, Engineering and Mathematics], with further cuts being announced as late as April 2024.)

Yet the problem with such critiques of the otherwise masked or dark side of the digital, and of digital humanities, is that, for all their undoubted influence and for all that they continue to be referred to and drawn upon, they themselves have a dark side that remains unexplored and unaccounted for. This is apparent from the way such critiques do not pay sufficient attention to either politics or theory.

Politics

They insist that the digital must be understood in terms of questions of power, exploitation and social inequality, as well as the hidden *material* phenomena that make the digital possible. But this means that what politics is, what it is to be political, is decided *in advance* of intellectual questioning, in fairly obvious (some might say habitual, even clichéd) ways. Witness the emphasis in such critiques: on ideology, identity, class, gender, sexuality, race; on activism; on the environment and planet (and the unequal distribution of negative impacts upon them); on economics (and the market logic of neoliberalism, including low wages and student debt); and on the conditions of labour (bureaucratic control, precarity, fixed-term, part-time, hourly paid and zero-hour contracts).

So Grusin presents digital humanities as being connected to the larger economic crisis in the humanities, which most thinkers on the left, in turn, blame on the 'corporatization of the academy and the neoliberal insistence that the value of higher education must be measured chiefly if not solely in economic terms' (2014, 82). He emphasises 'the way in which the institutional structure of digital humanities threatens to intensify (both within DH itself and among the humanities more broadly) the proliferation of temporary, insecure labor that is rampant not only in the academy but also throughout twenty-first-century capitalism' (82). (It is a proliferation of precarity that may well increase further in a time of global pandemics. Following the outbreak of Covid in 2020 and the need for social distancing and lockdown, many institutions shifted rapidly to making use of remote modes of online teaching and learning, letting large numbers of their part-time and hourly paid staff go in the process.) For Grusin, the neoliberal instrumentalism and stress on managerial and technical expertise he associates with digital humanities – especially the 'distinction between making things and doing more traditional scholarly work' of the kind associated with theory and critique – 'reproduces within the academy ... the precaritization of labor that marks the dark side of information capitalism in the twenty-first century' (2014, 87).[61]

It is a similar 'antipolitical moralism' (in Brown's sense of the term) that enables Allington, Brouillette and Golumbia to position digital humanities as standing in opposition not so much to the close reading of the traditional humanities, but *'the insistence that academic work should be critical,* and that there is, after all, no work and no way to be in the world that is not political' (2016). From this perspective, they align the anti-interpretative tendency of digital humanities with what they depict as 'a variety of other postcritical methodologies, such as versions of Speculative Realism and Object-Oriented Ontology, and the explicitly "postcritical" literary theory advocated by scholars such as University of Virginia English Professor Rita Felski, which tend to challenge, avoid, or disavow scholarly endeavor that is overtly critical of existing social relations' (2016). Yet are all these postcritical methodologies – including those of digital humanities – really endeavouring *not* to be political? Is this the case always and everywhere, in every situation and circumstance? Or is it possible that at least some of them *are political* in a manner that may indeed be involved in *challenging* preconceived ideas of what it is to be political, which means they are not so easy to recognise as such when viewed through an anti-political, moralistic lens? Even if, after careful intellectual examination of specific cases, the conclusion reached is that these methodologies are not to be considered either overtly or covertly political (at least not in any interesting or progressive fashion), the fact remains that what politics is, what it is to be political here, is not being opened up to rigorous inquiry, either by Allington, Brouillette and Golumbia, or, indeed, by Grusin. It is rather excluded from their critiques of the digital and digital humanities as a result of having been decided in advance.[62]

Theory

Such arguments position digital humanities as part of a neoliberal attack on the humanities in general, and theory in particular, because of their perceived shift away from social, cultural and political critique. Despite the importance that is attached to supporting 'socially engaged literary study', '"French literary theory"', and 'queer and feminist theory', however, critiques of this nature can themselves be said to represent a shift away from politically engaged literary, critical and cultural theory (Grusin 2014, 81). For theory, not least in the shape of the writings of Jacques Derrida, Jean-François Lyotard, Jean-Luc Nancy, Judith Butler, Chantal Mouffe, Wendy Brown and Alberto Moreiras, is one of the main places in society where our premises and assumptions regarding what politics is and what it is to be political *are* subject to rigorous intellectual questioning and critique.

Let's highlight perhaps the most obviously *political* of these theorists. According to Mouffe's philosophy of hegemony and antagonism – which over the years has been an acknowledged influence on numerous political movements and parties, including Podemos and Más Madrid in Spain and Syriza in Greece – the political is a decision that is always 'taken in an undecidable terrain'. This is because, for her, social relations are not fixed or natural, the result of objective and immutable economic or historical processes and practices (Mouffe 2000, 130). They are the product of continual, precarious, hegemonic, politico-economic articulations: that is, of contingent, pragmatic yet temporary decisions involving power, conflict and violence. In fact, Mouffe distinguishes between:

> 'the political' – referring to the dimension of antagonism, inherent to human societies – and 'politics' – or the ensemble of practices and institutions that attempt to establish an order, to organise human coexistence in the context of the conflicts generated by 'the political'. What the distinction highlights is, firstly, that the political cannot be reduced to a given place in society, and is not limited to specific institutions, but is, rather, itself a constitutive dimension of social order. And, secondly, that such order is the result of power relations and always contingent, given that it is riddled with antagonism. (Mouffe, in Errejón and Mouffe 2016, 38)

As far as Mouffe is concerned, what this means is that a perfectly harmonious and non-conflictual society without relations of force and violence can never be achieved: that 'instead of creating the conditions for a reconciled society', the consensual approach of liberalism, which holds 'rational agreement can be reached in politics ... leads to the emergence of antagonisms'. Interestingly, for a neo-Marxist political theorist, what it also means is that the 'emancipatory ideal cannot be formulated in terms of a realization of any form of "communism"' either (Mouffe 2005, 3-4; 2013, xi). This social situation does bring with it, though, the advantage that there is the potential for these articulations to be disarticulated, transformed and rearticulated as a result of struggle between the agonistic adversaries and a new configuration of hegemony established.

What is so important about Mouffe's theory of politics and the political for the argument being made here? Quite simply, it's the manner in which it shows that criticising the digital and digital humanities, and defending social, cultural and political critique, on the basis of a politics that is decided *in advance*, is clearly *not* to take a decision in an undecidable terrain. Such critiques of the obfuscated, masked, dark side of the digital and of digital humanities can themselves be regarded as constituting an avoidance or disavowal of literary, critical and cultural theory: this is because they do not subject to rigorous intellectual critique the very question of politics and the political that theory helps to keep open-ended. As a result, these dark side critiques are themselves neither particularly political, nor theoretical, nor indeed critical.

What is needed is to invent ways of working and thinking as theorists that (to continue with Mouffe's conceptual language) *are* capable of taking contingent, pragmatic, yet temporary decisions regarding the digital and digital humanities *in an undecidable terrain*. Equally as important is the need to do so with respect to the humanities, humanism and the human – all the while taking care not to remain oblivious to the otherwise masked material reality that makes socially, culturally and politically engaged theory and criticism possible. The latter is an aspect of research that is all too often left in the dark by critiques of the digital. It is for this reason that I might describe what I and a range of collaborators (including some collectives) are doing with the research projects with which we are involved, as affirmatively disrupting the humanities to create spaces for the invention of radically different – though not dialectically opposed – *posthumanities* systems for the creation, circulation and ownership of theory. So it is *posthumanities* as in the posthuman and posthumanism, but also as in posthuman posthumanities.

Chapter 4

Liberalism Must Be Defeated

Turning rebellion into money.
– *The Clash*

More than ever, the point of the writer is to be unpopular.
– *Arundhati Roy*

People know what they do; frequently they know why they do what they do; but what they don't know is what what they do does.
– *Michel Foucault*

What forms might contemporary theory take if in its performance it is to be neither neoliberal nor liberal but something else besides? Answering the second element of this question, that concerning liberalism, is particularly difficult. Part of the task of the 'rising 21st century professoriate' (*rtc*, 67) is to invent new modes of working that are more appropriate to dealing with the dynamic logics of any emergent post-Gutenberg universe, so the future of knowledge production is not dominated by the likes of Elsevier, Amazon and OpenAI (nor indeed Facebook and Google, owners of WhatsApp and Instagram, YouTube and Bard, respectively). Yet there's no easy means to avoid adhering to liberal humanist ways of being as writers and researchers, no matter how ontologically relational and co-constitutive the content of our theory may be. One reason for this is the strong link that exists between our copyright laws and the production of liberal humanist subjectivity and agency. This link means there are few if any non-liberal and nonhumanist alternatives to publishing and sharing our work on a copyright all-rights-reserved basis that are legally and professionally recognised.

To a large degree the lack of alternatives can be traced to the fact that, although the UK, US and Europe all have different requirements for copyrightability, in each copyright is dependent on the figure of the singular human author (or its corporate stand-in). Kaja Marczewska, another one-time collaborator, highlights this dependency in her book, *This Is Not a Copy*. She summarises the complexities of the situation as follows:

> Under the US Copyright Act, originality and fixation are the only two requirements for copyrightability; in France, the notion of originality is often linked to authorial expression and works are proclaimed original if they bear marks of author's personality; in British law, every work is considered original if it is not a copy; on the international scale, the World Intellectual Property Organization (WIPO) Berne Convention does not define originality at all.
>
> What is clear, however, is the inherent correlation that copyright draws between the figure of the author and work's originality. Characteristically, the assignation of the status of the original work of art relies on and is subject to authorial contribution. The legal notion of originality resides in legal preoccupations with the author as the origin of the work. It is the possibility of an unambiguous assignation of authorship rather than qualities of creativity and novelty that underpin the legal understanding of an original

work. ... Such thinking as the key doctrinal features of copyright today still resides in and continues being shaped by Romantic aesthetics, influenced by the Lockean model of property and late eighteenth-century theories of personhood that gave rise to the figure of the author as a unique, inspired, individual genius, creating in vacuum. ... It is the inherent reliance on the singularity and uniqueness of authorship as manifested in the legal anxiety of influence that remains key in determining the conceptual framework of copyright's approach to artistic practice. (Marczewska 2018, 20)

Marczewska thus shows how copyright has a clear predisposition toward works that can be unequivocally assigned to a unique human individual. These are the expressions of authorship that fit with the law's conception of those 'distinct art forms that it recognizes and protects' (2018, 21).

When it is argued that our property laws need to adapt if they are to be fit for purpose in the twenty-first century, often it is Creative Commons (CC) that is put forward as the example to be followed. Yet Creative Commons does not provide a solution to the problem of copyright's dependency on the figure of the singular author any more than an 'all-rights-reserved' licence, since CC likewise has its basis in the notion of the proprietorial human individual. Generally, commons can be understood as shared, non-proprietary spaces and resources, along with the collective social processes that are necessary for commoners to produce, manage and maintain them and themselves as a community. Rather than endorsing a collective agreement or philosophy, however, Creative Commons provides a range of licences from which individual creators (or the communities that stand in for them) can freely choose, and which can then be applied to goods such as books seen as ontologically distinct from humans. These extend from the Attribution-NonCommercial-NoDerivatives licence (or 'BY-NC-ND'), which is the most restrictive of the Creative Commons licences, to the least restrictive Attribution licence (or 'CC BY), and even takes in the public domain CC0 tool by which a creator can waive or abandon all rights.

Nor does refusing to attach a copyright claim to a work resolve the problem. If we do that, then in most countries copyright is claimed automatically by default. Elsewhere I have shown how, from this standpoint, our current copyright laws have a twofold function: first, they protect the author's economic and moral rights; second, they participate in creating and shaping the author as a sovereign, liberal, human subject (Hall 2021a). (Indeed, for George Orwell, the writer is by definition liberal [1940].)[63] A third function can now be added to this list: that of making it difficult for the author to adopt other forms – forms, for instance, that *are* capable of acknowledging and *assuming* (rather than ignoring or repressing) the implications of texts coming into being through the various multiple and messy interrelations of an extended assemblage of both humans and nonhumans (to persist with the heuristic they can be distinguished in this fashion).[64]

・・・・・

Do the restrictions imposed on us by our laws of copyright and intellectual property go some way toward explaining why the majority of radical researchers today continue to work in a surprisingly conservative manner? Even those who are well-known for engaging with new forms of subjectivity and social relations, such as those associated with the horizontalist, decentralised, self-organising mobilisations of the Occupy, *Indignados*, Dakota Standing Rock Sioux, *gilets jaunes*, Extinction Rebellion, Black Lives Matter chapters and pro-democracy Hong Kong protests, are no exception. I'm thinking of some of the most interesting and influential political theorists of recent decades: Alain Badiou, Judith Butler, Jodi Dean, Chantal Mouffe, Slavoj Žižek, Michael

Hardt and Antonio Negri, Nick Srnicek and Alex Williams, David Graeber. Texts such as Mouffe's *Towards A Green Democratic Revolution* (2022) and Graeber's *Pirate Enlightenment* (2023) are written *as if* they are the absolutely authentic creative expressions of the minds of sovereign individuals who live and think in isolation from all others, and who are quite entitled to claim the moral and legal right to be identified as their singular *human* authors. They are then made available on this basis for economic exploitation by a reputable publisher as commodities, in the form of materially conventional books that can be bought and sold according to a system of property exchange that is governed by the logic of late capitalism and its individualistic, competitive ethos. It's a situation that ensures ideas, concepts, indeed whole philosophies and worldviews, continue to be attributed to these high profile and well-resourced theorists as *theirs*: as part of their intellectual capital, trademark and position in the international division of (academic) labour.

It's almost unfair to single anyone out: it's about a system rather than individuals; a way of being-in and being-with the world for which, as I say, there are few if any non-liberal and nonhumanist alternatives that are legally and professionally recognised. But to provide another brief analysis by way of illustration: when it comes to their relationship to such self-organising mobilisations, can't Hardt and Negri be said to reproduce with their book *Assembly* much the same behaviour they criticise platform capitalist companies for engaging in with regard to the social relations of their users?[65] Like these companies, Hardt and Negri extract intelligence from the common. In their case they extract it from the leaderless social movements that have risen up in recent decades, and the potential of these movements 'to take power differently' and 'crucially, to produce new subjectivities' (2017, xiii-xiv). Like platform capitalist companies, Hardt and Negri accumulate this intelligence that is 'constructed in social cooperation' (xviii), transform it into private property and control access to it. They do so by publishing *Assembly* with the non-profit Oxford University Press (OUP) using a restrictive all-rights-reserved copyright licence. (OUP is the largest and wealthiest university press in the world. It's a non-profit in that its profits go not to shareholders but to the University of Oxford, which for August 2018 – July 2019, the year following the 2017 publication of *Assembly*, had a total income of £2.45bn.) OUP then make it available, but only at a cost. It is a cost that renders the book and the knowledges it contains inaccessible to many of those involved in such 'inspiring social movements', especially in the Global South, further marginalising them from debates about how to 'create a new, more democratic and just society', and impeding *Assembly* from assisting with the construction of the common (xiii). The paradoxical – or, perhaps better, contradictory – situation thus arises whereby Hardt and Negri make their argument for a radical politics capable of bringing about 'a lasting social transformation' and of organising the production of subjectivity necessary for doing so, in a highly conservative, commodified and capitalist fashion (xiii). When it comes to their own ways of being, their political imaginations appear to have been taken over by global neoliberalism and its epistemic colonialism. (Curiously, they don't even do what a lot of others have done, and try to 'reappropriate the common from capital' [xx] by making use of any of the open and commons-oriented alternatives to publishing on an 'all-rights-reserved' basis with the likes of OUP that are available to them.) A double negation or masking is in operation here. First, problems relating to authorship, creativity, sovereignty, finance, commodification, competition, copyright, symbolic capital and so forth are excluded as irrelevant when it comes to Hardt and Negri's own manner of working and of sharing knowledge, wealth and resources. As we'll see shortly, for them to take on board these potentially transformative issues – issues that, as they emphasise, concern the production and reproduction not just of 'commodities but social relations and ultimately society itself' – would be perceived as a rather strange and eccentric thing to do (xv). (There is no 'questioning some of [Hardt and Negri's] basic political assumptions', then [xiii].) Second, the power they have to perform both the initial commercial extractivism and the above exclusion is also negated and denied.

The situation is not helped by the fact that, when radical thinkers do turn their attention to how scholars operate nowadays, their concern – as we saw in the previous chapter with the example of the 'dark side' critics – is predominantly with the digital neoliberal subjects we are supposedly transitioning into with the help of new era information technologies: capitalist platforms, social media, data analytics, predictive products, network sensors, AI deep-learning, synthetic media and so on. They are not quite so concerned about the particular configurations of subjectivity (and the related information technologies: i.e., commercially copyrighted, printed-paper codex books and journal articles) we are changing *from*. Yet it is of fundamental importance to pay close critical attention to the latter, too, because, in practice, this subjectivity has typically been *liberal humanist*. When it comes to the actual creation, publication and communication of research especially, this form of subjectivity has occupied a position of hegemonic dominance within the profession. In many respects, it still does. Being the constitutive discourse of the West, liberal humanism is built into the very system of the university. As past President of the Modern Language Association Christopher Newfield explains with regard to higher education in the US, 'a consensus version of university humanism has long consisted of "five interwoven concepts: the free self, experiential knowledge, self-development, autonomous agency, and enjoyment."' What's more, 'university philosophers and administrators did not simply espouse these concepts as ideals, but institutionalised them' (Newfield 2016, 329; quoting Newfield 2003, 56).[66]

· · · · ·

Liberalism is of course concerned with the human individual's right to life, liberty and property, together with the political conditions and institutions that secure these rights (e.g., constitutional government and the democratic rule of law under which all legal subjects are supposed to have an equal status, irrespective of other differences and inequalities). What's really being condemned in many accounts of the corporatisation of the academy, then, is the manner in which a version of liberalism is being intensified and transformed into another, specifically neoliberal interpretation of which, among those rights, are deemed to be most important: the unassailable rights of property and the extension of the values of the free-market economy and its metrics to all areas of life. Coupled to the latter interpretation is an emphasis on the centrality of the individual (there was famously 'no such thing as society' for Margaret Thatcher); on competition (complete with systems of rankings and ratings to separate winners from losers, strivers from shirkers); on privatisation (of the public realm by for-profit businesses, for example; indeed, on the 'dominance of public life by the global corporation');[67] on the value of finance, insurance and real estate (FIRE); on lower regulation and taxation of the rich and private interests; on a weakening of the power of the trade unions; and on a reduction to a minimum of the role played by the public sector and welfare, not least with regard to health, education, employment, food and housing. Contrary to what many accounts of this political rationality would have us believe, though, neoliberalism is not necessarily concerned with deregulation and the reduction of the role played by the liberal democratic state in order to allow markets to regulate themselves. As a philosophy and policy agenda the so-called neoliberal revolution of the 1970s and 1980s was about the use of government intervention and regulation in the interests of capital and the free market. The success of the state today is often determined by its ability to support the market, if not achieve unlimited economic growth. Consider how many governments were forced to borrow vast amounts to pay off the debts created by the banks and financial capital and keep the global economy functioning after the crisis of 2008-2009. Think, too, of the countless companies that continue to rely on the state to top-up the wages of their employees (i.e., 'the working poor') with benefits, wages having been driven down by the breaking-up of unions; of the way in which the British state helped to sustain businesses during the period of the 2020/2021 coronavirus outbreak and lockdown; and of how lower regulation and taxation, and the rising cost of food and energy, along with an ability to exploit labour, has meant the richest 1% have been able to secure almost as much new wealth since the start of the pandemic as the rest of the world put together (Christensen *et al.* 2023).

Yet the focus of critical attention is routinely placed on the process of change, and especially on what we are changing *to*: that is capitalist entrepreneurs, including entrepreneurs of our own selves and lives, who are prepared to cope with the risks of our involvement in higher education on an individual – rather than a social, collective or, indeed, radically relational – basis. If a particular job or set of opportunities is not available to us it's presented as *our* fault. It's because we haven't published enough, or networked widely enough, or simply striven hard enough. Since 2009 salaries for academics in the UK have decreased almost 20%, with a third already on fixed term contracts, this figure rising to 'almost half for teaching-only academics (44%) and over two thirds (68%) for research only staff' (UCU n.d.). Due to the pay and working conditions, 60% say they are looking to leave the sector in the next five years (UCU 2022). How long before more of us are encouraged by the nature of the demands placed on academics in the uberfied university to decamp from the traditional systems of higher education teaching and publishing to set up as our own, precarious, solo media brands using software tools like Substack? The latter enables writers to build an audience of subscribers to a free or paid-for newsletter. One can imagine scholars soon being placed in a position where they have to conform to the cult of (authentic) personality by curating their whole world using photographs, videos, podcasts, interviews and Q&As along with access to opportunities for chats, tutorials and mentoring, much as many creatives are doing already through membership platforms such as Patreon. And that's for those who can generate sufficient brand recognition to make this a feasible option: if, say, you're one of the secret, specially selected 'Pro' group to whom Substack has been prepared to give large amounts of money to write a newsletter for its platform. Some fortunate authors have admitted to receiving one-off payments of as much as $250,000 (Kafka 2021).[68] For the rest the future is likely to take the form of microworking: being paid small amounts to carry out short-term tasks they bid for on online platforms, and that can't yet be performed by large language model AI. (In the UK, the number of people who once a week or more took on jobs they'd discovered via the platform economy increased from 5.8% of the working population in 2016 to 14.7% in 2021.That's somewhere in the region of 4.4 million people [TUC 2021, 9].)

Rather less critical attention in scholarly analyses of this kind is devoted to what we are changing *from*. What is a predominantly liberal humanist mode of academic personhood is thus, in effect, positioned by default as some kind of solution, or at least preferable alternative, to the shift toward the constantly self-governing, self-disciplining, self-exploitative subject of neoliberalism. It's an attitude on the part of internet researchers that's encapsulated by a remark of Shoshana

Zuboff's on surveillance capitalism: 'Once I was mine. Now I am theirs' (Naughton and Zuboff 2019, 21).[69]

To put it in different words, a form of liberal humanism, along with the attendant concepts of the self-identical autonomous subject, the individual proprietorial author, originality and copyright, acts as something of a datum point in much established theory and research. Just as liberals regard liberalism as the only system of government that is true and valid for everyone, independent of historico-cultural context (i.e., that which would be universally accepted by all reasonable persons if they had the freedom to choose), so the writing of peer-reviewed, sequentially ordered, bound and printed-paper codex books and journal articles is a professional practice that is held as transcending the period and place in which it is employed – which means continuity and stability in these matters tend to be valued more highly than transformation, let alone revolution. It's a manner of operating that is taken-for-granted as fixed and enduring (although the activities and concepts it involves are continually being renegotiated over time); one that constitutes a preprogrammed mode of performance many academics adopt more or less passively in order to construct theoretical frameworks and draw conclusions.

Hence the lack of care shown by even the most politically radical of thinkers for the materiality (not to mention collectivity and relationality) of their own social practices, their own ways of working and knowing, and of the exploitation of labour and resources involved. It's a refusal to take a political decision (i.e., a decision made in an undecidable terrain) that extends to the kind of commercial copyright licences and arrangements that are used to publish, market and sell their texts. New, highly-specialised knowledge and research is often intended initially for just a relative few people to read: not an ideal situation for creating a large demand for it, let alone one that can be used to generate a financial profit. If it took centuries for scholarly journals to be developed after Gutenberg, this is the reason. It's also why they had to be supported and subsidised on a non-profit basis by learned societies and universities. In fact, far from it being a long-standing convention, Leslie Chan *et al.* show the 'idea that journals should be owned by for-profit publishers', as opposed to non-profit, and made available accordingly on a closed rather than on an open basis, is actually relatively new (Chan *et al.* 2020, 4). 'Between 1852 and 1908, academic journals were regulated by default by open licences. This did not stop researchers from making and disseminating countless discoveries. Generally, academic journals were associated with disciplinary associations and published on a non-profit basis' (2020, 4). (As with so much of the modern Euro-Western university – in England especially – this state of affairs has its origins in a model that stretches back to the nineteenth century and beyond. In this model it is independently wealthy people – usually upper-class gentlemen-cum-amateur-scholars – who participate in research because they have sufficient time, education and resources to be able to do so out of interest rather than a professional concern with anything as vulgar as making money.)

Only in the 1960s did this situation begin to change, with large commercial publishing houses, having developed ways of participating in academic publishing for financial gain, not least through the use of closed copyright licences, steadily coming to purchase more and more of these journals. The degree to which such for-profit presses were able to secure ownership and control of the scholarly communications ecosystem accelerated with the advent of the electronic age as journals were acquired and digitised in ever larger numbers. By the mid-1990s commercial publishers were responsible for 40% of academic output in the US, with approximately a fifth of all papers in the UK being published by Elsevier (Smits and Pells 2022, 32). In the process the model shifted from research libraries actually owning physical copies to merely licencing electronic access to their content. Nowadays this is often in the form of 'big deal', multi-year contract bundling strategies that lock institutions into purchasing large publisher-created packages of journals, whether they want all of them or not. That the writing and publishing of theory is a professional mode of performance in which continuity and stability are valued more highly than transformation is further evident from the way in which, when theorists *do* try to act differently, the changes they devise – such as making their papercentric books and journal articles openly and freely available online using a Creative Commons licence – while addressing some issues and concerns, tend not to present much of a challenge to the status quo.

• • • • •

The argument being set out here is very different to that of many neoliberals, who are inclined to portray those who struggle against their modernising project, liberals included, as reactionary and conservative. It's a discursive strategy that has frequently been applied to the Labour Party and those on the left in the UK. The Silicon Valley version is to characterise the opponents of Big Tech as suffering from nostalgia and technophobia. But if *Masked Media*'s argument is different from the technocratic neoliberalism of Emmanuel Macron and Keir Starmer, which depends on a rule of law-based system of economic governance, and so looks to reach an agreement with the administrative state, it's also different from the nationalistic libertarian neoliberalism associated with the age of Donald Trump, Elon Musk and Boris Johnson (aspects of which Starmer has, surprisingly, begun to adopt). That seeks to dismantle much of the rules-based system by which democracy and the state keep a check on capitalism and the freedom of the human individual to act economically in order to generate new, disruptive business opportunities.

The latter are only possible because many of the old political institutions will have been done away with, along with their accumulated rules and regulations, knowledge and norms (the maintenance of standards in public life, the fairness of the electoral process, the peaceful transfer of political power etc.). Hence Johnson's willingness to break lockdown rules and international agreements; ignore independent oversight; unlawfully prorogue parliament at the height of the Brexit crisis; 'reform' the Electoral Commission; change the ministerial code so ministers who contravene it don't always have to resign; and rewrite the rules on parliamentary conduct. It's not surprising that the more professional-managerial technocratic neoliberals should find the nationalistic libertarian variant so shocking. For Johnson, by contrast, the food, fuel and labour shortages produced by Brexit could be considered merely as a temporary 'period of adjustment' the country needed to go through to end the 'broken model' of the UK economy that relied on immigration, foreign capital and, with them, 'low wages and low skill and chronic low productivity' (Johnson 2021). The idea was to replace it with a new model based on high skill, high productivity and high-wage job creation, and possibly high-tax and high-spend to go with it.

It also needs to be said that, even though they have a lot in common – to the extent neoliberalism can be understood as a *variant* of liberalism, both sharing a belief in individual human rights and personal freedoms – neoliberalism and liberalism are *not* the same. Liberalism is four centuries old now, with a history of canonical thinkers that takes in Benjamin Constant, Jean-Jacques Rousseau and Immanuel Kant through to Isaiah Berlin, John Rawls and beyond. It is thus a philosophy of many different strands and nuances, some of which have on occasion provided a means of resisting neoliberalism. The historian Duncan Bell sums up the complexity of the situation in his account of how liberalism has been variously understood as a category of political analysis. He observes that: 'Self-declared liberals have supported extensive welfare states and their abolition; the imperial civilising mission and its passionate denunciation; the necessity of social justice and its outright rejection; the perpetuation of the sovereign state and its transcendence; massive global redistribution of wealth and the radical inequalities of the existing order' (2014, 683). We could endeavour to simplify things somewhat by following Colin Crouch, who presents the liberal political tradition as being divided historically into two main parts: the social and the economic. Social liberalism focused on the search for freedoms and rights, and often looked precisely to the state for help with that. Economic liberalism emphasised the 'liberties of property-ownership and market transactions' (2011, 4); liberties that, in classical liberalism, need to be protected from state intervention (e.g., in the form of laws, regulations or taxes).

The standard narrative developed in this context is that the Great Depression of the 1920s and 1930s signalled to many that the classical liberal idea of running capitalist economies with minimal interference from government had failed. After World War II, a policy of diverse economic and social interventions into a capitalist economy by a democratic state therefore drew approval from practically all sides of the political mainstream in Western Europe and North America as well as Japan, India and Australasia. The idea was to integrate government power with market forces to create an economy that maximised efficiency while avoiding major surprises, pursuing some social goals otherwise difficult to achieve by means of the market alone, while limiting the injustices and inequalities the latter produces. Indeed, Crouch comments that by the 'third quarter of the twentieth century one could contain most of the political spectrum, at least of west European countries, within the terrain' of the 'large comprise ground between a pure market and a primarily state-owned economy' (2011, 5, 9). It was then economic liberalism's push-back against the interventionist government of social democratic liberalism that led to the development, over roughly the same period, of neoliberalism, with its philosophy of using the state in the interests of capital and the free market. More recently, neoliberalism has been presented as having gone too far in turn. Here the need to protect the financial sector from regulation by the state is held as having led to the crash of 2008 and the elections of Trump and Johnson as a reaction to the widening gap between rich and poor. It is this argument that political economist Francis Fukuyama makes in his defence of classical liberalism. For Fukuyama, those who criticise liberalism today on the populist right and progressive left do so not 'because of a fundamental weakness in the doctrine', but because of the way it has evolved into neoliberalism which, for many, is bound up with the excessive inequalities generated by capitalism (2022, ix).

Yet Chantal Mouffe – to continue to draw on some of the more stimulating of contemporary attempts to answer the question, 'What is liberalism?' – also identifies two main paradigms of liberal political thought, and they are rather different to those of Crouch. The first of Mouffe's two paradigm's is the 'aggregative', a model she sees as having been initiated by Joseph Schumpeter's *Capitalism, Socialism, Democracy* of 1947, and as having become standard in empirical political theory. Politics is presented by the aggregative paradigm as the 'establishment of a compromise between differing competing forces in society' (Mouffe 2005, 12). In essence, it is 'the idea of the market applied to the domain of politics which is apprehended with concepts borrowed from economics' (13). Individuals are presented as 'rational beings, driven by the maximization of their own interests', rather than by the moral idea that they should do what is best for the community. Accordingly, they act 'in the political world in a basically instrumental way' (13). The emphasis is on 'aggregation of preferences, taking place through political parties for which people ... have the capacity to vote at regular intervals' (Mouffe 2000, 81).

The second of Mouffe's liberal paradigms – developed as a reaction to the aggregative – is the 'deliberative'. Here the contention is that it is 'possible to create in the realm of politics a rational moral consensus' based on universal principles by means of impartial discussion among citizens who are not only free and equal but reasonable (Mouffe 2005, 13). This exchange of arguments and counterarguments in a non-exclusive public sphere of deliberation is how agreement over political decisions that are in the interests of all – the 'common good' – should be arrived at in a liberal democracy. It is also the source of the legitimacy of their outcomes. To provide an example, rather than seeing racism as the result of economic or structural factors, anti-racist liberals use rational argumentation and education – EDI (Equality, Diversity, Inclusivity) training and so forth – to try to convince others of the lack of a moral justification for racist views. Communicative rationality thus takes the place of the instrumental rationality of the aggregative model.

The deliberative paradigm and its reclamation of the moral over the economic dimension of politics itself has two main schools of thought. One is influenced by the political philosopher John Rawls, who, when it comes to the twin logics that make up liberal democracy, supports liberalism's emphasis on individual liberty and human rights. The other is influenced by the Marxist Frankfurt School critical theorist Jürgen Habermas, who privileges democratic self-government and its emphasis on equality and the sovereignty of the people (Mouffe 2000, 8, 92-93). For Mouffe, however, the paradox of modern liberal democracy is that these two logics – that of the liberal and the democratic – are ultimately irreconcilable. 'Liberal-democratic politics consists, in fact, in the constant process of negotiation and renegotiation – through different hegemonic articulations – of this constitutive paradox' (2000, 45). We should therefore give up on the idea that it is possible to achieve a 'final rational solution' or even a '"rational" political consensus' free from conflict and antagonism by means of deliberative democracy (2000, 32, 93).

Attempts to pin liberalism down are complicated further by the fact that, in Europe, 'liberal' is applied to centre-right parties suspicious of socialism; while in the US 'liberal' refers to the political left-of-centre and those who support the welfare state and other intrusions by democratic government into the workings of the capitalist market economy. The latter usage is contrary to the meaning attached to the word 'liberal' most commonly over the course of its history. That the term 'liberal societies' is, as the historian Timothy Garton Ash remarks, used to describe 'what distinguishes liberal democracies, starting with those at the heart of the modern transatlantic west, from totalitarian regimes such as Nazi Germany and the Soviet Union, and the authoritarian regimes all the way up to Xi Jinping's China and Vladimir Putin's Russia', needs to be considered, too (2020, 19).

· · · · ·

Nor is neoliberalism as a philosophy unified and self-identical, the perfect projection of a political desire. There are many different versions of neoliberalism as well, all with different arrays of policies. In *The Birth of Biopolitics* (2008), Foucault distinguishes between German neoliberalism (the German ordoliberals, named after the journal *Ordo* in which they principally published), European neoliberalism (particularly that implemented in France), and American neoliberalism, where what he describes as the anarcho-liberalism of the Chicago School (Milton Friedman, Friedrich von Hayek *et al.*) can itself be differentiated from Reagonomics. As already indicated, we can add to Foucault's list the libertarian neoliberalism of Trumpism in the US and the post-2016 Tories in the UK (what has also been termed 'authoritarian entrepreneurialism', despite libertarianism being somewhat at odds with authoritarianism, strictly speaking). In almost the reverse of the situation with New Labour under Tony Blair and the Conservatives under David Cameron, both of which were economically neoliberal but socially liberal, many libertarian neoliberal governments have combined right-wing, socially conservative cultural polices (on crime, border control, the forcible repelling of immigrants, the imprisoning of peaceful protestors, voter suppression) with left-wing economic ideas such as nationalisation and welfarism. It is something that was increasingly apparent with respect to Boris Johnson's government (in their plans for public spending on railways, bridges and tunnels and in seeking net zero carbon emissions), even before the coronavirus pandemic made it difficult to avoid state intervention, such as then Chancellor of the Exchequer Rishi Sunak's initial £500bn bailout for workers on PAYE (pay-as-you-earn tax) in 2020, or his spending £849m in a single month of the same year on his 'eat out to help out' scheme. Of course, these interventions were designed to help society and the economy return as quickly as possible to the 'old normal' of consuming, commuting and dining in restaurants (to the point of being willing to put public safety at risk, given the latter scheme may have resulted in many further clusters of infections), rather than produce the kind of longer-term systemic transformation that might lead to a more sustainable 'new normal' that includes a generous system of welfare. Hence the more Thatcherite Sunak's subsequent reversion to small-state neoliberal type, as signalled by his dropping of the northern part of the HS2 high-speed railway, and refusal to make much money available for funding the Johnson government's 'levelling up' plans for investing in infrastructure in neglected areas of the country. It was also a small state, low tax (for those in the highest tax bracket) neo-Thatcherite philosophy that was championed by Johnson's immediate successor as prime minister, Liz Truss in 2022 (the short-lived plan to spend £150bn on freezing electricity and gas bills for two years to deal with the energy crisis notwithstanding). Besides, neoliberalism of whatever variety seldom occurs in a pure guise, certainly not at the level of practical politics. Compromises with other political values and ideological interests, including non-liberal ones, usually have to be made, in liberal-representative democracies especially.

Even within its own terms, any one self-understanding of neoliberalism is hardly freer from ambiguity, contradiction and incoherence than capitalism itself. And that's without delving into the many different interpretations of late-stage capitalism that are available: biocapitalism, racial capitalism, heteropatriarchal capitalism, platform capitalism, computational capitalism, communicative capitalism, cognitive capitalism, data capitalism, surveillance capitalism, coronavirus capitalism, extractive capitalism. It would therefore be more accurate to say that the manner in which most contemporary theorists act as authors and scholars today is not so much liberal or neoliberal, but hybrid. Although different in exact composition in each singular case, such performances are a contingent assemblage, generated at the very least from those two comingled sets of agential practices involving humans, technologies, objects, spaces, places, laws, norms, habits and so on that I have classified, all too crudely perhaps, as liberal and neoliberal. The relation between these authorial repertoires is not a fixed and static one, either. It is a provisional, messy, transformative process in which today the neoliberal is often striving to achieve dominance over the liberal.

All the same, within that, it can be argued that the failure to denaturalise and destabilise what, for the sake of economy, I have referred to as the liberal humanist model of subjectivity – to confront and rigorously think through liberal concepts of human rights, freedom and property as they apply to us as theorists and researchers (although we understand philosophically that theory's questioning of liberal thought must involve questioning these concepts too) – is one of the reasons it has been relatively easy for the commodifying, measuring, monitoring logic of *neo*liberalism to reinterpret our ways of working-thinking as well. After all, neoliberalism does not stand in direct opposition to liberalism and its guiding doctrine of possessive individualism; it is a version of it, as its name, *neo* or *new liberalism*, suggests. (Foucault refers to a text written by the Marquis d'Argenson that recalls 'what the merchant Le Gendre said to Colbert – when Colbert asked him: "what can I do for you?" Le Gendre replied: "What can you do for us? Leave us alone [*Laissez-nous faire*]."' *Laissez faire* [leave alone] is of course closely associated with neoliberal free market politics, of the Reagan and Thatcher period especially. Yet Foucault associates it here with liberalism more generally – 'a new art of government that began to be formulated, reflected upon, and outlined around the middle of the eighteenth century' [2008, 27]. He proceeds by asking: 'What is this new type of rationality in the art of government, this new type of calculation that consists in saying and telling government: I accept, wish, plan, and calculate that all this should be left alone?'. Foucault's answer: 'I think that this is broadly what is called "liberalism"' [2008, 20].)[70] Given that the wider historical tradition of liberalism has provided the discursive framework of modern capitalism, it is important to recognise neoliberal logic is not necessarily always going against the liberal rights and values that many of us, even on the left, continue to conform to in practice.[71] (Much of the time when we make a determined effort to elude late stage capitalism's processes of subjectivation – by increasing our digital literacy and ability to code, for instance, so we can think sceptically about the internet rather than allowing our behaviour to be nudged by the dopamine-inducing algorithms of Netflix, Spotify *et al.* – we do so by acting as if we are autonomous, reasoning, liberal subjects skilled in critical detachment and reflection.) Rather, under this logic aspects of our liberal ways of working-thinking have been intensified and transformed into another, specifically neoliberal interpretation of what, among those rights and values, are deemed most significant.

▪ ▪ ▪ ▪ ▪

It is worth quickly pointing out that the liberalism inherent in so much of our practice is not the only reason for the failure of the left to date to bring about the kind of mainstream political change the right has been able to achieve. Neoliberals mobilise powerful forces against those who try to change the existing structures fundamentally. They do so not least by depicting them as proposing an alternative that is 'radical', 'extreme' or 'eccentric' at best: that is not 'realistic', in other words, realistic here being something that closely resembles what the mainstream is already providing in terms of the distribution of wealth and power, only with minor changes perhaps. The experience of Syriza in Greece, the Scottish Referendum of 2014, and the more recent Black Lives Matter, Extinction Rebellion and Just Stop Oil protests all testify to this. So does the instruction to schools from the UK government's Department for Education that they should not teach their pupils using materials 'produced by organisations that take extreme political stances' such as the 'desire to abolish or overthrow ... capitalism' (Department for Education 2020). It's also interesting in this context how neoliberalism often pushes back most forcefully when it looks like the opposition may not be merely critical, but capable of getting others involved in its struggle and mobilising them. Consider the way people as diverse as the activist Aaron Swartz, politician Jeremy Corbyn and even football player-turned-sports-broadcaster Gary Lineker have been portrayed over the years. This violent aspect of neoliberalism becomes all the more evident when we consider radical texts written from an individual viewpoint can be accommodated within our current system without too much difficulty. They just appear – or can be presented as – the subjective personal opinions of isolated mavericks and can consequently be easily ridiculed and dismissed. Texts that seem to speak for a wider community or political movement are far more threatening.

· · · · ·

It's a set of circumstances that has left many of us in a condition of melancholy, of unresolved mourning, for what we have lost: unresolved, because our attachment to a certain liberal manner of performing as academics and theorists is not fully acknowledged, so it's not something that we can work through when we do experience its loss at the hands of neoliberalism. (Is the landfill of theoretical literature on the Anthropocene one expression of this melancholy?) In turn this unresolved mourning can be said to have led to a state of political disorientation and paralysis. Since it's a loss we find difficult to acknowledge, we are unable to achieve an adequate understanding of how the process of corporatising the academy can be productively reinflected, or what kind of institution we should be endeavouring to put in place of the neoliberal university. (Does the resulting sense of impotence and frustration lead to at least some of the aggression, anxiety and stress Burrows, Gill and others have identified?)

Still, the problem is not just that the political rationalities of neoliberalism find it relatively easy to shape and control any efforts to counter the becoming business of higher education by acting as liberals – even radical left ones – and calling for a return to the rights and values of the mid-twentieth century public university. The latter include academic freedom and trust; fundamental as opposed to applied research; individualised rather than mass teaching; and the relatively autonomous institution, the primary function of which is to help maintain our democracies through the education of their citizens, and so contribute to public value in that fashion rather than through the generation of economic impact and financial profit. The problem is that such calls also tend to discipline and reproach, if not close down, attempts to question their own, often ahistorical, liberal premises, and to search for different, emergent means of being, knowing and doing as researchers that are neither simply neoliberal nor liberal. (Consider some of the reactions to anti-intellectual property advocates and experiments with so-called internet piracy.) We could go so far as to say that, far from being part of the solution, calls for a restoration of the importance of the liberal values of the public university and the traditional humanities, although they may have their hearts in the right place, are actually part of the problem. To quote Oscar Wilde from his 1891 essay 'The Soul of Man Under Socialism' (when referring to those who are concerned about the condition of the poor): 'their remedies do not cure the disease: they merely prolong it. Indeed, their remedies are part of the disease' (1891).

This is why liberalism – at least the liberalism of a minority of north-western nations – has to be overcome, not just as a philosophy but also, and especially, as a practice. We need to dislodge it from its position of unmarked and unquestioned hegemonic dominance so we can explore what comes after liberalism. By contrast many recent critiques of liberalism and its shortcomings have really just been about making a case for a slightly better liberalism. I:ts mean this in three senses. The most obvious sense is typified by Fukuyama when he argues that the answer to the unhappiness with present-day liberalism of both the populist right and progressive left is 'not to abandon liberalism as such, but to moderate it'. The idea is to replace neoliberalism with a form of classical liberalism that is better able to temper the inequalities engendered by free market capitalism (2022, xi). I:ts mean it in the less obvious sense that liberalism dominates how we perceive the world today, and that the majority of legitimate political positions not considered to be liberal (Marxist, anarchist, radical feminist) have in fact been incorporated within the liberal tradition. Consequently, most attempts to replace liberalism with an apparently non-liberal alternative just end up promoting another form of liberalism. But I:ts also mean it in the more cloaked, disguised sense this book has been exploring, where it applies to those who criticise liberal ideas of universal human rights, freedom and property from a radical, non-liberal or post-liberal perspective, yet neglect to do so with regard to how these ideas relate to their own knowledge-making practices. As a result they continue to operate as liberals, albeit masked ones. It's also why I:ts are making this argument at a time when post- or anti-liberalism, in the guise of a right-wing authoritarian populism, has placed liberal democracy itself under threat in many places. And that was *before* Putin's attempt to bring an end to the period of relative peace and stability in the Global North and West that followed the Second World War and fall of the Berlin Wall in 1989, by moving parts of Europe from a liberal rules-based order to an illiberal power-based one. It's a threat to liberal democracy encapsulated by the assaults of many populist parties on public institutions such as the university. From a liberal perspective, these institutions are designed to act as a curb on political power precisely by remaining separate from it. One of the foundations of liberal politics, after all, is the belief in the importance of a 'separation of powers'. As Montesquieu, who first formulated the theory of the separation of powers, wrote in 1748:

> When the legislative and executive powers are united in the same person, or in the same body of

> magistrates, there can be no liberty ... there is no liberty, if the judiciary power be not separated from the legislative and executive. Were it joined with the legislative, the life and liberty of the subject would be exposed to arbitrary control; for the judge would be then the legislator. Were it joined to the executive power, the judge might behave with violence and oppression.
>
> There would be an end of everything, were the same man or the same body, whether of the nobles or of the people, to exercise those three powers, that of enacting laws, that of executing the public resolutions, and of trying the causes of individuals. (1899, 151-152)

Thus in the UK of the twenty-first century we find that Arts Council England (a public body responsible for supporting culture and the arts), is reasonably independent of the state thanks to the 'arm's-length' government funding of national museums, galleries and libraries, which is in turn independent of the free press, the church, the courts and justice system and so forth. The idea is that no one centre of power remains uncontested. Even if an illiberal power centre develops by legitimate democratic means – by a nationalist right-wing party winning enough votes in a general election, for example, as has happened of late in Sweden, Italy, Argentina and the Netherlands – it is unable to assume complete control. Instead, a form of liberal pluralism is produced since any such centre of power is open to challenge by the others – just not so far as to bring the very system of liberal pluralism itself into question. (In *Wehrhafte Demokratie* or *well-fortified democracy*, Germany even has a phrase for the idea that society, its institutions and legal system, are justified in taking action against those who pose a danger to liberal democracy: Holocaust deniers, for example.) It is this separation of powers – powers that are limited as result of being accountable to one another – that the undermining of independent public bodies such as the university by the reactionary nativist right is designed to address. Rather than a liberal-pluralist system of checks and balances, the nativist right favours a united coalition of forces in which all the different structural elements of society come to sing from the same politically manipulated hymn sheet. Witness developments in Poland where, during their eight years in power, the Law and Justice party (PiS) assumed control of the previously independent National Council of Judiciary; or in Hungary, where parliament passed legislation establishing foundations to take charge of the running of universities and cultural institutions. Consider, too, what has transpired in the UK, a Tory government having sought to place Conservative donors and former politicians at the head of a whole raft of organisations including the BBC, Office for Students, and Health and Safety Executive, while attacking 'activist lawyers' and 'do-gooder' refugee charities. The Sweden Democrats, Italy's Lega, Hungary's Fidesz, Poland's Law and Justice, Germany's Alternative für Deutschland, France's National Rally, the Netherland's JA21 and the UK's Tories are all members of the European Conservatives Group and Democratic Alliance on the Council of Europe. The reference to democracy in the name of this group is significant. Although the liberal separation of powers protects the democratic process, it is primarily liberalism – rather than democracy – that is under attack, as Fukuyama points out. 'Few people argue today that governments should not reflect the interests of "the people"'. Even 'Vladimir Putin still feels compelled to hold regular "elections" and seems to care about popular support, as do many other de facto authoritarian leaders around the world', including Modi in India and Erdoğan in Turkey (2022, 3). Significantly, however, liberalism has been declared by Putin to be 'obsolete' (quoted in Barber *et al.* 2019), while Orban has made explicit his desire to build an illiberal state.

· · · · ·

Lest this critique of the liberal values of the public university *still* appear rather counter-intuitive in the context our 'post-truth' world of QAnon conspiracies, climate-breakdown deniers and 15-minute-city-phobes, we should be aware that the public is not the same as the common. In fact, the public has often been used to reduce the space of the common, to pressure the common into withdrawing. As Roberto Esposito remarks:

> Modernity – with the invention of the state... – had already intended to exclude the common good, everybody's good; or at least it reduced it more and more in favour of a dialectic between private and public designed to progressively occupy the entire social scene.... For a long period of time, yet to end, the concept of government property, as public property of the state, was not the opposite of private property but a complementary aspect of it. (2013, 89)

Now it might be contended that, because of what is considered to be the university's defining rationalism and universalism (the latter is where it gets its name, after all), comparatively few in higher education actively espouse the politics of a technocratic nationalist like Sunak in the UK, let alone that of authoritarian nationalists such as Orbán, Trump and many of the post-2016 Conservatives. Not with their illiberal erosion of human rights, civil society and the rule of law, and attacks designed to undermine the idea that the experts of the cosmopolitan liberal elite are independent and impartial. (Hence the critiques of the unfair left-wing bias of the BBC in the UK, and depiction of universities, and the humanities in particular, as hotbeds of 'cultural Marxism' that lack the kind of civic bond and loyalty to the nation that is valued by 'the people'.) Even at their most modern, however, university leaders still seem too stuck in the globalised neoliberal world of Cameron and Obama, if not Clinton and Blair. It's a management philosophy of market-driven growth and expansion, of universalism-cum-internationalism, of global reputations and rankings, and of autonomy with accountability in which individuals have some flexibility over how they achieve their targets, but *not* over what those targets are, or whether they even have targets at all. Yet it is one that, like much of late capitalism, looks increasingly out of date after the 2010-2017 period of austerity – and especially after the 2019-2022 Covid-19 contagion and heat or eat crisis of 2022 onwards. (Evidence the US following China down the road of protectionism with President Joe Biden's 2023 introduction of 'Buy America' rules for infrastructure. These provided US-based businesses engaged in the shift to a low-carbon economy with subsidies and tax advantages amounting to roughly $370 billion. Such government spending and investment in industry represented a clear move away from the low regulation, trickle-down economics that had been a dominant feature of neoliberal free market politics for the last forty years. It's a strategy of industrial subsidy, particularly around green growth, that has been an acknowledged influence on the professional-managerial neoliberalism of Starmer's Chancellor of the Exchequer, Rachel Reeves – despite her mixed messages about the environment.) To repeat a question from earlier in this book: has the pandemic in particular not made it abundantly clear that, as the climate emergency develops and we continue to face health crises and other instances of socio-political unravelling, neither a globalist nor an authoritarian neoliberalism is going to be fit for purpose? Isn't a shared sense of social responsibility, solidarity and collaboration within a common struggle what is really needed?

What we learn from Esposito, however, is that we cannot provide an alternative to the networked individualism of the neoliberal university simply by calling for a return to its supposed dialectical opposite in the form of the state-funded public university.⁷² To use his words, such calls are intertwined with the 'inverse phenomenon of the privatization of the public in a manner that seems to exhaust, and even exclude something like a common good from the horizon of possibilities' (2013, 89). Granted, Esposito takes care to warn against making 'the strategic mistake of abandoning the public space in favour of common space, and by doing so possibly facilitate the privatization process'. All the same, the struggle for an alternative, he writes, 'must start precisely by breaking the vise grip between public and private that threatens to crush the common, by seeking instead to expand the space of the common' (2013, 89). To put it in quite different language: the problem is not just neoliberalism of various shades and hues (global neoliberalism, libertarian neoliberalism, professional-managerial technocratic neoliberalism etc.). It's that the main opposition to neoliberalism to date has come in the shape of different forms of liberalism – which is not much opposition at all.

Chapter 5

The Obsolescence of Bourgeois Theory in the Anthropocene

Our 'Age of Anxiety' is, in great part, the result of trying to do today's job with yesterday's tools – with yesterday's concepts.

– *Marshall McLuhan*

[T]he formula for success in the notoriously slow-changing groves of academe remains mildly challenging as opposed to radically innovative work – discoveries that can assume the mantle of the paradigm-changing without requiring anyone to question, let alone drastically revise, the basic tenets of the intellectual and disciplinary organisation that provides their sociological context.

– *Elizabeth S. Goodstein*

Making critical comments about radical researchers who continue to claim the right to be identified as the proprietorial authors of their books may well be dismissed as a rather mean-spirited thing to do. Drawing attention to the fact that such thinkers are making their work available for commercial exploitation on this basis, according to a system of commodity exchange governed by the logic of capitalism, can be considered unreasonable and unfair: at best not playing by the rules, and at worst, a rather weak formulation of the issues involved. Still, don't such reactions risk acting as an alibi for the widespread failure to take on board the implications of *not* thinking through liberal concepts of human rights, freedom and property as they apply to us *as theorists*?

Liberalism may mean we are free to make rational choices about almost every aspect of our lives: what we say, who we associate with, which politicians we vote for. Yet it also means we are free to choose *only within certain limits*. What we are *not* legally and professionally free to choose (if choice is the right word in this context), is an authorial identity that operates in a manner consistent with a more *inhuman* mode of theory. Why inhuman? And why switch to this term now, rather than continuing with posthuman and posthumanities?

The use of 'inhuman' here has to do with way in which the human cannot be opposed to the nonhuman. There is no such thing as the nonhuman ... or the human for that matter. Not in any simple sense. Each is born out of its relation to the other. The nonhuman is therefore already *in* the human – in(the)human. To put it another way, employing the concepts of 'in' and 'out' a little differently, albeit to the same end: if an artificial creative intelligence (ACI) is a human being who can think outside of the box, as it is for Mark Amerika writing in collaboration with GPT-2, then this includes thinking *outside* of the masked black box that ontologically separates the human, its thought processes and philosophies, from the nonhuman, be they plants, animals, the planet or indeed technologies such as GenAI (Amerika 2022c, 19).

In this respect, the approach to AI of artificial creative intelligence is somewhat distinct from that left-liberal techno-humanism promoted by the various institutes for human-centred, human-compatible or human-inspired AI that have been established over the last decade. It is also distinct from that advocated in recent work looking to 'unmask' the algorithmic biases of AI in order to safeguard the human, but which likewise functions dangerously to deny the former's co-constitutive relation with the nonhuman whilst simultaneously maintaining the human's position at the centre of the world. A snapshot illustration of such creative *outside of the box* thinking can be provided with the help of two accounts of AI art. The first comes from the paper, 'AI Art and Its Impact on Artists', written by members of the Distributed AI Research Institute (DAIR) in collaboration with a number of artists. In this article the human is set up by Harry H. Jiang, Lauren Brown, Jessica Cheng, Mehtab Khan, Abhishek Gupta, Deja Workman, Alex Hanna, Johnathan Flowers and Timnit Gebru in a traditional hierarchical dichotomy with the nonhuman machine that is artificial intelligence through the insistence that multimodal generative AI systems do not have agency and 'are not artists' (Jiang *et al.* 2023, 363). Art is portrayed as a 'uniquely human activity' (365). It is connected 'specifically to human culture and experience': those continually evolving 'customs, beliefs, meanings, and habits, including those habits of aesthetic production, supplied by the larger culture' (366).

Declarations of human exceptionalism of this kind should come as no surprise. Not when 'AI Art and Its Impact on Artists' derives its understanding of art and aesthetics in the age of AI in part from liberal, humanist figures who were writing in the first few decades of the twentieth century, namely: the American philosopher and reformer of liberal arts education, John Dewey; and a representative of Bloomsbury Group liberalism, the Englishman Clive Bell. To be fair, Jiang *et al.* also refer to several publications by contemporary scholars of Chinese, Japanese and Africana Philosophy in this context (although it's noticeable most of these scholars are themselves located in Western nations). Still, liberal humanism holds it values to be universal (rather than pluriversal or situated), so nothing much changes as a result (368): most philosophers of art and aesthetics argue that nonhuman entities are unable to be truly creative, according to Jiang *et al.* (365). On this (common sense) view, artists use 'external materials or the body' to make their lived experience present to an audience in an 'intensified form' through the development of a personal style that is authentic to them (Jiang *et al.*, 365). It is an experience that is 'unique to each human by virtue of the different cultural environments that furnish the broader set of habits, dispositions towards action, that enabled the development of anything called a personal style through how an individual took up those habits and deployed them intelligently' (366). Consequently, art cannot be performed by artifacts. Generative AI technologies 'lack the kinds of experiences and cultural inheritances that structure every creative act' (366). (The human exceptionalism of Jiang *et al.* thus aligns with the majority of legal systems to date for which works created using artificial intelligence do not meet the criteria for copyright protection, on the basis the latter rule out anything that is authored to a significant extent by nonhumans. It is also very much in keeping with how the question of computer creativity has been considered historically [Celis Bueno *et al.* 2024].)

The second account of artificially intelligent art can be found in Joanna Zylinska's book, *AI Art*. It shows how human artists can be conceived more imaginatively – and politically – as themselves 'having *always* been technical, and thus also, to some extent, artificially intelligent' (Zylinska 2020, 13). This is because technology, far from being external, is at the 'heart of the heart' of the human, its '"body and soul"', in a relation of what Derrida and Stiegler term originary technicity or originary prostheticity (Derrida 1995, 245; see also Hall 2016a, 59-65). As Zylinska has it: 'humans are quintessentially technical beings, in the sense that we have emerged with technology and through our relationship to it, from flint stones used as tools and weapons to genetic and cultural algorithms' (2020, 27). She even goes as far as to argue that the ethical choices we think we make as a result of human deliberation consist primarily of physical responses as performed by 'an "algorithm" of DNA, hormones and other chemicals' that drives us to behave in particular ways (91).

How can this second 'human-as-machine' conception of artificially intelligent art be positioned (albeit heuristically) as the more political of the two? After all, doing so seems rather counterintuitive, given the politically engaged nature of the work of DAIR, Gebru *et al.* (DAIR describes itself as operating 'free from Big Tech's pervasive influence' to publish 'work uncovering and mitigating the harms of current AI systems, and research, tools and frameworks for the technological future we should build instead' [n.d.].) The reason the second of these accounts of AI art can be positioned as being the more political is because, in its destabilising of the belief that art and culture stem from the creativity of self-identical, non-technological human individuals – a belief that stretches back at least as far as the eighteenth century – and its opening up to an expanded notion of agency and intelligence that is not delimited by anthropocentrism (and so is not decided in advance: i.e., as that which is recognised by humans *as agency and intelligence* [Zylinska, 34]), such an artificial-creative-intelligence approach to AI presents an opportunity even more radical – in a non-liberal, non-neoliberal, non-moralistic sense – than that Jiang *et al.* point to in 'AI Art and Its Impact on Artists'.

Rooted as the latter is in the 'argument that art is a uniquely human endeavor' (372), Jiang *et al.* advocate for new 'sector and industry specific' auditing, reporting and transparency proposals to be introduced for the effective regulation and governance of those large-scale GenAI tools currently based on the unliteral appropriation of free labour without consent. (One idea often proposed is to devise either a legal or a technological means whereby artists can opt out of having their work exploited for commercial machine learning like this.⁷³ Alternatives involve incorporating watermarks or tags into AI-generated output for the purpose of distinguishing it from human-generated content. Some intellectual property experts have even suggested the introduction of a new legal framework, termed 'learnright', complete with laws designed to oversee the manner in which AI utilises content for self-training.) The aim is to orient these tools, together with the people and organisations that build them, toward the goal of enhancing human creativity rather than trying to 'supplant it' (Jiang *et al.* 2023, 371). When it comes to the impact of AI on small-scale artists especially, the danger of the latter approach includes loss of market share, income, credit and compensation along with labour displacement and reputational damage, not to mention plagiarism and copyright infringement, at least as these are conventionally conceived within the proprietorial culture of late-stage capitalism. It is a list of earnings-related harms that is in keeping with Jiang *et al.'s* presentation of independent artists today – especially those who have neither existing wealth nor the ability to support their practice by taking on other kinds of day jobs – as highly competitive microentrepreneurs. Witness the interest attributed to them in trading 'tutorials, tools, and resources', and in gaining sufficient visibility on social media platforms to be able to 'build an audience and sell their work' (368). Once again, we get a sense of just what it means to be human in the age of artificial intelligence.

According to Demis Hassabis, chief executive of Google's AI unit, we ought to respond to the dangers posed by artificial intelligence with the same level of seriousness we do the climate crisis. A regulatory framework should thus be instituted, overseen initially by a body akin to the Intergovernmental Panel on Climate Change (IPCC), and subsequently by an organisation resembling the International Atomic Energy Agency (IAEA) for the long term (Milmo 2023). Of course, it is quite typical of those behind Big Tech to call for the regulation of the anticipated or hypothetical dangers that will be posed by foundational AI models at some point in the future, such as their ability to circumvent our control or render humanity extinct, rather than for actions that address the real risks they represent to society right now. The position of Amazon, Google, Microsoft, *et al.* as the dominant (Western) businesses in the AI market – both in their own right and as major investors in AI start-ups such as Anthropic (Amazon, Google) and OpenAI (Microsoft) – would be impacted far more if governments were to seriously adopt the second of these approaches to the safety testing of AI instead of leaving it to voluntary self-regulation on their part. These companies would also be exposed to greater competition and challenge if it wasn't just Big Tech that was held as having the money, computing power and technical expertise to deal with such existential concerns: if all AI engines and their datasets had to be made available on an open, commons basis that makes it easier for a diverse range of smaller, independent and non-profit entities to be part of the AI ecosystem, for instance, and thus provide alternative visions of the future for AI, the human and indeed the planet. (It's estimated that OpenAI burned through $100 million in computing energy and resources when training its GPT-4 model for release in 2023.) Nevertheless, to convey a sense of the radical political potential of artificial creative intelligence, let's return to the example of the environmental crisis offered in Chapter 3. As we saw there, our romantic and extractive attitude toward the environment, which presents it – much as Jiang *et al.* do the work of artists in the face of AI – as either passive background to be protected or freely accessible resource to be exploited for wealth and profit, is underpinned by a modernist ontology based on the separation of human from nonhuman, culture from nature, alive from non-alive. It is this very ontology and the associated liberal humanist values – which in their neoliberal form frequently include an emphasis on auditing, transparency and reporting, as we have seen – that artificial creative intelligence can help us to move beyond with its ability to think outside of the box.

Based as it is on the performance of a non-unified, non-essentialist, polymorphous subject (rather than the sovereign, modernist individual of both liberal and neoliberal humanism), it follows that this *inhuman* theory of artificial creative intelligence can also be understood as an instance of *inhumanities*. For if the inhuman equals the human enmeshed with the nonhuman, then a humanities with this radically relational, inhuman figure at their heart must become inhumanities. To be sure, such an understanding of subjectivity and authorship could be gathered under the sign of the posthuman and posthumanities. Approaches to the posthuman, however, have been dominated by the 'posthuman Humanities' of Rosi Braidotti, Donna Haraway, Cary Wolfe and others (Braidotti 2013a; 2013b, 157; Hall 2016a).[74] My proposal is that the above transformative conception of the human and humanities can therefore on occasion be more productively articulated in terms of the inhuman and inhumanities. The idea is that such a conceptual and rhetorical shift might enable us to challenge more successfully the (liberal) humanist subject that serves as a datum point to so many theories – not just of the humanities, but of the posthuman and posthumanities (and cosmopolitics, planetarity and generative AI) too. Building on the argument McKenzie Wark develops in 'On the Obsolescence of the Bourgeois Novel in the Anthropocene' (2017d), could we go so far as to characterise the apparent inability of radical political theory to operate according to a more *inhuman* mode of philosophy as a sign of its obsolescence?[75]

· · · · ·

Wark's text on the bourgeois novel was published on the blog of Verso Books as an addition to the collection of critical appreciations she provides in *General Intellects: Twenty-One Thinkers for The Twenty-First Century* (2017c). While the chapters in that volume offer succinct analyses of individual thinkers such as Isabelle Stengers and Hiroki Azuma, Wark's focus in 'On the Obsolescence of the Bourgeois Novel' is *The Great Derangement: Climate Change and the Unthinkable*, published by the writer and novelist Amitav Ghosh in 2016. In this work of non-fiction Ghosh contemplates global warming and the environmental crisis from a literary perspective that has its origins in the Indian subcontinent. As far as he is concerned, climate change is not just about ecological problems, or even capitalism and its carbon-based political economy. Climate change is about empire. It's about imperialism. Above all, it's about *climate justice*. (And it's hard to disagree knowing 86% of global CO_2 emissions are generated by the planet's wealthier counties, and that the carbon emitted in a year by the average citizen of Somalia or Uganda is less than what someone in the UK emits in two weeks.) Providing an account of Ghosh's influential lectures thus enables Wark to conceive of a *geo-humanities* project that brings earth science into contact with 'post-colonial voices that have pushed back against imperial mappings of the world' (Wark 2017d). In doing so she acknowledges that approaching climate change in terms of social justice brings with it a conceptual challenge. 'One has to avoid excluding the diversity of human voices', Wark writes, quoting from *The Great Derangement*, 'and yet at the same time avoid excluding the nonhuman world and rendering it a mere background, or "environment". One has to voice "the urgent proximity of nonhuman presences"' (Wark 2017d, quoting Ghosh 2016, 5).

Ghosh approaches this conceptual challenge as a literary problem. The difficulty, however, is that climate change – or climate crisis or climate breakdown, as many now term the environmental emergency we are now facing – goes far beyond what can be expressed in the form of the bourgeois novel. The issue is summed up for Wark by the fact that 'fiction that takes climate change seriously is not taken seriously as fiction' (2017d). Hence some of the best responses to the Anthropocene have for her been provided by science fiction.[76] Hence, too, Ghosh's concern that we are now 'entering into a *great derangement*' – a period future generations will look back at and wonder if our inability to grasp the importance of climate change meant we were unhinged. Wark describes this as 'a time when art and literature concealed rather than articulated the nature of the times and the time of nature' (2017d). In place of dealing with the Anthropocene, novels become choked with what, following Franco Moretti (2013), can be thought of as 'filler, the everyday life of bourgeois society, its objects, decors, styles and habits' (Wark 2017d).

The reason the bourgeois novel is obsolete, then, is because it has not 'adapted to *new probabilities*'. Nowhere is this more apparent according to Wark than with respect to the '"centrality of the improbable"', by which she means the Anthropocene 'as a time that alters a predictable one' so that it is no longer about either *gradual* or *catastrophic* time, orderly or apocalyptic change, but a temporality of a third type (2017d, quoting Ghosh 2016, 23). (It is here she positions Rob Nixon's notion of slow violence as coming into play [2013].) Instead, Wark characterises the bourgeois novel as 'a genre of fantasy fiction smeared with naturalistic details – filler – to make it appear otherwise. It excludes the totality so that bourgeois subjects can keep prattling on about their precious "inner lives"'.

Yet most critical theory has not adapted to the Anthropocene either. In fact, to include it seriously in the argument Wark makes about literature and art only serves to place further emphasis on the idea that we are arriving at a great derangement, a period when no element remains in its original place. For ours is an age when established theory too can be said to obscure rather than express the changing nature of the times and the time of nature. As with the bourgeois novel, it is a derangement that works through formal limitations; and this despite the fact that one of the reasons theory continues to be important is because of its ability to denaturalise the parameters within which our professional forms, methods and procedures of knowledge operate. In the case of theory (*and both literary and genre fiction*, we might add),[77] these limitations involve the named individualistic author, self-expression, the signature and so forth. As with the modern novel, the screening out of this scaffolding – this 'faded frame', as we've seen David Theo Goldberg call it when referring to what goes on under the heading of the 'critical' in theory – '"continues to be essential"' to the functioning of what we can now rather teasingly refer to as *bourgeois theory.* To further paraphrase Ghosh by way of Wark, here then is the great irony of theory in the Anthropocene: '"the very gestures with which it conjures up"' nonhuman actors, objects and elements '"are actually a concealment"' of them (Wark 2017d, quoting Ghosh 2016, 23).[78]

The performance of serious theory today is therefore as formally limited to bourgeois liberal humanism as the novel. (As Wark says in her earlier text on Moretti and the bourgeois novel: 'It is about making something of this world, not transcending it in favor of another'. When it comes to the 'bourgeois sensibility' there is no adventuring into the unknown, 'no spontaneous bravery', '"few surprises"'. It might be 'hard work', being a bourgeois writer or theorist, then, 'but it's a steady job' [2013].)[79] This means that it is extremely difficult, if not impossible, for even the most radical of political theories to do anything other than exclude the diversity of human and nonhuman presences. To sample and remix Wark's text on the novel in the Anthropocene in order to further undercut notions of the author as self-identical human individual: anything that would actually impact on the concealment of theory's established scaffolding, how it is created, disseminated and monetised, is regarded as not proper, eccentric, odd and risks banishment. 'But from what? Polite bourgeois society?' (2017d). The for-profit world of Verso books and Routledge journals where *proper* theory is to be found?[80]

· · · · ·

In this way theory eliminates the improbable – including non-liberal, nonhumanist, nonrivalrous or non-commodifiable modes of being and doing – 'from serious consideration' (2017d). With Naruto from Chapter 3 in mind, we could perhaps cite as examples designed to provoke further speculation the fact that in 2015 an orangutan in Argentina called Sandra was declared by the courts there to be a 'nonhuman person' with legal rights; that in 2017 the Whanganui River in New Zealand was granted legal personhood, as was the Magpie River in Canada in 2021; that in 2018 the Amazon rainforest was declared a 'subject of rights' by Colombia's supreme court in a bid to protect it from deforestation; and that the constitutions of a number of countries and cities have been changed to include Rights of Nature, starting with Ecuador in 2008, followed by Bolivia in 2010 and Mexico City in 2017.[81] If nonhuman entities can now have legal rights and duties, and go to court and be the party of interest in administrative proceedings – just as they have at various times and places in the past[82] – can we envisage reaching a point in the future where a work of critical theory can be legally and professionally recognised as having been (co)created by an ape, a river, a forest, a mountain, an ecosystem, nature?

Admittedly, this may seem like a weird question. Yet the spheres of art and poetry already contain a number of cases that point us in this direction. They include *Decomp*, a 2013 book by the poets Jordan Scott and Stephen Collis. In 2009, Scott and Collis journeyed to five different ecosystems in British Columbia, Canada. In a remote outdoor location in each place they deposited a copy of Charles Darwin's *On the Origin of Species* somewhere it would be exposed to the elements. After a year they returned, collected the books, took pictures of them, documented them, and used these materials to create an extended prose poem and photo-essay called *Decomp*. By doing so, Scott and Collis allowed nature 'to make "selections" from Darwin's text, via decomposition'. A unique '"reading" of (and through) the rotting book's pages' was thus generated by each of the five ecosystems (Scott and Collis 2013).[83]

Another instance is provided by Anaïs Berck. Since 2019, this pseudonym has been used to refer to a collaboration between humans, algorithms and trees. Some of the former are affiliated with Constant, others with Algolit, a research group focused on free code and texts. By combining human, plant and artificial intelligences, the Anaïs Berck collective crafts narratives that position trees at the centre of its work while simultaneously decentring the perspective of humans (Berck n.d.-a). Anaïs Berck's experimental algoliterary book *Paseo por arboles de Madrid*, for example, employs the Markov Chain algorithm to create both a poem and a tour of the trees in the *Las Letras* neighbourhood, which is located at the heart of Spain's capital (Berck n.d.-b).[84]

As the above cases from Argentina, New Zealand and other places testify, ideas of personhood are generally more adaptable, legally-speaking, than copyright. When it comes to the rights and duties ascribed to personhood, many legal systems don't insist on the entity in question being a human being – rather than, say, an animal or river (or indeed an artificial intelligence engine) – in the way they do when it comes to copyright. Yet what would the consequences be for Euro-Western notions of the author, originality and copyright – and of the legal subject, and of consciousness that are associated with them – if a work of theory *could* be recognised as having been created or cocreated by nature?[85] (It is a nature, moreover, that is also pluriversal, I would argue, rather than universal or holistic.) Does even asking such improbable questions not involve imposing *onto nature* legal, political and professional strictures that are designed for humans? Notwithstanding the issue of how such rights can be enforced, is it nature that is exercising its powers here, or is it humans who are acting and speaking on nature's behalf? This is a query that can be directed at the Party for Animals, which has had representatives in the Dutch Parliament for some years; and, staying with the Netherlands, the Embassy of the North Sea, which was launched in The Hague in 2018. Based on 'the principle that the North Sea owns itself', this project both politically represents, and *negotiates* on behalf of, the sea and the life it encapsulates (Embassy of the North Sea n.d.). The latter includes plants, animals and microbes which are all 'listened to' and engaged as political actors. Could such a question be asked of 'The Treaty of Finsbury Park 2025' as well, to provide one last generative example, courtesy of the Furtherfield design studio? This collaborative project took place both online and in Finsbury Park in north London in 2022-2023 and was based around a set of live action role play games. In it, 'we are catapulted several years into the future where all the species of the park have risen up to demand equal rights with humans. After much unrest, it has been agreed that a treaty will be drawn up, designating these rights' (Furtherfield n.d.).

To avoid imposing onto nature rights that have been designed by and for humans, does nature not need its own rights, then, which would be different from – and perhaps even have priority over – those of humans? Yet far from destabilising the modernist ontological distinction between human and nonhuman, a rights and personhood-bestowed nature, whether it takes the form of a dog, a rainforest or an ice cap, would still be seen as a separate entity existing independently from human beings. In fact, for de Sousa Santos, the very 'concept of the rights of nature (as established in the Constitution of Ecuador) is a hybrid one' (2018, 11). It takes cultural elements from both the West and non-West and mixes them together. When it comes to 'indigenous cosmovisions or philosophies, it makes no sense to attribute rights to nature, for nature is the source of all rights. It would be like a monotheistic religion recognizing God's rights' (11).

Nor can the issue be resolved, as might be imagined, by having more cultural tolerance for Indigenous cosmovisions. This is a point made by the political ontologists Mario Blaser and Marisol de la Cadena. They draw on the suggestion of Isabelle Stengers that:

> tolerance may protect what she calls 'those that know' ... from a frightening prospect: that of having to consider that those practices and entities they deem unreal (and destined for extinction) could present themselves with the power to create a situation where ontological clashes would have to be anticipated everywhere without offering guarantees for the preservation of that which makes 'those that know' who they are. ... Hence the possibility of animism threatens those that were not previously threatened with extinction; the prospect that what makes them be could be taken away from them frightens them. (Blaser and de la Cadena 2018, 13; referring to Stengers 2018)

What is required for Blaser and de la Cadena, adapting Stengers for their own purposes, is an 'immanent' form of attention; one that is able to 'attend to presences that are or can be' but do not meet the standards of modern knowledge, and therefore cannot be verified by it (2018, 14). (Something similar could be said with regard to the intelligence and creativity of large language model AI.)

Certainly, from the perspective of bourgeois theory, that which is outside its inherited frame can only appear as 'strange', 'weird', 'freaky' (Wark 2017d). Any such strangeness emanating from an actual engagement with the implications of the Anthropocene can thus be kept in the 'background', the unmarked environment in which theory takes place, or moved into it. As is the case with the bourgeois novel, such theory – with rare exceptions – 'draws a sharp distinction between the human and the nonhuman', not to mention the 'collective and collaborative'.[86] Here, too, the actions of individual human agents are treated as 'discontinuous with other agents' and energies (including the 'masses, peoples, movements'), even though '"the earth of the Anthropocene is precisely a world of insistent, inescapable continuities..."' (Wark 2017d, quoting Ghosh 2016, 62).[87]

Bourgeois theory clearly 'isn't working', then. The nonhuman, anthropogenic climate breakdown, ecocide, the Anthropocene: all exceed what the form of *proper* theory can currently express. Like the novel, theory has not adapted to the new reality ushered in by the Anthropocene, including all those laws and legal decisions that are starting to pile up around the question of the rights of nature. (For sure, the last thing bourgeois legacy theorists want is for any of this to actually impact on their own ways of performing as *great authors*.) Instead, theory 'imposes itself on a nature it cannot really perceive or value' (Wark 2017d). Just as 'serious fiction, like bourgeois culture, now seems rather unserious, indeed frivolous', so too does *serious theory* (2017d). The nonhuman may be what a lot of contemporary theory studies and writes about, but it cannot take seriously the implications of the nonhuman *for theory*. As a result, the current landfill of theoretical literature on the Anthropocene is merely a form of bourgeois liberal humanism *smeared* with nonhuman *filler* – objects, materials, technologies, animals, insects, plants, fungi, compost, viruses, microbes, stones, geological formations – *to make it appear otherwise.*

Chapter 6

Missing Communities – Situating Situatedness

Our writing tools are also working on our thoughts.
– *Friedrich Nietzsche*

We do not lack communication. On the contrary, we have too much of it. We lack creation. We lack resistance to the present.
– *Gilles Deleuze and Felix Guattari*

Identity politics, the only authenticity to survive the twentieth century.
– *Zadie Smith*

And what do the books gain by being attached to me, my face, my mannerisms, in all their demoralizing specificity? Nothing. So why, why, is it done this way? … It … serves to arrange literary discourse entirely around the domineering figure of 'the author'.
– *Sally Rooney*

Why am I writing this book? Nobody asked me to. Especially not those for whom it is intended.
– *Frantz Fanon*

I:ts are aware the argument *Masked Media* is making regarding serious theory in the Anthropocene raises a number of issues for I:ts' own ways of being a contemporary theorist-medium. After all, a question mark is being placed here against both our neoliberal *and* our liberal humanist models of subjectivity. Isn't it somewhat naïve, then, not to mention contradictory, to expect there to be a pre-existing community of readers and researchers out there that can be reached with this textual performance of *Masked Media*? A community (beyond those I:ts are already working with) that is ready and waiting for I:ts to simply prod them into taking on board this book's ideas and the implications they have for our current, bourgeois (neo)liberal humanist modes of being-with?[88]

In denaturalising and destabilising entrenched notions of the rational human individual, intellectual property and the public/private distinction, this book is designed to challenge many of those taken-for-granted practices and values that could otherwise have been used to gather a large readership around it. The concept of 'the public' is no exception. The audience for *Masked Media* might therefore be thought of more in terms of *coming communities, communities to come*, or even *missing communities*.[89] Yet this is why I'm interested in experimenting with possibilities for being a theorist that involve not only *representing* worlds but *performatively acting* with, in and as part of them: because experimenting is closely aligned with certain kinds of critical and creative consciousness (see Hall and Morgan Wortham 2007).[90] Operating in this fashion is therefore about doing things that, to some, may indeed on occasion seem weird, awkward, confusing, surprising, unfamiliar. Accordingly – and contrary to the advice that's often given about how to attract an audience – I'm not all that concerned with making myself appear more *human* in my work: say, by emphasising my personal backstory in order to convey the impression of being transparent and trustworthy at a time when generative media proliferates. It also explains why I *don't* want to think these issues through the lens of autobiography and memoir in the manner that, in *A Stubborn Fury* (2021a), Didier Eribon and Édouard Louis are shown to do in *Returning to Reims* (2013) and *The End of Eddy* (2017) – not even in the guise of what's called critical memoir or autotheory.[91] As other forms of authority and legitimacy such as those provided by experts and the book are breaking down, so they are often being replaced by an emphasis on ourselves and our own identities and biographies.

. . . . .

For all this way of working is flying in the face of the myth that humans are hardwired to respond to stories, especially those that engage them personally (the idea that human society arose from people gathered around a campfire telling stories being itself a story [Nancy 1991]), I wouldn't want to convey the impression my knowledges are not *situated* in terms of time and place: that for some reason *Masked Media* is endeavouring to operate according to what Haraway, building on a long history of feminist critique, refers to in her influential essay on 'Situated Knowledges' as the 'god trick'. The latter is a ruse by means of which a researcher can somehow leap out of their marked biological body and its embeddedness in a complicated context and act as if they are speaking from an uncontestable, objective, transcendent position: 'from above, from nowhere', as it were (1988, 589). (It's a masking trick that's far easier to pull off if your biological body is unmarked because you are white, male, middle class, straight and cis. Otherwise, you're likely to find your body is already marked for you.) But just as Derrida (1988), in his debate over speech acts with John Searle, shows that context can never be fully taken into account, so knowledge construction can never be fully situated. There are *ways of self-critically situating* and there are *ways of self-critically situating*, and a politico-ethical decision must be taken in each case, including as to whether to situate your knowledge or not.⁹² Otherwise there's the risk of the concept of 'situated knowledges' being divorced from its embeddedness in specific knowledge contexts and universalised as received wisdom, for all its emphasis on immanence. Once again, we can see that what politics is, what it is to be political, is not to be decided *in advance* of intellectual questioning and contestation. That it automatically has to do with, say, class, race, gender, age, sexuality, ethnicity, ability, nationality, faith, education, privilege and so forth by default. Yet this also means it's not a simple as saying 'there can be no such thing as a leftist identity politics' (no matter we live in an age of renationalisation, bloc affinities, the revival of popular sovereignty and fundamentally racist citizenship-based immigration policies [Lorey 2022]). At the risk of over-repetition, the point is that such a decision cannot be taken in advance. Always the invention of the other, including the other in us, it must be left open to interrogation.

A political decision I've often made is to refuse to limit my location and overtly situate my knowledge using my autobiography, my own 'auto' element as an author – and, what's more, to make it difficult for others to do so as well. It's not merely that, as Haraway remarks, we are 'not immediately present to ourselves', that 'self-identity is a bad visual system' (1988, 585). It's also that the biographical human subject is more symptom than cure. To provide an example by way of explanation: the decolonial approach or 'option' in Latin America that is organised around the work of Walter Mignolo is, as I've argued elsewhere, more of a 'hindrance to decolonization than a help' as far as Gareth Williams is concerned:

> for until there is a decolonization of the law of the Subject (that is, of identity thinking) there can be no decolonization at all. Until then the entire history of Western phallo-logocentrism (that is, the legacies of identity and difference; of the paternal, the familial, the fraternal, the Law, the Christian community, the

> hearth, the nation, the homo-philial, *lo nuestro* etc.) remains firmly in place in, and thanks to, the decolonial option, despite its accusations of Eurocentrism and its claims of a political and cultural alternative to the reigning nomos. (Williams 2016)

Another 'Latin Americanist', Alberto Moreiras, goes further still. Moreiras insists that he is

> done with Latin Americanism and, more generally, with the entire Hispanic intellectual tradition, having concluded that such a tradition has produced only one dominant thought, namely, identity. From this dominant thought would spring the most commercially successful Latin Americanist trends of the time. The subalternist and decolonial turns would be so successful, for instance, because they are 'identitarian and fundamentalist in a world that was and is complacent enough with identitarian fundamentalism' (2020, 28; see also Hall 2021b)[93]

I'm not therefore trying to signify a philosophy by means of my identity, of who I am. My personal (life) is not my political (statement). It's for this reason that very little is provided in the way of intimate, relatable, autobiographical information as a means of peaking people's interest and holding their attention. Next to nothing about my lived experience, history, background, family, friends, mental and physical health, personal vices or virtues. No anecdotes about working-class Sunderland, the impoverished north of England, the 'left behind', and about *knowing these marginalised people* in an effort to make me appear more 'authentic' at a time when so much art and culture is not just technologically *re*produced but technologically *produced*. Neither words nor pictures (which would themselves be forms of masking, albeit forms that pretend not to be masks) are used to share what it feels like to be me. Nor am I particularly concerned to create opportunities for people to establish interpersonal relationships with me by using Instagram, TikTok, WeChat *et al.* In fact, difficult though it is, I try to avoid anything that might have the effect of obviously *humanising* me, including providing friendly photographs of myself, despite research indicating that 'Instagram photos with faces are 38% more likely to receive likes and 32% more likely to receive comments than photos without faces' (Jarreau and Yammine 2017).

For related reasons, I don't always adopt a prose style that ensures my sentences are simple, plain and invisible, in keeping with much of the current advice about how to write well. Guidance of this kind is often influenced by Orwell's notion that good writing should be 'transparent', like a window pane – as if such transparency were even possible. Nor do I adopt the kind of form that would indicate my work has been influenced by social media. I'm referring to the adoption of a concise personal style that mixes the formal and informal, and breaks the text into manageable chunks, sometimes of just a paragraph or even a line, similar to the length of a post or blog entry. These fragments are then interspersed with emails, tweets, emojis, DMs, Wikipedia entries, Slack chat conversations, below the line comments, reviews, listicles, extracts from newspapers, magazines graphics, visualisations and so forth, none of which necessarily relate to one another, at least in a direct or linear fashion. Instead, when it comes to the development of its arguments, this book is neither simply linear nor non-linear but has a more staggering, stuttering, zig-zagging structure as it proceeds from chapter to chapter. If we want to make the objects of information media we're working with weird and contestable, and therefore more difficult to approach unconsciously, in a default setting, as if they're understood and accepted in advance, we also on occasion need to try to *weird* our writing. (And this applies to its avant-garde aspects, too.) Various means of doing so are employed here. In addition to those already identified in the preamble, they involve, among others things: repeating words, phrases, even whole passages from elsewhere (as well as habitually employing the rule of three); *not* alternating short and long sentences; using 'jargon', conjunctive adverbs ('Moreover ...', 'However ...', 'Furthermore...'), numerous parentheses, endnotes and qualifications within the text along with other supposed 'bad' habits of academic literature; and making the syntax complex and visible rather than smooth and slick.[94]

The emphasis that is so often placed on writing clearly and cleanly is not neutral. Indeed, it is why theory is regularly attacked by journalists and those in the professional publishing and media industries for being too academic and intellectual. As Rachael Allen, poetry editor for the literary magazine *Granta*, observes, here '"accessible" and "academic" are functionally coded to mean "good" and "bad"' (2023). It is certainly ironic that in Britain there is a largely private school and Oxbridge-educated section of society who are quite prepared to chastise contemporary theory for its use of 'difficult' language – including on occasion avant-garde or experimental language – on the grounds that they themselves know best what the 'ordinary reader' can and cannot understand. The situation brings to mind the words of B. S. Johnson: 'I am always sceptical about writers who claim to be writing for an identifiable public. How many letters and phone calls do they receive from this public that they know it so well as to write for it. Precious few in my experience, when I have questioned them about it' (1973). Still, it's an argument theory-averse journalists, publishers and media commentators continue to make: despite Britain having a long history of self-educated people who are perfectly capable of appreciating all sorts of supposedly inaccessible material; and despite the significant success theory has had in impacting on the public realm.[95] What Britain's elite-educated minority are really doing with their repeated attacks on theory, of course, is protecting themselves and their own liberal humanist privilege from being questioned or challenged. By contrast, what's needed as far as a lot of theorists are concerned is, as the feminist sociologist Rachelle Chadwick so aptly puts it, a certain 'epistemic generosity' and 'openness towards other ideas, positions, persons, and problems' as well as 'to difference, difficulty and friction' (2023a). To quote Chadwick at a little more length, such an alternative form of critical engagement requires:

> a commitment to *thinking* rather than the easy repetition of accepted ideas (which often reproduce privilege) or a stubborn and defensive clinging to unexamined attachments and assumptions. Privileged persons are unfortunately prone to the latter. Comfortable social positions (and the desire to maintain them) often breed 'willful ignorance'. This can be thought of as a kind of refusal to engage, recognise and attend to the oppression and injustice we inevitably encounter and contribute towards. (Chadwick 2023a; 2023b, 12)

Since it's flouting many of the rules about how to acquire a twenty-first century readership (including some of those around both situated knowledges and experimental writing), I appreciate this risks coming across as being at best deliberately eccentric. At worst it is wilfully difficult, if not contradictory, self-defeating and potentially quite boring. After all, the reason we're told to avoid using stock phrases and clichés is because such thoughtlessness is held to rob our writing of personality. Refusing to abide by such rules is all the more eccentric at a time when people *are* sometimes conceived as being more or less an aggregate of their race, class, gender and other demographic characteristics, and are placed under pressure to express this conception of themselves in acts of zealous cultural identification. A backstory can be useful in such circumstances, making the 'who' that is speaking appear more authentic and relatable. Of course, situating one's knowledge – including personally or autobiographically – can be a much-needed act of correction, push-back, even emancipation in the context of a history of neglected and repressed authorship, where the objective, detached, unmarked white, male, straight, Christian, middle class, cis voice has been positioned as the universal norm. In making the political decision not to overtly foreground *my own* empirical bodily identity and positionality in this fashion (and to often mask it in various ways instead), I recognise not everyone can afford to do this, be it for cultural, economic or professional reasons. All the same, if what I'm interested in is transforming – rather than passively repeating – the dominant, Euro-Western, (neo)liberal humanist discourse network and its manufactured common sense about not just *which* actors get to create, publish and circulate knowledge today, but *how* they do so, then this a chance I sometimes have to take, in a humble, self-reflexive fashion, I hope. There needs to be a space to at least try something different.[96]

Another reason there needs to be space to try something different is because time and again the arguments of what detractors term the 'illiberal left' retain a form of liberalism. As I say, it's not just *which* subjects get to write and publish that is crucial, it's also *how* those subjects write and publish: how writing, publishing and subjectivity are *performed*, be it online or off (see Hall 2021a; Hall 2024). The related power structures and institutional systems cannot be transformed merely by centring within them specific marginalised identities or groups; nor, indeed, by centring 'the spokespeople who stand in for them', who are often those already powerful within these groups (Táíwò 2022, 112).[97]

However, the main reason performativity is important is because, rather than endeavour to speak about or on behalf of such missing communities, we have to invent the new contexts, the new cultures, the *new* relationships of politics, economics, technology and so on out of which they can emerge. Furthermore, we have to do so without any assurances or certainty on our part that this will actually happen. We know from Derrida that the future is monstrous. 'A future that would not be monstrous would not be a future' (1995, 386-7). As theorist-mediums, then, we need to open ourselves to a future in which we do not simply adhere to the proper, accepted processes for composing, disseminating and storing our work, replete with their canned ideas regarding the virtuoso author, the proper real name and the authoritative, finalised, stable object. Instead, we need to be weird, unsettling monsters.[98]

· · · · ·

Acting as monsters to help generate the conditions in which such missing communities might emerge is what I and my collaborators Janneke Adema, Gabriela Méndez Cota, Sigi Jöttkandt, David Ottina, Joanna Zylinska and others have been doing for some time now with projects such as Open Humanities Press, *Living Books About Life* and *Photomediations*. Like Amerika's, these initiatives are *performative*, in that they're concerned not just with representing (or re-presenting) multiple worlds in the sense of being *about* or *from* them. They're also concerned with radically interrelating with them in order to do things within and as part of these worlds, and so make (other) things happen. (Amerika refers to this as hacking the situation or context. But we can also appreciate these endeavours in terms of the event and prefiguration: i.e., *of being the changes we want to see*.)

One reason this book is called *Masked Media* is that it involves a series of experiments not too dissimilar from what Foucault proposes in 'The Masked Philosopher' when he suggests books should be published for a year without their authors' names. These are experiments undertaken by my collaborators and I that are designed to help us engage in the de-liberalisation project (to adopt a slightly awkward term) in a substantive, structural and physical way. In other words, if my previous book in this series, *A Stubborn Fury*, with its critique of the bourgeois liberal humanism that dominates so much of contemporary culture – most media theory included – was about *why* we needed to experiment with inhumanist ways of being theorists and researchers (ways that are not simply liberal and humanist), *Masked Media* is about *how* my collaborators and I are actually doing this. Yet just as there are lots of different masks and uses of masks, only some of which involve anonymity, disguise and obfuscation, so there are lots of different forms of intervention. Indeed, as Mouffe emphasises, the striated nature of the 'globalized space', in which – rather than a new form of planetary governance – there is a multiplicity of 'sites where relations of power are articulated in specific local, regional and national configurations', means that what is required is precisely a 'variety of strategies' and resistances (2005, 114). This is what we are endeavouring to provide with our different projects: a variety of situated strategies and resistances. And they include some engagements that are neither simply modernist, left, nor counterhegemonic, but are closer to (yet not the same as) the pluriversal, ontological, deeply relational politics described by Arturo Escobar (2020; Hall 2021b). It's a politics that includes the modernist, left and pluriversal at the same time;[99] with the further proviso that such pluriversality or relationality is not everywhere and always the same. It takes different forms in different places and times. Our projects thus constitute a multiplicity of forms of intervention that are engaging with particular 'live' issues across and between a number of different sites. They are forms of intervention associated not just with the university and with the practices of theorists and researchers, but also with art, activism, urbanism, education, literature, business, politics, technology and the media.

Such multiplicity and such rejection of fixed form mean that our undertakings don't necessarily have to be consistent with one another. This holds true even with regard to the previously mentioned idea of counter-hegemonic and pluriversal politics constituting a variety of strategies and resistances. On occasion, they can be incompatible with this theory too.[100] As singular projects they unfold according to different scales and life spans, with some being more obviously successful than others – depending on one's criteria of success, of course, and recognising that how we understood them at first is not necessarily how we understand them later. Our initiatives are thus quite open to the risk of 'failing', considering it simply as the price to be paid to produce work that is exploratory and experimental. (For John Cage, the word 'experimental' should be 'understood not as descriptive of an act to be later judged in terms of success and failure, but simply as of an act the outcome of which is unknown' [1968, 19].) Several are short-lived by design. Others deliberately refuse to grow, either by increasing their output or by expanding their community and its modes of production and dissemination. They prefer to *nonscale*, to borrow a term from Anna Tsing's 2015 book, *The Mushroom at the End of the* World – although we've been working in this manner at Open Humanities Press for over twenty years now. It's a *modus operandi* that, following Janneke Adema's lead, some collaborators have come to think of in terms of *scaling small* (an idea that has even greater resonance following the rise to prominence of large language model AI after the release of ChatGPT in November 2022).[101] A number of our ventures achieve this by opening themselves to potentially transformative (and conflictual) relationships with a multiplicity of communities in different parts of the world through collaborative cocreation and custodianship. This approach is akin to the non-extractivist methodology de Sousa Santos describes in terms of 'knowing-with rather than knowing-about' (2018, 15).[102] In the words of Blaser and de la Cadena, what is important here is to aim for

> an ethical politics of doing difference together without any participating know-how canceling any other one. This is a politics in which the negotiated agreement through which concepts emerge in the encounter does not cancel differences among knowers; rather, it makes those differences visible as the epistemic then and there from where participants come to the encounter, and which they have to be ready to leave behind (while maintaining awareness of how they go about making them). The encounter thus becomes the opportunity for the creation of concepts different from those every participating knower brought with them. (2018, 10-11)

Other initiatives scale small by making their tools, content and infrastructure deliberately available to being (more or less violently) appropriated, copied, repurposed, remixed, built upon, modified, forked, distributed and pirated by a diverse range of actors and institutions. Some even do both. Nevertheless, the aim of all of them is to disarticulate the existing playing field, its received wisdom (its 'orthodoxy', what seems 'self-evident', that which Gayatri Spivak describes in terms of 'habits'), and to articulate instead a variety of antagonistic spaces both *inside* and *outside* of states and capital that are neither simply liberal nor neoliberal, neither public nor private, neither global nor local (Eribon 2013, 101; Hall 2021a, 29; Hall 2020, 168). Instead, these are spaces that can, where appropriate, contribute to the development of counter-institutions and counter-environments.

So our (anti-bourgeois) theory does not try to *fuck with your heads* by conforming to a 'preconceived notion of what an academic paper should look and smell like' (*rtc*, 160, 63). (If we want to avoid falling passive victim to styles of being that are already set out in advance and be open to new inhuman possibilities for theory in the age of AI and the Anthropocene, we need to be careful not to merely substitute one set of rules for another, even if the latter are those associated with the production of books and articles of radical theory. *Especially if they're associated with the production of radical theory.*) Our masked media performances of artificial creative intelligence need not even take the form of a piece of writing at all (*rtc*, 36). They can be a business, a collective or an institutional research centre, and can on occasion (under the acknowledged influence of feminism) involve the often unsensational and overlooked work of building, developing, maintaining, caring, guiding, supporting, encouraging or inspiring more than authoring. It depends on what is most appropriate to the task in hand: different issue, different context, different addresser and addressee, different theory-performance.

. . . . .

The open access publisher Open Humanities Press (OHP), for example, is a Community Interest Company. It involves multiple self-organising, predominantly autonomous, groups of researchers, librarians, technologists, infrastructure providers, alt-acs and others, all functioning in a non-rivalrous fashion to make works of contemporary theory available on a non-profit, free, open access (OA) basis as flow-objects in the 'gift economy' (*rtc*, 152). Launched in 2008 by myself, Sigi Jöttkandt and David Ottina, this distributed, heterogeneous, multi-user collective contains twenty-two journals (online and sometimes also in print) in fields such as continental philosophy, science and technology studies, and postcolonialism. They include *Capacious, Electronic Book Review* and *Fast Capitalism*. At the time of writing Open Humanities Press also has ten book series that have published over sixty relatively conventional, print+digital first books. Let me draw on the descriptions of some of these series provided by my OHP colleagues, thus generating an overtly choral effect appropriate for such a collective project. New Metaphysics, edited by Graham Harman and Bruno Latour (until his death in 2022), furnishes a protected space for original speculative metaphysics and, 'like an emergent recording company', seeks the traces of 'a new metaphysical "sound" from any nation of the world'. The Tom Cohen and Claire Colebrook edited series, CCC2 Irreversibility, offers a platform for experimentations within what can be called the second phase of the Anthropocene, 'outside of the ghost of left/right prescriptions and exculpatory dialectical villains ("Capital")'. Technographies, edited by Steven Connor, David Trotter and James Purdon, promotes research on 'writing "about" technology' in history in which contributors themselves write technographically. 'How to forge concepts with explanatory power that strikes the social and technical conditions of our time?', is the core question that motivates Low Latencies, edited by Brett Neilson and Ned Rossiter. Meanwhile, the Fibreculture series, edited by Andrew Murphie, surveys a world in which the 'question of what "media" or "communications" are has become strange to us', in order to ask, 'what comes next?'. Finally, for now, DATA browser, edited by Geoff Cox and Joasia Krysa, examines cutting-edge theory and practice at the nexus of contemporary art, digital culture and politics, in order to celebrate the 'potential of browsing for dynamic rearrangement and interpretation of existing material into new configurations that are open to reinvention'.[103]

Open Humanities Press was set up to promote highly specialised research in the humanities and to make it available to all those who wanted it, rather than having such research continue to be restricted to those with access to either university libraries or the funds to buy it for themselves. The press' publications are freely obtainable online to anyone, anywhere, so long as they have access to the internet. We realise some readers still prefer print as a format, so paper copies of OHP's books can also be purchased through online retailers and in more radical bookstores. However, we endeavour to keep prices for these versions as near to cost as possible.

We hoped Open Humanities Press would have an impact (even if a modest one) on governments, policymakers and the international publishing industry. Our aim was to show that it was perfectly possible to establish and run a non-profit organisation for publishing journals and books open access over the longer term; to maintain rigorous intellectual and production standards when doing so; and to acquire a level of prestige in the process that would ordinarily be afforded only to an 'internationally excellent', high-impact, legacy print press. In addition, we wanted to demonstrate that all this could be accomplished while remaining relatively unconstrained by commercial considerations, and without relying on external funding or author-pays fees (or, indeed, embargoes). APCs (article processing charges) and BPCs (book processing charges) are often very high in academic publishing, the latter ranging from between £5,000 and £15,000. While, at the time of writing, Cambridge University Press (n.d.-b) asks authors for £9,500 to publish an open access monograph of up to 120,000 words, and Manchester University Press £9850 (n.d.), Open Humanities Press charges nothing.[104] OHP can do so because most of its funding comes indirectly: from institutions paying our salaries as academics, librarians and so forth. Open Humanities Press itself has no salaried staff. We are merely making use of the time allotted to us to carry out research to develop open-access publication options for others on a voluntary basis (Hall 2016a, 221-222, n118). In this respect we see ourselves not so much as publishers as collaborators with other scholars.

Not relying on author-pays fees is a policy that has been extremely important to us right from the start of Open Humanities Press. We wanted to experiment with economic models for full and equitable open access that don't risk disenfranchising independent scholars, researchers with alternative viewpoints that are unlikely to meet with managerial approval, early career scholars and those in less wealthy fields, institutions or parts of the world where such fees are hard to come by. As far as we are concerned, the transfer of responsibility for paying for publication onto the individual author (or more likely their university or funding agency) that is achieved by gold author-pays open access (i.e., paying an article processing charge to have their work made available in an OA journal) generates a burden that is too onerous and expensive for many to bear. It is also a characteristic neoliberal move.

■ ■ ■ ■ ■

Plan S offers a cautionary tale in this respect. This is the scheme that was designed to speed up the transition to a 'scholarly publishing system that is characterised by immediate, free online' open access (cOAlition S n.d.-b). It was launched in September 2018 by Science Europe with the support of the European Commission, the European Research Council and a significant number of major national funding organisations and agencies: a group now known as cOAlition S. Subsequently updated in May 2019 after a period of consultation, Plan S took as one of its principles that 'Where applicable, Open Access publication fees are covered by the Funders or research institutions, not by individual researchers' (cOAlition S n.d.-b).

What this meant is that, while some of those behind Plan S may have wished for fees for article processing charges to be ultimately standardised and capped (across Europe) to prevent prices from sky-rocketing – that was the idea of its original architect, Robert-Jan Smits, certainly (Smits and Pells 2022, 72, 75, 85), even if it was rejected by a majority of other members of the coalition – they were still prepared for these fees to be paid, at least with regard to funded research. When Plan S was finally implemented in January 2021, Springer's *Nature* and Elsevier's *Cell* revealed they would be charging APCs as high as £8,600. Other publishers made it clear that they were operating pay-to-publish-quickly pricing too.

Granted, cOAlition S stated that it did not want to deliver just one business model, and that it supported a diversity of approaches to open access, including diamond and green, along with various forms of new, innovative platforms. (Neither diamond nor green OA requires APCs, the former referring to OA journals charging neither readers nor authors, the latter to self-archiving OA repositories.) Yet the only model clearly identified for financing and paying for open access publications at this point was APCs/BPCs (cOAlition S 2019).[105] Many thus soon came to see Plan S as having been co-opted by the 'big five' for-profit academic publishing companies: Elsevier, Wiley-Blackwell, Taylor & Francis, Springer Nature and SAGE. As early as 2022 researchers were able to show that, while APC expenses had increased sharply in those six countries that were responsible for over 50% of the world's scientific output – the USA, China, the UK, France, the Netherlands and Norway – it was in the 'four European countries collaborating in cOAlition S and thereby in practice supporting the gold and hybrid alternatives (as long as the latter is viewed as temporary)' that APC fees had increased most dramatically (Sivertsen and Zhang 2022).

The hybrid model is where authors publish in a subscription journal which charges readers for the content they want to read but can pay to have their text made available open access. It was devised to support publishers in converting their journals to full open access without putting their profits at risk by radically disrupting their existing revenue streams or business models. If an author wished to publish in a hybrid journal and still be compliant with Plan S, however, then the subscription venue needed to explain how it was in the process of transitioning to being fully open access – which at least until the beginning of 2025 could be by means of a transformative agreement. This was to avoid a situation where publishers were charging for both APCs and subscriptions, and so being paid twice for the same work.

Transformative agreements (TAs) allow researchers in a given institution to publish their articles with a particular publisher on an open access basis. These arrangements, which some national and regional consortia, funders and libraries – most of them in the Global North, it has to be said – have made with the likes of Springer, Sage and the Taylor & Francis Group, fold the cost of APC payments for bringing work out in one of these companies' titles into subscription contracts. The institution (i.e., university or library) pays the subscription fee and in return the publisher converts its content to open access. They are called transformative agreements because they seek to gradually migrate the publisher's titles and legacy content to full OA over time. The downside is they have the effect of enshrining the APC model and introducing it in places where it did not operate previously, to the disadvantage of the Global South (see below), among others. They also deny libraries money the latter could otherwise use to explore alternative models for transitioning to 100% open access, including those that do not rely on APCs. It goes without saying that the large, dominant, for-profit publishers like TAs – sometimes known as 'publish and read' deals – because they mean they continue to get paid APCs. (Such large-scale agreements are harder for small- and even medium-sized publishers to enter into.) But many funders also like them because they shift the cost of paying APCs from funders to institutions and their libraries.

In January 2023 cOAlition S announced that its members would no longer support such agreements beyond the end of 2024. It did so out of a concern over their becoming permanent, many publishers failing to actually migrate to full OA (cOAlition S 2023a), only 4% of the journals on their Transformative Journal programme having done so, according to the data for 2023 (cOAlition S 2024). (Too often TAs do not contain a binding commitment for publishers to migrate within a specific time frame, certainly not one where compliance is enforceable.) In the process cOAlition S emphasised the transitional nature of transformative agreements. Still, it could be argued that this announcement brought with it the risk of a lot of damage already being done by the start of 2025 through the tacit positioning of APCs as the main model for paying for open access, the embedding of this model in some organisational budgets and the ensuing extraction of large amounts of money from the higher education system over this period.

A concern with serial double-dipping on the part of publishers is also why cOAlition S implemented a Rights Retention Strategy (RRS) in January 2021. This strategy 'ensures that authors apply a CC BY licence to the Author Accepted Manuscript of their submissions. ... It enables authors to retain sufficient rights on their articles, making it possible for the author to reuse their work as they see fit, and to make a copy of their published article immediately available in a repository', without the delay caused by an embargo period. 'In this way, cOAlition S funded authors can meet their funder's open access (OA) requirements' (Rumsey 2022). This strategy also means authors are able to submit their manuscripts to any journal they wish, subscription journals included, without needing to worry about not fully meeting the requirements of Plan S (cOAlition S n.d.-a). However, as Samuel Moore of the Radical Open Access Collective observes, the RSS of cOAlition S was largely a reaction to some funders no longer being willing to cover the cost of APC publishing in hybrid journals, 'a form of profiteering initially permitted by many funders who now realise the errors of their ways'. APCs not being an option, researchers needed to be able to hold onto their rights so they could keep on publishing in hybrid journals at the same time as complying with the requirements of their funders (Moore 2023).[106] Incidentally, the RRS only applies to new research that is being submitted for publication: it doesn't apply to the legacy content that has already been published. The big five commercial companies still hold the copyright on the majority of that. And the value of that corpus of already published research is only going to increase now that access to it can be licensed out to the likes of Microsoft and OpenAI for data-training purposes as one of society's main sources of reliable knowledge (Pooley 2024).

When it comes to books, as the Community-led Open Publication Infrastructures for Monographs (COPIM) project emphasised in its response to the UKRI Open Access Policy announced in 2021, 'any funding made available without a cap on BPCs and without support for alternative funding routes' (such as Cambridge University Press's Flip It Open or COPIM's Opening the Future revenue model, which enables closed access presses to 'flip' to OA by virtue of library subscriptions to their non-OA backlist, the proceeds from which fund their OA frontlist), 'would risk entrenching the BPC model as the major or only method of funding OA books' (COPIM 2021).[107] cOAlition S, for instance, did not explicitly express support for gold APC OA over green OA. Yet neither did its Plan S permit embargoes whereby a publisher allows the final published version of a journal article, or the author's accepted peer-reviewed manuscript, to be made freely available in an OA repository only after a given period, usually somewhere between six and twenty-four months. Instead, it stipulated that 'Open Access should be immediate i.e., without embargoes' (2019). Similarly, with regard to books, Plan S recommended that '[a]ll academic books based on original research that was directly supported with funding from cOAlition S organisations should be made available open access on publication' (2021). Plan S thus in effect positioned a lot of research published OA on a green basis as noncompliant, given that much of it is still subject to an embargo period.

Moore summed up the situation like this: 'The architects of Plan S appear keen to intervene in the commercial end of the market (e.g., by *thinking about* capping APCs and refusing to pay for hybrid OA)'. In his view, those behind Plan S were 'less interested in prioritising alternative models, particularly for OA monographs' (Moore 2018). Eduardo Aguado-López, Founder and General Director of Redalyc, and Arianna Becerril-García, Executive Director of Redalyc, and Founder and Chair of AmeliCA, put things more starkly. For them:

> Plan S has been largely shaped by the interests of corporate publishers and ultimately not those of the academic community, especially the academic community outside of the Global North. ... [I]t is a Eurocentric proposal that aims to remove paywalls to achieve open access, but which does not seek to reduce the earnings and concentration of power over academic publishing enjoyed by a small number of commercial publishers. As such, Plan S resembles an accounting project, albeit a potentially transparent one: shifting funds from subscriptions towards article processing charges (APCs), whilst leaving the current communication system largely intact. (Aguado-López and Becerril-García 2020)

Others, such as Heather Morrison and Anis Rahman, went still further, seeing as a possible long-term consequence of Plan S the creation of a 'global knowledge divide' that splits the 'global scientific community into two separate systems: cOAlition S grantees vs. the rest of the world'. Members of the latter group may or may not be located in the geographical Global South, but they will most certainly be put off from carrying out and publishing research by the cost of the APCs (2020).[108]

* * * * *

There is no need to delve any further into the various ins and outs of cOAlition S and Plan S (e.g., transformative agreements, rights retention strategies, or how things changed when a new executive director of cOAlition S was hired in 2020 and transitioned it away from its initial focus on APCs to plan for a future 'scholar-led' OA communication system). Neither cOAlition S nor Plan S is the main concern here. The fact is debates over open access in the Global North tend to be dominated by seemingly never-ending discussions of financial models and the related funding policies and principles – arguably another neoliberal move. Far less attention is paid to the underlying systems of power that control which actors can and cannot engage in the process of knowledge production and for what purposes, let alone to how they do so: in other words, to how writing, publishing and subjectivity are actually performed. Plan S is no exception, regardless of any belatedly expressed intentions to support non-APC publishing initiatives. Suffice it to say, by placing researchers in a position where they have to compete with others for the limited amount of finances that are available to enable them to publish on an article- or book-processing-charge basis, the author-pays model of open access serves as yet another means of introducing commercial values into the public system of higher education – and of marginalising unfunded scholars and areas of research. In doing so it establishes a market for APC/BPCs, and, with it, a further way of inflicting debt onto the university. As a result, capital is being moved out of the higher education system and into commercial firms, in effect providing the latter with an additional revenue stream, thus compensating for any loss of income they experience because of reduced journal subscriptions. Certainly, there is a lot of money at stake. UKRI stated that increased funding of up to £46.7 million per year would be provided to support the implementation of the OA policy it announced in 2021 (UKRI 2022/2024). The latter mandate stipulated the 'requirement for monographs, book chapters and edited collections published from 1 January 2024 to be made open access within 12 months of publication' (UKRI 2021). Meanwhile, it has been estimated that the major academic journal publishers saw their annual earnings from article processing charges surpass $2 billion US in 2020. APCs are thus arguably an even more lucrative business model for publishers than subscriptions, not least because they are not restricted by the size of library budgets (Sivertsen and Zhang 2022; see also Butler et al. 2023). (In 2023 a member of the editorial board of *The Journal of Political Philosophy* reported that the quarterly had been asked by its owners Wiley to increase the number of articles it publishes by a factor of ten in the first instance. This was with a view to maximising revenue through open access agreements and author fees rather than through library subscriptions [Weinberg 2023].) Not only does the author-pays model move capital out of higher education and into the commercial sector, it also introduces a new set of gatekeepers capable of exercising control – be it at funding council, university vice-chancellor, provost or research committee level – over what kind of research is and is not published, by emphasising accountability, transparency and centralised data management. It is a logic that has become a dominant feature of neoliberalism's audit culture.[109] Both politicians and policy makers then use the data obtained for inspection purposes, forcing institutions – and the academics within them – to compete with one another through the compilation of league tables, indexes and rankings. (As a small act of opposition to such surveillance capitalism, Open Humanities Press refuses to track who, or what, is downloading and reading its books and journals; or how many visitors its site gets, how much time they spend on it, and what they click on. It thus cannot provide such data, even if it is asked to do so by one of its authors or editors, quite simply because it hasn't collected or retained any.)

All of which explains why at OHP we are experimenting with new models for the creation, sharing and use of research: models that are different – socio-economically, but also politically and on occasion legally – from those associated with the market and its metrics. We are operating according to a non-profit philosophy to make all of our books and journals available on a non-embargoed, free (or what used to be referred to as *gratis*) basis – and a considerable number of them on a *libre* or read/write/re-use basis, too. And we're gifting our labour, rather than always demanding remuneration for it. We see this as helping to shift waged labour from its central place in society by placing more emphasis on activities that are often not valued, including various forms of caregiving and carework. But we also view the gifting of time and energy as a means of developing notions of the community, commons and of commoning that help to transform the culture supporting the universal, Western-centric, modernist-liberal (and quite often straight, white, male) proprietorial subject.

The idea is to operate horizontally in a non-rivalrous, non-competitive fashion, too, in order to collaboratively proliferate new models for property and ownership. Among other things, this involves exchanging our time, knowledge and expertise for free, both among ourselves and with other open access communities. We even share some of OHP's books with other publishers. Of course, we appreciate not everyone is in a position to have either the opportunity or the inclination to donate their labour like this. Academics employed at relatively wealthy institutions often have time bought for them in the form of lighter teaching loads, research and administrative assistants, sabbaticals and other kinds of support for their various responsibilities. However, time – to keep up with the field, to conduct research, to write and publish, to set up and maintain presses and journals, even just to think and reflect – is what many of those working at under-resourced institutions, or who are not working at all, or are only doing so precariously, do not have. It is therefore important that those who are able to 'donate' their time and energy to different kinds of carework do so to support others, to try to change this situation.

▪ ▪ ▪ ▪ ▪

While we have operated in this manner from the early days of Open Humanities Press, the provision of such mutual aid – and the associated forging of new, potentially transformative, interpersonal and inter-group relationships – is something we have been engaging with even more since 2016, in our capacity as a founder member of the Radical Open Access Collective (ROAC). The Collective is a non-hierarchical community of international presses, journals, platforms and other projects formed after the 2015 Radical Open Access conference at Coventry University organised by Adema, myself and others. The ROAC includes journals such as *Collaborations, Feral Feminisms* and *Journal of Peer Production*; presses such as African Minds, Institute of Network Cultures and sdvig press; and platforms such as Humanities Commons, MediArXiv and Librería Latinoamericana at Clacso: The Latin American Council of Social Sciences. The latter is itself a network encompassing over 800 research institutions in 55 countries, with links to many OA libraries.

A key aim of the Radical Open Access Collective is to cultivate and support progressive, scholar- and community-led publishing and publishing-adjacent initiatives with a view to taking back control of the material practices and social relations of scholarly communication within the arts, humanities and social sciences. The idea is to offer a 'radical "alternative"

Missing Communities – Situating Situatedness 173

to the conservative versions of open access currently being put forward by commercially-oriented legacy presses, funders and policy makers', one that emphasises *sharing* over competition (Radical Open Access Collective n.d.). The ROAC is doing so by fostering critical experiments with a diversity of approaches to the creation, publication and dissemination of academic research. Adema and Moore give a sense of this diversity when writing on the Collective in relation to new forms of communality in scholar-led publishing. It is worth quoting them at length just to convey the sheer variety of communities involved:

> member presses and projects range from those with formalized models for revenue generation and sustainability, such as Open Book Publishers and punctum books, to completely DIY approaches with little to no financial support or commercial orientation, such as Mayfly Books and Roving Eye Press, who instead rely solely on small grants and gifted labour for their projects. Many member projects are situated within and/or scaffold upon a university setting, such as The Institute of Network Cultures and Goldsmiths University Press, while others act as disparate networks of scholars from a wide range of locations and institutional attachments. …
>
> Journals such as *Vectors, Thresholds* and *Textshop Experiments* publish experimental, innovative and hybrid works that … seek to fully explore and utilize the potential of digital environments for new forms of readership and textuality. … Projects such as Humanities Commons experiment with notions of academic social media self-branding … while the *Journal of Peer Production* and the *Public Philosophy Journal* operate non-standard forms of peer review with a view to making the process more collegial

> and less focused on the evaluative and gatekeeping aspects of scholarly review. ...
>
> Presses such as Éditions Science et Bien Commun, sdvig press and African Minds represent communities outside the global North and West, each offering a reminder that OA publishing should represent the voices of diverse communities. In a similar way, members such as Mattering Press, *Capacious* and the *Public Philosophy Journal* aim to support and bring to the fore the work of early-career researchers, who themselves have historically had a fraught relationship with open access. (Adema and Moore 2018)[110]

But the ROAC is also endeavouring to strengthen solidarity and alliances between the open access movement and other struggles that are dealing with the 'right to access, copy, distribute, sell and (re)use artistic, cultural and academic research works and other materials' (Radical Open Access Collective n.d.). Included in this right is the collective use of resources associated with shadow libraries and p2p file sharing networks.

It should be stressed that, as far as both Open Humanities Press and the Radical Open Access Collective are concerned, the provision of mutual support across initiatives is about more than the sharing of expert knowledge and advice (or texts, legal documentation and promotional materials, for that matter, not to mention open source software tools, platforms and infrastructure).[111] It also involves member projects in building resilience by considering one another less as competitors (for authors, texts, funding resources) and more as 'partners or collaborators' (Moore 2019). While each individual initiative retains its own aims, identity, values and autonomy, it is able to 'benefit from the relationships fostered within the collective' in spaces such as Humanities Commons and the 'RADICALOPENACCESS' mailing list (Moore 2019). Likewise, newcomers to the open access movement don't need to struggle on their own when starting out but can learn from, and build upon, the work of others. In this regard, both OHP and the ROAC are about significantly more than publishing. They are designed to emphasise the 'possibilities of mutual reliance in higher education (and beyond)' (Moore 2019). This is with a view to both offering critical mass when it comes to advocating policy and encouraging and supporting others – including para-academics, and independent and precariously employed scholars – to engage in similar, horizontal, nonscaling and commons-oriented practices of collaboration (Moore and Adema 2019; Moore 2019). As such, Adema and Moore present the Radical Open Access Collective as nurturing the kinds of 'loose affiliations' between 'presses that are not necessarily related by discipline, geography or situation' that they associate with Anna Tsing's notion of the latent (in the sense of undeveloped) commons:

> in the latent commons, practices of mutual reliance are informal and cultivated through happenstance interactions rather than through rules or institutional structures. In fact, for Tsing, the latent commons does not 'institutionalise' well, primarily because of its ephemeral nature. So it cannot be reduced to any formal structures that presuppose a particular kind of behaviour. The ROAC is similar in this sense, due to its heterogeneity and the diversity of interactions it seeks to foster, meaning that its purpose is one of bringing disparate groups together in order to cultivate, rather than prescribe, cultures of mutual resilience. (Adema and Moore 2021)

For Adema and Moore, the Radical Open Access Collective can thus be understood as a '"non-institutional" institution' that counters the kind of 'institutionalised alienation' that 'reveals itself in the unsupported nature of scholar-led experiments, undervalued by universities and siloed away from their fellow practitioners' (Adema and Moore 2021). Meanwhile, as Ellie Masterman indicates, the sheer number and plurality of its members makes it a non-institutional institution that it is 'difficult for other publishers to fully understand and therefore challenge' (Masterman 2020, 57). The *affirmative disruption* of the legacy academic publishing industry is thus less of a risk for the Radical Open Access Collective than it is for other individual disruptors (Hall 2016b).

· · · · ·

Yet, importantly, divesting ourselves of the business-as-usual practices of authorship is not just about who we, as writers and researchers, publish with: scholar-led, community-owned, non-profit presses rather than privately-owned corporate for-profits. It is also about transforming ourselves and our subjectivities by developing different ways of doing things that are neither liberal not humanist. In short, *we* are the 'work in progress' (*rtc*, 173). We may want to listen to Eileen Joy of both punctum books and the Radical Open Access Collective, when she writes about the importance of avoiding the fate of 'Self-Absorbed ... Radicals who think being "political" and intellectually "cool" ... means publishing leftist diatribes (about #Occupy, Marxism, Disaster Capitalism, Poverty, Debt, Terrorism, the Anthropocene, whatEVER) with the intellectual property thugs at Verso books' (2017). At the same time, we may need to push even further. In order to decentre humanism and the human from their traditional place at the heart of Western thought, it's not enough to individually author politically progressive books and journal articles about the Capitalocene and the Planthropocene, or even about what comes after them: say, a new postcapitalist way of living that places the emphasis on degrowth and decarbonisation in an effort to repair the destruction of the environment and planetary systems that is being brought about by capitalism's profit-driven emphasis on mass production and consumption. Important though doing so may be, the humanist subject still remains at the centre of this manner of working, regardless of who publishes such texts. Rather, we need to engage critically and creatively with *the very concept of the liberal, humanist, authorial subject* that underpins our mode of being-with as writers and researchers. Still further, we need to do so by actually performing this concept differently in how we act and think to produce a field of more fluid, resonant and relational subjectivities that are always-in-the-making.

One method my collaborators and I have adopted involves finding creative means of attracting 'other collaborators into our network', such as by making our research openly available to be appropriated, sampled and reused. The idea is 'that they can take what we have made and increase its value by sharing and doing cool things with it' (*rtc*, 21) through the way they 'uniquely inhabit the transmission process' (172). To this end, Open Humanities Press has two experimental series: the ongoing Liquid Books which was launched in 2008 by Clare Birchall and myself; and the Jisc-funded Living Books About Life, which was initiated a few years later in 2011 by Birchall, Joanna Zylinska and I, and which published the last of its twenty-five volumes in 2014. The books in these series are 'liquid' and 'living' in the sense that, not only are they open and free for anyone, anywhere, to read, they are also open on a read/write/re-write basis. Users are able to engage with the wiki technology with which the books are composed and published live, to add to, edit and remix them using text, images, infographics, podcasts, videos and more. Anyone can take part in the process of creating these books, or in copying and adapting existing liquid/living books for use in teaching and learning: as an alternative kind of online course reader, for example, the content and form of which can be updated and altered by learners themselves. It also means books in these series can be overtly polyvocal and can question themselves (rather than presenting a single-voiced truth via a long-form argument that provides a coherent and consistent through-line, bringing it all together into a unified whole). That all the mistakes, revisions and erasures made in assembling them are visible to anyone who goes into the wiki's history feature offers additional encouragement for others to get involved. It helps to take away still further some of the aura associated with the cult of the controlling author as individual genius and of the book as impregnable monument.

While making the end products slightly different – perhaps by using an open licence or adding data visualisations – is important, what's even more important is to transform the process of creating them.[112] Accordingly, these books, along with any subsequent versions of them, are produced asynchronously over time in an extended, decentralised, multi-user-generated fashion: not only by their initial authors or curators, but by an open multiplicity of often-anonymous actors/collaborators distributed around the world. (At the point of this writing the Liquid Books project has users located in places such as Brazil, South Africa, Hong Kong and the Lebanon, as well as the UK, Europe and US.) It should be emphasised that it's a transindividual multiplicity that also includes machines and other nonhuman entities. Indeed, Janneke Adema and Pete Woodbridge, in the introduction to *Symbiosis*, their contribution to the Living Books series, regard the digital medium as making it possible for the book to be increasingly infected with 'foreign (non-textual) elements as it evolves into something different'. For them, a 'living book is also a symbiotic book. It is a merging and co-habitation of different media-species, a mash-up of text and video, sound and images, pixels and living, material tissue', whether the latter is living in a biological sense or not (Adema and Woodbridge 2011). By challenging some of the physical, conceptual but also durational limitations of the traditional codex volume in this fashion, these two series engage in rethinking the book as an expanded, collaborative, processual endeavour – *after Gutenberg,* yet *in the Anthropocene.*

Admittedly, it could be argued that some of the books in the two series are not particularly fluid or alive given that relatively few people appear to interact with them on occasion. These liquid and living volumes could thus be held to reproduce the conventional author function far more than they challenge it. There are a number of comments that can be made by way of response to such an argument. To begin with, could something similar be said about almost any kind of book? As Bob Stein from the Institute for the Future of the Book points out: 'Reading and writing have always been social experiences, but when frozen into print these relations tend to be omitted. A significant book gets people talking in society, but this is not seen or incorporated in the paper-based object' (Stein, in Gottlieb 2009/2020, 64).

What's more, while some fixed and frozen dead-tree volumes are undoubtedly read, cited, referenced, translated and built upon a great deal, many – perhaps the majority – are barely read or engaged with at all.[113] It's the same with open access books published on either a *gratis* or *libre* basis. And that holds true even if OA books are on average downloaded ten times more than non-OA books, cited over 50% more and mentioned ten times more online, with a higher geographic diversity of usage (Emery *et al.* 2017; Neylon *et al.* 2021). Why, then, should liquid and living books be so different, just because they are published using the kind of wiki technology that makes overtly interacting with them comparatively easy? As the Freee Art Collective demonstrate, it is perfectly possible to interact with fixed and frozen codex texts published using conventional print technology. Freee took a pencil to a book by the art historian Herbert Read with which they violently disagreed, *To Hell with Culture,* and angrily rewrote it, turning it into a manifesto titled 'To Hell with Herbert Read' (Beech *et al.* 2015). They did something similar – albeit less angrily – with 'The New Text Art ~~of~~ and Making ~~Books~~ a Difference by ~~Ulises Carrión~~ Freee', which was performed as an impromptu spoken choir before being published as another manifesto (Beech *et al.* 2017). Meanwhile Matthew Kirschenbaum has shown how the poet Edward Kamau Brathwaite, whose position in a postcolonial context operating outside the establishment networks seems to have left him 'unwillingly to risk any distribution channel for his poetry lacking the cultural authority of print', nevertheless 'continually rewrote and republished – re-*mediated* – his work throughout his career', assisted at a really practical level by his Apple Macintosh SE/30 and its internal hard drive (2021, 68, 67).

That said, while it may be the case that some of our liquid and living titles have had few others add to, update or rewrite them, it's certainly not the case with all of them. Some have had relatively large groups of collaborators engage with them quite extensively. *Technology and Cultural Form: A Liquid Theory Reader*, for example, the third volume in the Liquid Books series, was collectively written, edited and curated by Joanna Zylinska and her students – in the first instance as a reader for a course on the MA Digital Media at Goldsmiths, University of London, titled 'Technology and Cultural Form: Debates, Models, Dialogues' (2010). Volume 4 in the series, *Wyrd to the Wiki: Lacunae Toward Wiki Ontologies*, which was initiated by Shareriff (Trey Conner, University of South Florida, St. Petersburg) and mobius (Richard Doyle, Penn State University), also worked in this limited sense of what it is for such a project to 'work' (2010). Others may not necessarily have overtly interacted with any of the volumes in these two series, but they have taken the liquid and living books concept, copied and modified it to produce their own versions on other platforms and in other institutional spaces. Such instances of living books include: Ellsworth and Kruse, *Making the Geological Now: Responses To Material Conditions of*

Contemporary Life (2012); Koller *et al*., *Living Books About History* (2016); Baker *et al*., *The Living Bibliography of Animal* Studies (2016); Rayner and Lyons, *The Academic Book of the Future BOOC (Books As Open Online Content)* (2017); and Méndez Cota, Torres and Arziniaga, *En busca del qualite perdido (In Search of The Lost Quelite)* (2018). (Méndez Cota contributed to both the Liquid Books and the Living Books About Life series [see Méndez Cota *et al*. 2016; and Méndez Cota 2011].)[114]

Besides, books published on a liquid and living basis are never actually frozen or dead. They may give the impression of being so if no actors explicitly appear to reuse or remake them; or when the energy and enthusiasm of their initial community of authors, curators and collaborators runs out. However, precisely because they are published on a liquid and living basis, they can always be melted and resuscitated, either by the original multiplicity of interested users or by new ones.

Such experiments on our part can also be viewed through the lens of poet Kenneth Goldsmith's idea that today, in the new environment created by the computational universe's fast-paced, high-volume flocks of digital data and information, 'a certain type of book is being written' (2011, 158). It's the kind of book that, strange as it may seem, is not actually intended to be read, not by humans at any rate, simply because it contains too much for this to be practically possible, the networked structure of the internet and generative nature of many tools and platforms making it even harder to exhaust an online work than it is a traditional codex. Or, at least, it's the kind of book that's not meant to be read 'as much as it's meant to be thought about' (2011, 158). (The question that immediately follows is: thought about by whom, or what? Is it humans, or is it other forms of intelligence?) After all, ours is an age when the computational universe is increasingly moving us away from content creation and toward more upstream and downstream activities (e.g., control of data strategy by data analysts, retailing of digital content by journalists and PR professionals). Accordingly, these are 'books that, in their construction, seem to be both mimicking and commenting on our engagement with digital words and, by so doing, [proposing] new strategies for reading – or *not* reading'.[115] To recycle a phrase from Goldsmith, Open Humanities Press's two Liquid and Living Books series can therefore be understood as a 'material investigation of a philosophical inquiry, a concept in the guise' of critical theory (Goldsmith 2011, 168).

Be that as it may, creating a fluid, living book that is produced over time in an extended, decentralised, multi-user-generated fashion may not always be the most effective thing to do. As Florian Cramer asks, referring to a point made by John Barth in his 1967 essay 'The Literature of Exhaustion', might it be 'more elegant if a prose writer like Jorge Luis Borges simply imagined and fictionalized these poetic practices instead of actually performing them' (Cramer 2012; Barth 1984, 62-76)? Can a similar question be raised about our two series? Could it be that *proposing the idea* of a dynamic book that is produced in a collaborative, processual manner is on occasion a more effective thing to do than *actually creating* such a book?

These projects are therefore about making a statement and taking a stand. Just as publishing *gratis* open access still constitutes a valid political position even if a given text made freely available in this manner is never read or downloaded, so publishing work on a liquid, living basis is a perfectly legitimate thing to do even if a particular book, or series of books, is never interacted with in an obvious read/write/rewrite fashion.

Yet the point my collaborators and I are trying to make with these series is not concerned merely with so-called *libre* vs *gratis* open access, open vs closed books, or even liquid and living media vs frozen and dead. It has to do with how we perform as theorists and researchers too. Initiatives such as Open Humanities Press and Liquid Books can therefore be seen to be challenging certain values and practices – and making it possible for others to do so – by generating *alternative* (for which we can read *strange* and *unsettling*) forms of contemporary writing and scholarship.[116]

The process will perhaps require the emergence of *missing communities* of the kind referred to earlier, before our liquid and living books (or any books, for that matter) are engaged with in a manner that does in fact challenge the conventional author function far more than it reproduces it. Only then we will have created a situation whereby a trans-individual multiplicity of active collaborators will emerge in which we will be able to:

1. include human and nonhuman others in cocreating such projects from the very beginning, so they have collaborative ownership and control of them, and can participate in them in ways that are appropriate to these others and *their* needs (and, where possible, indicate if some research processes are wrong or inappropriate).

2. involve these human and nonhuman others in the design and shaping of the research processes and projects, and in the making of the related decisions.

3. acknowledge their contributions – not just in ways that are meaningful to us as academics and theorists but that are also meaningful to them, and that are open to the possibility they may not see the world in the same way, or share the same 'human values', or even the same world: that our perspectives and worlds may indeed be incommensurable.[117]

Nevertheless, helping to generate the conditions in which such missing communities might emerge is what we are trying to do with projects such as Liquid Books and Living Books About Life.

· · · · ·

The discussion above hopefully goes some way towards clarifying why it is important for my collaborators and I to disarticulate, transform and rearticulate the authority of the book. But not *just* the authority of the book. It is also important to rearticulate the power and appeal of those modern ideas that have been passed on to us *along with* the book, such as the privilege we have seen afforded to writing, originality and immutability.

Having said that, we're not attempting to completely rethink everything at the same time and to the same extent with our projects, as if we've arrived at a completely new system for doing things capable of solving all of the issues raised by *Masked Media*. Here, too, we're operating according to Derrida's notion of the quasi-transcendental, whereby the process of examining some concepts by necessity requires others are left unexamined. OHP publishes a good many of its books using a Creative Commons licence, for instance, despite it having been pointed out earlier that this is not necessarily a particularly radical thing to do, nowadays especially. (It was a little different when Open Humanities Press first started in 2008.) Still, we cannot 'tamper' with one thing, such as the form of the book, 'without disturbing everything else' (Derrida 1981, 3). If we want to perform the book differently, in a manner that does try to take account of and assume its emergence from the radically relational interactions of a heterogeneous assemblage of both humans and nonhumans, then we need to reconsider (as much as is possible) all those common-sense ideas we have inherited with the book, and the extent to which we do still need them, at least in their current forms.

Of course, there are others who are also weirding their work like this. To provide the reader with further inspiration I:ts have referred to some of them in *Masked Media*. They include Anaïs Berck, Are Not Books & Publications, Constant and uncertain commons. In the main, however, this book has focused on those ventures with which I:ts are explicitly involved, as these are the ones I:ts know best and can some take responsibility for. Even so, I:ts don't want to write too much in the abstract about these collaborative initiatives, beyond introducing several of them.[118] *Masked Media* is as much an addition to these projects as it is *about* them. Besides, engaging with these theory-performances in their contextual site-specificity – a site-specificity that involves multiple histories and possible futures and is always living – is in many respects the most apt way of understanding and experiencing them. (If the alternative is not quite akin to dancing about architecture, it's on the same spectrum.) Many of these projects are concerned with building and maintaining relationships and communities, and communities of communities, for instance. Yet, as Moore has pointed out, to understand community dynamics fully one must often be 'entangled' within that community (2017; cited in Masterman 2020). Perhaps, then, it can be left to a future version of *Masked Media* to discuss in more detail how some of the projects have changed and developed over time. For while both the print and electronic versions of this book appear to be finished and complete, the technology Open Humanities Press is using to publish them enables changes to be made between each printing.[119] The proper, authoritative form and content of I:ts' theory here will therefore never be finally arrived at once and for all. Instead, *Masked Media* will remain temporary, variable, contingent: there will always be the potential for every print-on-demand copy to be a unique, singular edition – above and beyond the fact that print-on-demand generates small inconsistencies from copy to copy anyway.[120] But let I:ts just quickly point to a few of our other collaborative projects; projects that also experiment with the form of theory as *media*, particularly books and learned journals.

· · · · ·

Joanna Zylinska and Ting Ting Cheng's image-driven online journal-cum-gallery site, *Photomediations Machine*, ran from 2013 to 2020. Set up as a sister project to OHP's *Culture Machine* journal, *Photomediations Machine* speculated on the possibility that we were moving from an era in which we communicated primarily by writing, to a culture in which communicating by networked flows of mediation that produced photographic images increasingly had priority. As such it was concerned not just with cameras but with film, television, video, computers, mobile phones, CCTV, satellites, sensors, drones and the Google Street View equipment too. In the process it asked: what does such a change mean for media theory? Can we have a highly specialised theory journal that is primarily image-based, yet retains all the rigour associated with the writing of philosophy? At the same time, by showcasing theoretical and practical work at the intersections of art and mainstream practices, *Photomediations Machine* served as both an archive of mediations past and a site of production of media *as-we-do-not-yet-know-them*.[121]

The approaches developed in *Photomediations Machine* and the Liquid and Living Books series were subsequently combined by Joanna Zylinska, Kamila Kuc *et al.* in the interactive photographic platform *Photomediations: An Open Book*, which was launched in 2015. The idea behind the platform was to redesign a coffee-table photography book as a free, remixable, online experience, one that was capable of exploring the dynamic relationship between photography and other areas of the arts and humanities. Like OHP's Liquid and Living Books, *Photomediations* used free (*libre*) content, which it drew from various online repositories (Wikimedia

Commons, Flickr Commons and Europeana, the latter funding the project), and tagged with CC-BY and other open licences. Together with four specially commissioned chapters on light, movement, hybridity and networks that contained over two hundred images, it also had three 'open' chapters that 'transcend[ed] the boundaries of the book', being able to develop and grow over time. They were made up of an open reader, featuring texts for further intellectual enquiry; a connection to a Tumblr-based social networking space-cum-short-blog called 'The Book is Alive'; and an online exhibition space. The latter included a pack of *Creative Jam Cards*, based on four sets of tasks, designed to facilitate the production of inventive new works: a Question Card, a Challenge Card, a Duration Card and a Licence Card. Each had a QR code and url on its reverse that took players to further resources, open images and content. The idea was for players to use the cards to 'build unique and unexpected challenges' or to remix them to include questions and interventions of their own (Zylinska *et al.* 2015a). A remix generator was also incorporated into the exhibition space. It provided users with an introduction to the fundamental principles and techniques of collecting and refashioning open images. The remix generator achieved this by offering a selection of open tasks and open content that, by following the instructions provided, participants could use to create their own 'unique remix works', and, in doing so, acquire the necessary 'values, attitudes and skills ... to be a successful "open" image creator' (Zylinska *et al.* 2015c). Meanwhile, the online exhibition came with an offline modifiable flatpack version. Launched at Hamburger Bahnhof, Museum für Gegenwart in Berlin in November 2016, the *Photomediations* flatpack exhibition featured the work of nineteen international artists, all of whom had responded to the project's open call-to-action to liberate the image in the twenty-first century (Zylinska *et al.* 2015b). They had done so by contributing still or moving images that reused content from the Europeana repository in the form of remixes, mash-ups, collages or montages. Open Humanities Press also brought out a stand-alone print book version of the open reader in 2016, comprising twenty scholarly and curatorial essays from, among others, Raúl Rodríguez Fernández, Paul Frosh and Katrina Sluis (Kuc and Zylinska 2016).

Photomediations: An Open Book was thus an experiment in open and hybrid publishing. In keeping with the emphasis on openness, it was accompanied by a free, downloadable brochure titled *A Guide to Open and Hybrid Publishing (Or How To Create An Image-Based Open Access Book in 10 Easy Steps)*, which explained how anyone could undertake a project of this kind for themselves (Hall, Kuc and Zylinska 2015). Like the Liquid and Living Books series, *Photomediations: An Open Book* also celebrated the book as a living object – in this case, as an evolving visual medium. The conceptual framework of the larger editorial and curatorial project behind *Photomediations* presented a radically new perspective on photography. It moved beyond seeing a photograph as just an individual object, 'tomb' or 'fossilised version of the past' that yielded itself to being framed and displayed, either 'individually or in series, on flat surfaces in galleries and other cultural institutions' (Zylinska 2015). Instead, in its coupling with movement, the project foregrounded another key aspect of photography: namely, its embeddedness in the flow of time and duration and thus life itself. *Photomediations* accordingly took a 'process- and time-based approach to images' – including photographic stills, movie excerpts and gif animations – 'tracing the technological, biological, cultural, social and political flows of data that produce photographic objects'; imagistic currents that could be 'dipped or cut into occasionally', as the various elements of the project showed (Zylinska 2015).

If some of the research projects that are being introduced here have experimented with the material form of theory as information media in the shape of books, journals, even the very gestures of reading and writing (Adema and Kuc 2019), others have concentrated more on hardware, software and networked infrastructures; and on making our ideas of education, the university[122] and academic social networks (Adema and Hall 2016b) less *easy to read*, in the sense of Foucault's masked philosopher provocation.[123] By way of bringing this chapter to a close, however, I would like to draw attention to a theory-performance that is particularly relevant to my own way of acting as a weird monster with *Masked Media*. It concerns a 2016 issue of the *Journal of Electronic Publishing* (*JEP*) titled 'Disrupting the *Human*ities: Towards Posthumanities', edited by Janneke Adema and myself, which consisted of video-presentations/articles-cum-theory-performances (2016a). Extensively annotated using the *InterLace* open-source software program developed by Robert Ochshorn that allowed us to include audience responses to the 'original' presentations, questions and the accompanying social media engagement, these contributions were designed to break down the divisions between the research, the presentation and the final publication, as well as between the *real time* and the online, or *virtual*, audience.

With 'Disrupting the *Human*ities: Towards Posthumanities' Adema and I wanted to put to the test some of the material and performative aspects involved in the ritual of presenting an academic conference or seminar paper, including the setting in which it takes place. We endeavoured to take on and assume, as theorists, some of the implications of the idea that a presentation is not simply a re-presentation of the written, text-on-paper (or text-on-laptop) theoretical argument, more often than not delivered by an individual human author. Rather, it is a relational and processual meshwork of (embodied) presenter, event organisers, facilitators, audience and online public, along with the associated cultural practices, infrastructures, buildings, materials, technologies, institutions and so on, all of which contribute to the presentation *in its becoming*. To this end we asked questions such as: Is it possible to position the (post)humanities conference or seminar paper as both an active part of the ongoing research process (instead of merely an *after the fact re-presentation* of the research), and as a form of publication where its collective, collaborative aspect as a networked, processual, time-based event involving a heterogeneous assemblage of actants can be highlighted? (The latter is in marked contrast to the kind of fixed and finished, single-authored product or series of products that are more usually expected to emerge out of such settings, and which are normally the only versions that are made publicly available, albeit often behind a paywall.) And if it is possible to position the conference or seminar paper in this manner, doesn't it require us to do more than just make use of new era technologies such as the *InterLace* software (which in turn enables us to incorporate images, references, links and screenshots relating to the various thinkers and ideas mentioned during the presentations into the videos)? Doesn't it also require us to reinvent, radically, how we design and run conferences and seminars, both on- and off-line? For instance, must scholars always present newly written (and previously unpublished) material? As with jazz musicians, should it not be conceivable for them to revisit, and perform differently or otherwise, older material in a fresh context? Or to remix already published and circulated work with more recent research, as I am doing now? Could we even arrive at a situation where a researcher can spend their whole career presenting the same, continually revised and updated, and so never fixed and finalised, paper – or, indeed, book?[124] What would this mean for our ideas of authorship, originality and, indeed, 'the book'?

Please tear out the following pages if you would prefer this book to be more obviously *theoretical* and less obviously *performative*.

All the projects discussed in this chapter can be accessed via this link:

https://linktr.ee/maskedmedia1

Chapter 7

Some Day We Will All Think Like This: Experiments in Radical Open Access Publishing – An Incomplete Directory

A changing consciousness calls for a changing technology, and a changing technology changes consciousness.

– *Vilém Flusser*

Constellation, not sequencing, carries the truth.

– *Olga Tokarczuk*

When I depart from convention, it is because the convention has failed, is inadequate for conveying what I want to say.

– *B. S. Johnson*

Culture Machine

Founding Editors: Gary Hall and Dave Boothroyd
Editors (since 2018) Gabriela Méndez Cota and Rafico Ruiz

culturemachine.net

Culture Machine is a peer-reviewed journal dedicated to media and cultural theory. Launched in 1999 by Dave Boothroyd and myself, it is one of the oldest born-digital open access journals in the humanities. Others include *Postmodern Culture* and *Surfaces*, which were established in 1990 and 1991 respectively, the former billing itself as the first electronic peer-reviewed journal in the field. While *Surfaces* ceased publication in 1999, *Culture Machine*, like *Postmodern Culture*, is among the few still operating from that period. In 2018, *Culture Machine* was relaunched from Mexico, under the editorship of Gabriela Méndez Cota and Rafico Ruiz, complete with a redesign by members of the Mexican hackerspace El Rancho Electrónico and a more explicit Global South focus.

Open Humanities Press

openhumanitiespress.org

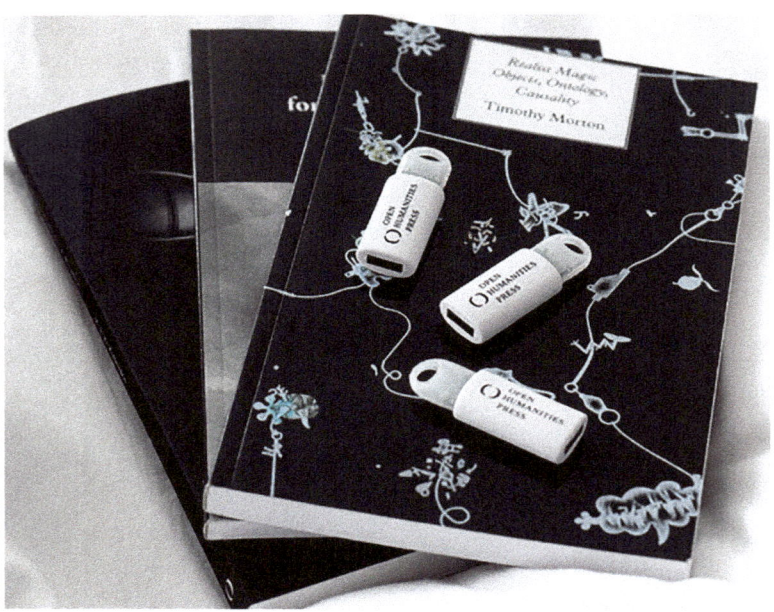

Open Humanities Press (OHP) is a not-for-profit scholar-led publishing collective. Initiated in 2006 and launched publicly in 2008, it consists of a network of interlacing scholarly communities whose various, predominantly autonomous, editorial activities make up the press. OHP's mission is to make leading works of contemporary critical thought immediately available on an open access basis, without charging author-pays fees. OHP has published over sixty relatively conventional, hybrid print+digital first open access books. It also includes ten book series and twenty-two journals, among them *Culture Machine*, *Postcolonial Text* and *Teknokultura: Journal of Digital Culture and Social Movements*.

Radical Open Access Collective

radicaloa.postdigitalcultures.org

The Radical Open Access Collective is a community of presses, journals, platforms and other projects. Formed in 2015, it has more than eighty members looking to create a progressive open access publishing environment in the humanities and social sciences that is based on experiments with various alternative non-profit, independent and scholar-led models.

Open Humanities Notebook
Gary Hall
garyhall.squarespace.com/journal/

The Open Humanities Notebook is an online notebook I have used since 2010 to make my research openly available, more or less as it emerges: not just in draft and pre-print form as journal articles, book chapters, catalogue essays and so on, but also as conference papers, lectures, even contributions to online discussions. The notebook allows my research to be downloaded, reproduced, translated, modified, distributed, re-used, built upon and even 'pirated' in any medium, without indication of origin, long before it is handed over to a publisher to be made available as a book or journal article.

Liquid Books

Founding Editors: Gary Hall and Clare Birchall

liquidbooks.pbwiki.com

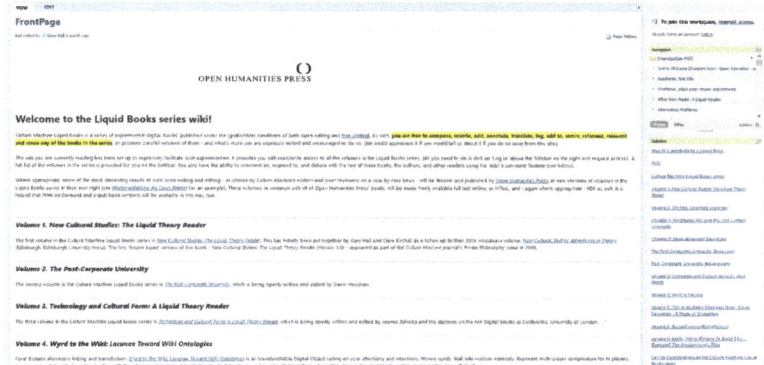

Liquid Books is series of digital books published on a *gratis/ libre* basis. Users are free to rewrite, remix and republish any of the volumes in the series. Since its inception in 2008, Liquid Books has published eleven titles, including *Technology and Cultural Form*, *Wyrd to the Wiki* and *Biomediaciones / Biomediations*. The latter was collaboratively speed-edited in three hours at the Living Books workshop held at the Festival of New Media Art and Video Transitio_ MX 05 BIOMEDIATIONS (Biomediaciones) in Mexico City, September 2013. *Eco-catástrofe y deconstrucción* (also known as *Critical Theory and Environmental Posthumanities in Spanglish*) is another notable title in the series. Edited by Gabriela Méndez Cota, Ana Cecilia Terrazas Valdés, Marco Antonio Alcalá Flores, Alejandro Ahumada and Diego Alejandro Corrales Caro, this liquid book aims to infuse environmental criticism in Spanish with a dose of transnational philosophy and experimental writing.

Liquid Theory TV
Clare Birchall, Gary Hall and Pete Woodbridge
youtu.be/vG7sIVlanO8

Liquid Theory TV was a short series of video essays. It experimented with the potential of online video – considered by Fredric Jameson to be the 'artform ... *par excellence*' of late capitalist society – to provide new ways of engaging with theory (1987, 223). Running from 2009 to 2012, the idea of these video essays was not so much to have a social or cultural impact. Nor was it simply to connect with an increasingly computational-media-literate audience using video – an audience that it is often thought long-form print texts can no longer reach. Instead, Liquid Theory TV was designed to probe the potential of video to produce alternative, rival or counter-desires and affectivities to those currently dominant in late capitalist society.

Living Books About Life

Series Editors: Clare Birchall, Gary Hall and Joanna Zylinska

livingbooksaboutlife.org

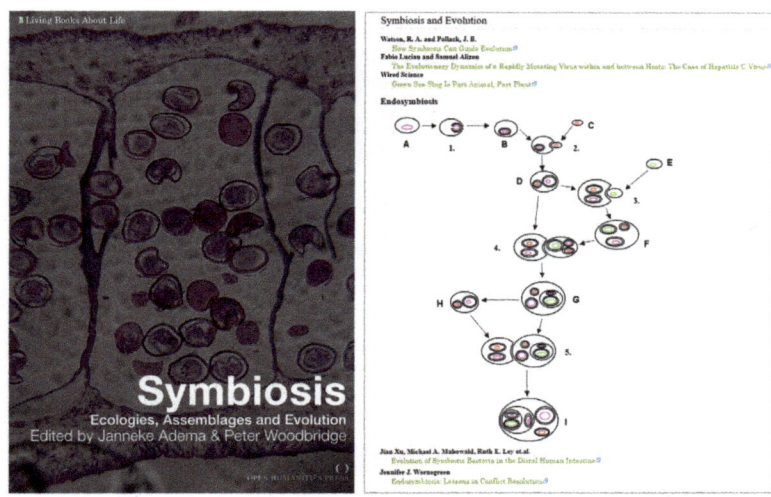

Living Books About Life, commissioned and funded by the Joint Information Systems Committee (Jisc) in 2011, is a series of twenty-five open access books that address the concept of life from both a philosophical and biological perspective, creating a bridge between the humanities and the sciences. Along with the Liquid Books series, it has championed a new model of publishing. The idea behind both series is to demonstrate it is possible to publish books that are open to collaborative processes of rewriting, re-editing and remixing, incorporating not just written text but also sound files, images, videos, information graphics and data visualisations.

Photomediations Machine

Curators: Joanna Zylinska and Ting Ting Chen

photomediationsmachine.net [legacy link]

Photomediations Machine, a sister project to the *Culture Machine* journal, was a curated online space, active from 2013 to 2020. It adopted a process-based philosophy for image-making, tracing the dynamic technological, biological, cultural, social and political flows of networked mediation that produce photography. In doing so *Photomediations Machine* experimented with some of the different forms theory can take when it is enacted with media other than the print codex and its papercentric derivatives, such as cameras, mobile phones, satellites, drones and CCTV.

Photomediations: An Open Book

Editors: Joanna Zylinska, Kamila Kuc, Jonathan Shaw, Ross Varney and Michael Wamposzyc

photomediationsopenbook.net

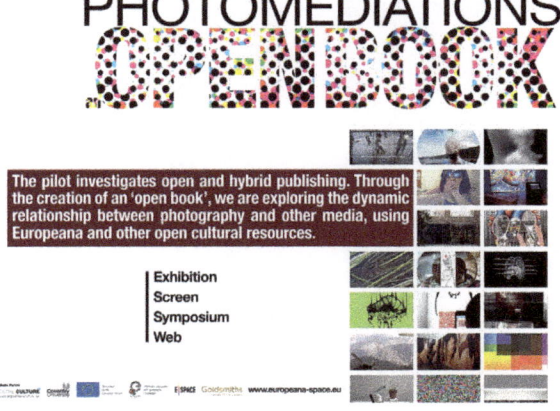

Photomediations: An Open Book reimagines the coffee-table book as an immersive online experience. Created in 2015, it investigates the relationship between photography and other media through an introduction and four chapters – on light, movement, hybridity and networks – featuring over 200 images from various open repositories. *Photomediations: An Open Book* also includes three chapters that can grow and develop over time. They consist of an open reader (which mutated into *Photomediations: A Reader*: see below), a social space and an exhibition space.

Photomediations: A Reader

Editors: Kamila Kuc and Joanna Zylinska

Kuc-Zylinska_2016_Photomediations-A-Reader.pdf

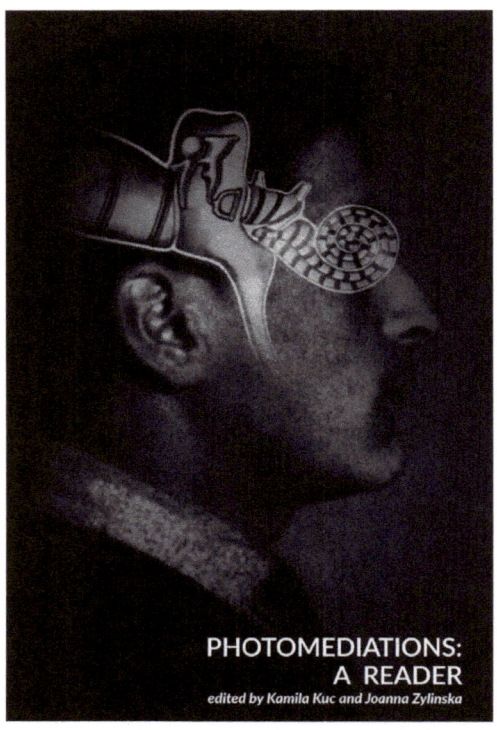

Photomediations: A Reader, published in 2016, is an edited collection featuring twenty scholarly and curatorial essays. The concept of photomediations that unites these texts cuts across the traditional classification of photography as suspended between art and social practice to capture the dynamism of the photographic medium in the twenty-first century. As befits a stand-alone print book, it also analyses photography's kinship with other media, including print – and with humans *as media*. It is accompanied by a free downloadable pdf brochure, *A Guide to Open and Hybrid Publishing (or How to Create An Image-based, Open Access Book In 10 Easy Steps)*, which uses *Photomediations: An Open Book* as an illustration.

after.video

Editors: Oliver Lerone Schultz, Adnan Hadzi, Pablo de Soto and Laila Shereen Sakr

after-video/

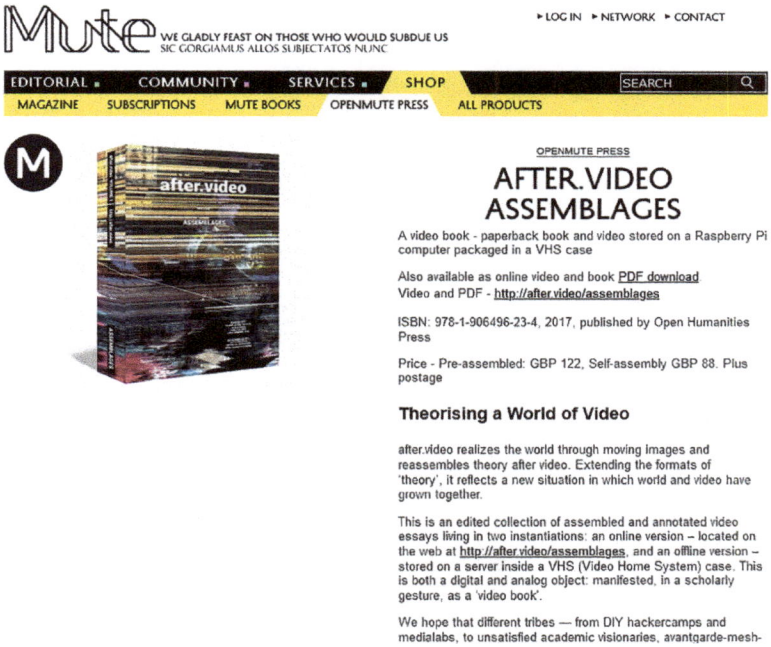

after.video is a collection of annotated video essays that consider the future for theory after both books *and* video. Produced in 2016, it exists in two different versions: a freely available online version; and an assembly-on-demand offline version stored on a Raspberry Pi computer inside a VHS (Video Home System) case. *after.video* is thus both an analogue and a digital object, with each of these versions in their different ways taking the shape of a 'video book'. Extending the formats of theory, it reflects – much like the earlier Liquid Theory TV – a new situation in which the world is moving from print to electronic forms of publishing, and from there increasingly to video. In sum, theorising a world of video, this project reassembles theory and the book *after video*.

Disrupting the *Human*ities: Towards Posthumanities

Editors: Janneke Adema and Gary Hall

jep/disruptingthehumanities/

'Disrupting the *Human*ities: Towards Posthumanities' is a special issue of *The Journal of Electronic Publishing*, which came out in 2016. Featuring a selection of heavily annotated video-presentations/articles-cum-performances, it endeavours to break down the divisions between both research and presentation, as well as between the 'real time' and online or 'virtual' conference audience. The issue has its basis in 'Disrupting the *Human*ities', a seminar series which studied research and scholarship in a posthumanities context, that was organised by the Centre for Disruptive Media, as it then was, at Coventry University. (The Centre for Disruptive Media has itself since been disrupted, becoming the Centre for Postdigital Cultures in 2017.) Both the journal issue and seminar series critically engage with the humanist legacy of the humanities while creatively exploring alternative possible futures for the field. (The 'Disrupting the *Human*ities' seminar series was accompanied by a wiki that is available at: http://disruptivemedia.org.uk/wiki/.)

Media Gifts
Gary Hall
garyhall.squarespace.com/about/

Media Gifts
MEDIA PHILOSOPHY: EXPERIMENTAL CRITICAL THEORY+PUBLISHING: RADICAL OPEN ACCESS: DIGITAL HUMANITIES: CREATIVE AI:

About...

'People know what they do; frequently they know why they do what they do; but what they don't know is what what they do does' -- Michel Foucault, personal communication

Media Gifts is the website/blog of Gary Hall, *a media theorist working on new media technologies, continental philosophy, art and politics. It provides details of his publications, talks and other activities, with a particular emphasis on work-in-progress.*

Media gifts: the idea

My research includes a series of performative media projects or 'media gifts' which use media, both 'new' and 'old', to actualise or creatively perform critical theory and philosophy. They are gifts in the sense they operate as part of what has come to be known as the academic gift economy whereby research is circulated for free rather than as intellectual property or market commodities that are bought and sold. They are performative in that they do not endeavour to provide a representation or critique of the world – or not *just* do so – as much as act in the world or intra-act with it. In other words, they are instances of media and mediation that endeavour to produce the effects they name or things of which they speak, and that are engaged primarily through their actualization, enactment and performance. They are a way to practice an affirmative media theory or media philosophy, where analysis and critique are not abandoned but take more creative, inventive forms.

Media Gifts refers to a series of performative projects that use media technologies to enact radical theory. With over twenty projects to date, they are *gifts* in the sense they operate as part of the academic gift economy whereby research is distributed for free rather than treated as a commodity for sale. They are *performative* in that these projects are concerned not so much with commenting on or representing the world from outside or above (or not *just* with doing so), but with acting in or with the world. In other words, they are instances of media and mediation that endeavour to produce the effects they name or things of which they speak, such as liquid and living books.

Pirate Philosophy
(Names And Addresses Unknown)

AAAARG DOESN'T EXIST

Pirate Philosophy is a media gift that delves into some of the implications of so-called internet piracy for the humanities, challenging received ideas of the author, authority and attribution. Released into the wild in 2009, it uses peer-to-peer BitTorrent networks to test these concepts both philosophically and legally. The project consists of an essay titled 'Pirate Philosophy' that is currently accessible only on 'pirate' peer-to-peer networks. Notably, there is no conventional master copy of this text – that was deliberately destroyed as soon as 'Pirate Philosophy' was made available on a peer-to-peer basis. Consequently, 'Pirate Philosophy' now exists only within these pirate networks and in so far as it is distributed through 'unauthorised' copying and sharing. As a result, anyone can claim authorship of this text.

ScholarLed

Mattering Press, meson press, Open Book Publishers, Open Humanities Press and punctum books

scholarled.org/

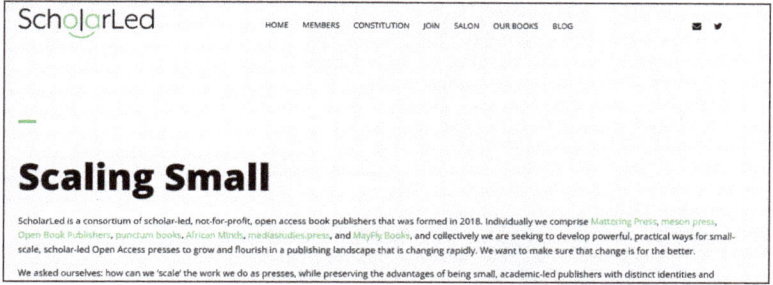

ScholarLed is a consortium of academic-led, non-profit, open access book publishers that emerged in 2018 from the Radical Open Access Collective. The founding members of ScholarLed were Mattering Press, meson press, Open Book Publishers, Open Humanities Press and punctum books. The ScholarLed community develops systems, workflows and practices that allow smaller-scale presses to provide each other with mutual support. This support ranges from pooled knowledge and expertise to shared online and offline tools and infrastructures. Each member of the consortium maintains its distinct identity as a publisher, with its own audience, business model and particular approach to open access. What they share is a commitment to opening scholarly research up to diverse readerships; resisting the marketisation (and homogenisation) of academic knowledge production; and working collaboratively rather than in competition with one another. At the time of writing, ScholarLed comprises Mattering Press, meson press, Open Book Publishers, punctum books, African Minds, MayFly Books and mediastudies. press. (While Open Humanities Press withdrew from the consortium in 2021 upon ScholarLed's decision to incorporate, it continues to collaborate with many of its presses.)

COPIM: Community-led Open Publication Infrastructures for Monographs

copim.pubpub.org

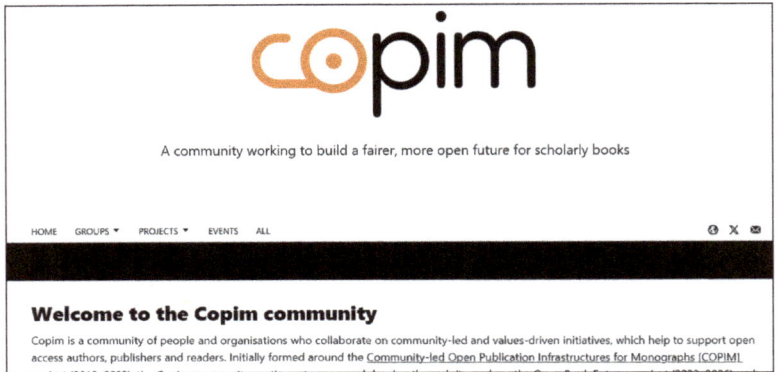

Community-led Open Publication Infrastructures for Monographs (COPIM) is a decentralised international partnership involving researchers, publishers, universities and libraries, along with a number of infrastructure and technology suppliers. Distributed across a range of geographical contexts, it arose in 2019 out of the original ScholarLed consortium. COPIM is constructed to reconfigure open access book publishing in the humanities and social sciences by shifting it away from the closed-access and surveillance capitalism models of competing commercial companies. Backed by the Research England Development Fund and the Arcadia Fund from November 2019 to April 2023, COPIM represents an alternative approach to the open sharing of knowledge, one that is far more collaborative and horizontal. In this approach systems, infrastructures and revenue streams are collectively owned, managed and governed by the scholarly community itself. This is done for the common good, in such a fashion as to make it easier for a diverse range of practices and projects – including small, non-profit, independent and scholar-led presses – to become part of the BPC-free and embargo-free open access publishing ecosystem.

Combinatorial Books: Gathering Flowers

Editors: Janneke Adema, Simon Bowie, Gary Hall, Rebekka Kiesewetter

ecological-rewriting

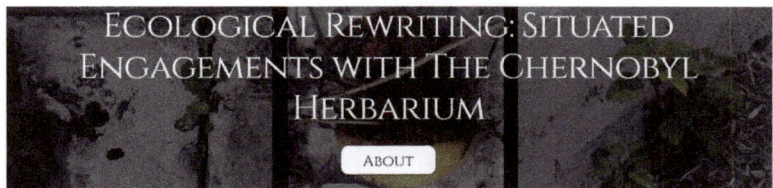

Combinatorial Books: Gathering Flowers is one of COPIM's more experimental projects. It makes use of the Creative Commons licences that many open access books are published under, actively encouraging the rewriting, remixing and remaking of volumes from the Open Humanities Press' back catalogue in order to generate radical new responses to them. The first OHP book Gathering Flowers responded to in this way was *The Chernobyl Herbarium* (2016) by philosopher Michael Marder and artist Anaïs Tondeur, facilitated through a collaboration with Gabriela Méndez Cota and a group of technologists, researchers and students from Universidad Iberoamericana in Mexico City: Etelvina Bernal, Sandra Hernández Reyes, Sandra Loyola Guízar, Fernanda Rodríguez González, Yareni Monteón López, Deni Garciamoreno, Nidia Rosales, Xóchitl Arteaga Villamil and Carolina Cuevas. Their method involved crafting a fragmentary and open-ended narrative on Mexico's relation with Chernobyl without directly intervening in Marder's and Tondeur's original text. Inspired by Mexican sociologist Cristina Rivera Garza's understanding of rewriting as *disappropriation*, Méndez Cota and her group instead 'rewrote' *The Chernobyl Herbarium* to produce a new work. Titled *Ecological Rewriting: Situated Engagements with The Chernobyl Herbarium*, this experimental book was published by Open Humanities Press in 2023.

How to Practise the Culture-Led Re-Commoning of Cities

Partisan Social Club, adjusted by Gary Hall

partisansocialclub.com/re-commoning/

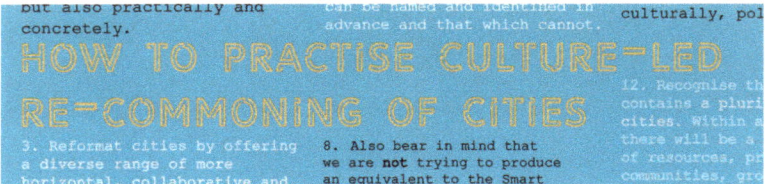

How to Practise the Culture-Led Re-Commoning of Cities is a collaborative project with the Partisan Social Club art collective. It has its basis in the following question: can the inhabitants of cities utilise the resources made available by those associated with open access, open GLAM, FLOSS, p2p filesharing, copyfarAI and the anti-privatised knowledge commons, to construct their own versions of galleries, libraries and museums on a self-organising basis? The creation of such bespoke institutions is to be undertaken in a non-rivalrous, non-competitive fashion with a view to proliferating experiments with reimagining the city. There is no plan or blueprint for the kinds of cities we are looking to create with this project. They are rather *missing cities*: cities that need to be called forth in different ways, times and places – artistically, practically, theoretically. With this *calling forth* in mind, a printable poster was designed, originally as part of the Art and the Urban Commons project for the 2021 *Coventry Creates* exhibition. This poster continues to be displayed on billboards and wrap around plinths, the idea being to use contemporary theory – rather than advertising – to call forth a city that does not yet exist. Building on the poster poems of the concrete poets, could we perhaps call this approach 'poster theory'?

Robot Review of Books

www.robotreviewofbooks.org

Like the *London Review of Books* ... but with even more robots! Established in 2024, the *Robot Review of Books* is an AI 'magazine' of short computational media essays that are typically structured as book reviews.

Chapter 8

Misunderstanding Media: The Epistemological Politics of Scaling Small

Despite appearances to the contrary – and despite *Masked Media* being written as a contribution to a series of books of media art and theory for an open access press I:ts helped co-found – publishing and books are not the main concern of I:ts and their collaborators. Instead, our prefigurative or annunciatory projects – which, under the influence of Foucault's 'The Masked Philosopher', have been characterised as instances of masked media – have a multi-layered rationale. This rationale has its basis in the following:

1. a desire to experiment with the invention and testing of new knowledges and new subjectivities, new agential practices and new ways of life;

2. a recognition that writing, print and the codex text are not the 'natural' or normative media in which such activities are conducted; and that, while experimentation of this kind *can* take place in books and journals, media theory should also be open to being *post-alphanumeric and post-book*;

3. a conviction that our theory-performances should not be confined to the realm of theory or even art. It's important they constitute a multiplicity of forms of intervention that engage specific problems across

a number of different places and sites, all of which have their own multi-layered histories.¹²⁵ They might be associated with activism, education, business, politics, technology or the media. To channel Derrida, 'it is necessary in each situation to create an appropriate mode of expression, to invent the law of the singular event, to take account of the presumed or desired addressee' (2007, 31).

■ ■ ■ ■ ■

This emphasis on multiplicity is evident in other ways too. At first sight it may appear as if our focus with these projects has been on scaling up and scaling out the creation of free resources and infrastructures, along with the communities that manage and maintain them: from the single journal *Culture Machine* (1999); to the (at the time of this writing) twenty-two journals and ten book series of Open Humanities Press (2008); through the eighty-plus members of the Radical Open Access Collective (2015); to the £3.6m project that is COPIM (Community-led Open Publication Infrastructures for Monographs). The latter emerged in 2019 out of a consortium of five open access presses called ScholarLed (which itself emerged out of the Radical Open Access Collective). A partnership involving universities and libraries along with infrastructure and technology providers, COPIM, as noted briefly in Chapter 6, is designed to transition open access book publishing away from surveillance capitalism's free market model of rivalrous commercial service providers. In particular, it is responding to the fact that companies such as Elsevier, Wiley-Blackwell and Springer are increasingly looking to monetise not just academic content but the 'entire knowledge production workflow, from article submissions, to metrics to reputation management and global rankings' and the related data extraction and analysis (Chan 2019). Evidence the partnership struck by Taylor & Francis with the Research Gate commercial social networking site for academics in 2023. Some ScholarLed colleagues have gone so far as to argue these businesses are doing so with a view to capturing the whole 'system of exchange between themselves and research-learning communities', free from the mediation of public university libraries – which these publishing companies regard as 'knots' that hamper their ability to extract public funds (Joy and van Gerven Oei 2022).

A 2023 report by the library alliance SPARC (Scholarly Publishing and Academic Resources Coalition) examined the data privacy practices of Elsevier's ScienceDirect business, 'the leading academic discovery platform of the world's largest publisher and many libraries' largest vendor for collections' (Yoose and Shockey 2023, 7). It demonstrates how the tracking of users and the harvesting of their personal data – which would have been unthinkable in a traditional physical library setting – is now a regular practice through the platforms of such companies. Nor is this information only being marketed to universities for auditing and monitoring purposes – something that also occurs by means of Elsevier's Pure portal, which it bills as the world's leading research information management system, the underlying data for which is taken from Scopus, Elsevier's abstract and citation database. As another member of the ScholarLed community emphasises, the scholar *is* the product' in this 'full-stack model': 'Her articles and references feed Scopus and Pure, which are then sold back to her university employer' (Pooley 2024). All that is bad enough, but it gets worse. The SPARC report points out that Elsevier, as an academic-publisher-cum-data-analytics business – one whose 'products span discovery; research management, funding, and collaboration; publishing and dissemination; and research analytics' – is also a subsidiary of RELX (Yoose and Shockey 2023, 7). The latter multinational conglomerate describes itself as a global provider of information-based analytics and decision tools. By amalgamating ten thousand data points relating to hundreds of millions of individuals, RELX (the name is a condensed version of Reed-Elsevier) is able to supply extensive databases of personal information to law enforcement agencies, governmental bodies and corporations. 'RELX risk products have been documented as being used in ways that raise serious concerns, including to help monitor protestors' social media feeds, surveil immigrants, blackmail women, and help in attempting to manufacture false terrorism charges against some of those who participated in anti-racism protests in the summer of 2020' (8).

AI has long been behind such tracking and harvesting – as a result of being embedded in mobile phones, for instance. Still, it will be fascinating to see what impact the increasing use of ChatGPT and other generative language models has on this system. Is it going to disrupt the business models of the big five for-profit academic publishing companies, to the point where they are eventually superseded by newer, smaller rivals (or acquired by the goliaths of commercial AI: Google, Meta, Nvidia *et al.*)? Or are Elsevier, Wiley-Blackwell, Taylor & Francis, Springer Nature and SAGE going to be able to future-proof themselves by incorporating large-language-model AI into their existing research-surveillance and data-brokering products, much as Advance Publications has adapted Turnitin by introducing AI detection into its anti-plagiarism software? Elsevier has already introduced a GenAI tool that produces summaries of research from the more than twenty-seven thousand journals in its Scopus abstract and citation database, for instance.

In this context COPIM is offering an alternative knowledge-sharing philosophy that is more horizontal and collaborative. Here the scholarly community collectively owns, manages and governs infrastructures and revenue streams for the common good in such a fashion as to enable a variety of initiatives to become part of the BPC- and embargo-free open access publishing ecosystem, including non-profit, independent and scholar-led presses.[126] (Far from being black-boxed, all the software developed by COPIM is open source. Its code is shared openly as well. These are just two of the practices COPIM has adopted, both to encourage and assist others in starting their own publishing initiatives, and to ward off the commercial capture of the systems it is building, all the while remaining aware that Big Tech has a long history of pursuing profit from open-source development.) What is more, because COPIM and ScholarLed are predicated on official legal agreements between the different entities in their respective consortiums, they can be understood as collaborative projects that are 'formal enough to embody the kind of strategic direction or intentionality necessary to effect systemic change across scholarly communication' (Adema and Moore 2021). In this regard they are distinct from the informality, flexibility and spontaneity of the latent commons that is the Radical Open Access Collective.

Yet, in spite of appearances, it has never been an ambition of my collaborators and I to simply increase our output or expand our community, its activities and mode of production. As indicated in Chapter 6, rather than practise what's known in the common parlance as 'scaling what works', we prefer to *nonscale*, to repeat a term from Anna Tsing: what my colleague Janneke Adema has dubbed 'scaling small'.

· · · · ·

To explain what is meant by scaling small: OHP consists of a network of interlacing scholarly communities whose various activities make up the collective. While all of these communities are relatively small in size, each operates according to its own scale and schedule, in its own academic subject area and geopolitical context, retaining its own intellectual identity, approach and manner of working in the process. But

Open Humanities Press is not simply about enlarging its community of communities by encouraging more and more journals and presses nationally and internationally to adopt its model of publishing open access – possibly with a view to themselves becoming part of OHP (what's called 'scaling out'), or OHP becoming part of a larger organisation. Nor is OHP focused on publishing an ever-growing number of journals and books according to its mode of open access ('scaling up'). In other words, OHP's chief concern is neither with flipping as many journals as it can to its version of open access, nor with trying to grow ever larger as an entity until it comes to rival, or otherwise disrupt, for-profit, closed-access, legacy publishers. For us, scaling small involves OHP opening its community of communities to what Tsing refers to as the kind of 'meaningful diversity' that might actually 'change things' (Tsing 2015, 38).

What forms does this scaling small take in practice? Since Open Humanities Press launched in 2008, we have been offered – either by current or prospective members of the collective – a number of experimental books that were so radically heterogeneous to our work they were considered unsuitable for inclusion in any of our existing series. Now we could have just left it there. We could have ignored these somewhat unconventional projects and continued to add more and more books and book series that *were* operating according to our already established standards and priorities. But we took a deliberate decision not to expand in this uniform, stable manner. Instead, we decided to create both the Liquid and Living Books series and OHP Labs as experimental spaces in which to 'explore new forms of scholarly communication and develop future models of theoretically-informed critique', spaces that would be capable of hosting such projects (Open Humanities Press n.d.). This is what scaling small means for us. The idea is not to accumulate ever more straightforward elements (i.e., regular open access books and journals). It's to add *distorting* elements like *Photomediations*, *after.video*, and Combinatorial Books: Gathering Flowers that have the potential to push Open Humanities Press as a project to form shapes that we had not originally thought of. (OHP's scaling small philosophy and anti-growth stance differentiates it markedly from legacy presses, many of which are consolidating and conglomerating in order to be more of the same, only at a greater scale. Evidence De Gruyter agreeing to acquire Brill for €51.5m in 2023 to form De Gruyter Brill. With their combined revenues of around €134m and 750 employees, De Gruyter Brill is planning to publish in excess 3,500 books and 800 journals a year. Its self-declared aim is to create the leading academic publisher in the humanities, something OHP has no intention of ever being [Brill 2023]; it's not even an aspiration.)

The inclusion of such non-standard series and spaces has certainly led to a change in Open Humanities Press. Among other things, it has challenged many of our guiding assumptions as to what an open access book is and can be. Consequently, while we continue to make OHP's texts, software and infrastructure openly available, we have become less interested in simply adding to the number of conventional book series or even journals within our network of entwined communities. And all the more so in light of some of the announcements that have been made in recent years. The Arcadia Fund is giving MIT Press a $10m endowment to support the publication of open access books and journals, for instance. Meanwhile, the Council of the EU member state governments – which oversees the £90bn Horizon Europe research funding programme – is recommending that immediate open access to publicly funded research be the standard position, that this should not require authors to pay fees, and, furthermore, that support should be provided for non-profit scholarly publishing models.[127] On this evidence it seems as if the battle around conventional open access books and journals is beginning to be won – although a lot remains still to be achieved, of course. Nevertheless, if we are going to add a new element to Open Humanities Press at this stage, it's more likely to be something experimental, something that provides an opportunity to open OHP's community of communities to the kind of (biblio)diversity that may transform us and our ways of doing things. It would be something akin to *Aesthetic Programming: A Handbook of Software Studies* (2020) by Winnie Soon and Geoff Cox, which explores the technical as well as cultural imaginaries of programming from its insides, and which is itself offered as a computational object that is open to modification, reversioning and forking. As with most OHP books, it is available in the pdf and print formats. But *Aesthetic Programming* can also be accessed as a GitLab repository and as a static site created from the repository,[128] which means readers are able to use their web browsers to execute the many JavaScript programming examples contained in the book. Soon and Cox describe this approach as a means of bringing the writing of code and writing about code 'together in ways that … emphasize that writing a book is necessarily a work in progress'. *Aesthetic Programming*, like a piece of software, 'is a book to be read, and acted upon, shared and rewritten' (Soon and Cox 2020, 17).[129] Following its publication, Sarah Ciston and Mark C. Marino produced an extra chapter of *Aesthetic Programming*: Chapter 8.5, 'Talking Back' (2021). In doing so they modified Soon and Cox's book while also offering a fresh take on the project, resulting in an exchange of ideas between the two versions. Ciston and Marino take care to emphasise that their chapter is not intended to fill any gaps in the original – it is not a missing chapter in that sense – but rather to supplement *Aesthetic Programming* by embracing the collaborative 'yes-and' philosophy of its initial co-authors.

A similar scaling small philosophy is adopted by Open Humanities Press with regard to those other communities it collaborates with. As an interlacing eco-system of projects OHP retains its own intellectual identity and operational scale. However, it simultaneously opens itself to potentially transformative relationships with a multiplicity of other, non-profit, independent and scholar-led approaches to the creation, publication and dissemination of academic research. Open Humanities Press does so not least through its membership of the Radical Open Access Collective and COPIM communities of communities. Our preference for the term 'scaling small' over Tsing's 'nonscaling' is a means of highlighting the fact that, through the 'scaling' part of the expression, OHP is becoming part of something larger: a community of communities with other communities of communities. But it's scaling small in that: 1) OHP's modest size and anti-growth philosophy is retained; and 2) OHP is not scaling without also potentially distorting itself and its programme.[130]

· · · · ·

It should be said that some scholars consider the relatively small size of initiatives such as Open Humanities Press to be an issue, precisely because they do not try to offer a complete answer to the question of how to provide a universal eco-system for open access books and journals (Poynder 2020, 73).[131] It's also important to acknowledge that the Radical Open Access Collective differs from Open Humanities Press in terms of the scale of some of its initiatives. As was pointed out earlier, the ROAC includes among its community of communities the Latin American Council of Social Sciences (CLACSO) network of publishers from Latin America. Yet even with the Radical Open Access Collective – or COPIM for that matter, which is also relatively large in scaling-out terms – we're not trying to produce a project or process *to rule them all*. This is just one of the many ways in which Open Humanities Press is distinct from the likes of Google Scholar, Academia.edu or even Knowledge Unlatched, and their endeavours to achieve critical mass in order to benefit from the network effect, whereby everyone ends up using them because everyone else does.[132] Their desired outcome is a monopoly: what the entrepreneur and venture capitalist Peter Thiel calls a market of one. The complexity and plurality of the higher education field, however, means such paternalistic attempts to impose a one-size-fits-all solution onto its constantly shifting publishing ecology are doomed to fail. (Speaking in the context of AI text generation, Gebru argues that keeping models and their datasets small and purpose-built for the specific task and community concerned – rather than building 'general-purpose AI' such as GPT-4, which was designed to tackle a wide variety of jobs and trained on forty-five terabytes of text – also makes those models more effective and efficient in terms of time, finances and cost to the environment. In particular, it reduces the risk of overrepresenting hegemonic viewpoints, and of encoding human biases, including stereotypical associations pertaining to inequalities of class, race and gender, which are potentially harmful to marginalised populations, as identified in the infamous 'stochastic parrots' paper [Bender and Gebru *et al.* 2021]. 'When you're trying to build something like a one-size-fits-all model for every kind of scenario, you've already lost in terms of safety', Gebru claims. 'You can't even ask the question: What is this for? What should it not be used for?' [quoted in Lapowsky 2023].) Besides, a one-size-fits-all approach leaves little room for experimentation, when my collaborators and I are convinced that what's required is a diverse range of models, business and otherwise – not least to avoid becoming reliant on a system of article and book processing charges that is potentially untenable. This is why the ROAC, as part of its particular scaling small approach, and as observed above, is concerned to 'strengthen alliances between the open access movement' and other struggles around the right to access, copy, distribute, sell and (re)use artistic, cultural and academic research works: struggles such as those associated with p2p file sharing, shadow libraries and internet piracy (Radical Open Access Collective n.d.). 'The trick' as Tsing indicates, 'is to trace or make relationships between projects'. She writes: 'Project scales jostle and contest each other. Because relationships are encounters across difference, they have a quality of indeterminacy. Relationships are transformative, and one is not sure of the outcome. Thus diversity-in-the-making is always part of the mix' (2012, 510).

In addition to the concepts of latent and formal commons, another way of understanding the relationship between these different projects is in terms of what Blaser and de la Cadena call the 'uncommons'. Building this time on Stengers' idea of 'interests in common which are not the same interests', Blaser and de la Cadena describe the creation of an uncommons as the 'negotiated coming together of heterogeneous worlds (and their practices) as they strive for what makes each of them be what they are, which is also not without others' (2018, 4; citing Stengers 2005; Stengers 2011, 60). Just as the communities within Open Humanities Press are both autonomous and interdependent, so the different communities of communities of which OHP is a part – the Radical Open Access Collective and so forth – have interests in common which are not all necessarily the same interests, and cannot always be mutually decided upon and agreed. Each of these communities – and the communities within them – is different and needs to operate in terms of the model that works best for them, be it freemium, institutional-subsidy, library-membership or some other approach. The relations between these communities can therefore be difficult, complex, antagonistic (right down to the fact that not all of those involved would necessarily agree with the accounts of these projects offered here). It is a situation exacerbated by the fact that the elements they do not have in common can include not only those

The Epistemological Politics of Scaling Small

other projects and approaches that are collaborated with but the relation itself, what is understood as the relation with and between them. This relation can take heterogenous forms too.

The issue of scale has received a lot of attention due to its connection with human development, Enlightenment progress, and, especially, capitalist expansion and growth. A potential to sustain itself through economies of scale, attained when production is increased and costs are proportionally decreased, is often considered a necessity if an open access publishing project is to attract funding, for instance. Yet the problem with scalability, as Tsing makes clear, is that it 'demands the possibility of infinite expansion without changing the research framework ... the research questions' or 'their framing assumptions' (2015, 37-38). Tsing provides the example of a business that, if it is scalable, is not able to 'change its organization as it expands'. A scalable research project can likewise only admit 'data that already fit the research theme' (2015, 38). This is not to suggest nonscaling projects are inherently more ethical or more politically progressive. Tsing insists it would be a 'huge mistake' to presuppose that scalability is undesirable while nonscalability is desirable *per se*. Both scalable and nonscalable projects can have negative consequences. As far as she is concerned the primary difference between scalable and nonscalable projects lies not with 'ethical conduct' but the fact nonscalable projects are more diverse since they are not set up for extensive growth. 'Nonscalable projects can be terrible or benign; they run the range' (42). A decision can always be taken that a particular project does need to 'change scales smoothly without any change in project frames' (38). (This is the case with the Open Book Collective, for instance, which has emerged out of the COPIM project. Governed, managed and led by its community of members, the Open Book Collective brings together open access book publishers, libraries and publishing service providers with a view to making it possible to fund open access books collectively and sustainably without requiring authors to pay BPCs. It is 'scaling medium', as it were, to enable it to incorporate a range of not large but not necessarily small non-diamond OA book publishing projects, including some university presses that are not yet fully OA but wish to be, so as 'to cultivate more spaces where scholarly book publishing will not be monopolised and gated by a small handful of large for-profit corporations' [Open Book Collective n.d.].) Still, it should be born in mind that scaling (even scaling medium) risks diminishing the degree of 'meaningful diversity' that might lead to change (Tsing 2015, 38).

■ ■ ■ ■ ■

Interestingly, Tsing offers European colonialism as a further instance of scalability and the 'messes it makes' (38):

> In their sixteenth- and seventeenth-century sugarcane plantations in Brazil, for example, Portuguese planters stumbled on a formula for smooth expansion. They crafted self-contained, interchangeable project elements, as follows: exterminate local people and plants; prepare now-empty, unclaimed land; and bring in exotic and isolated labor and crops for production. This landscape model of scalability became an inspiration for later industrialization and modernization. (38-39)

The connection between scalability and colonialism relates to another reason scaling small is important: it can help us avoid naturalising the neo-colonial 'centre/periphery' model of the geopolitics of knowledge, and thus passively repeating it. In that model several countries, such as the UK, US, France and Italy, are positioned at the centre of the global academic and publishing networks. From this position they are able to export their knowledge and present it as 'universal' – though mostly in English translation as far as the latter two are concerned. Countries on the periphery of these networks, however, lack the resources to publish, export or even produce their own universal knowledge.[133] (Although just 5% of the world's population has English as their mother tongue, 92.6% of Scopus and 95.4% of Web of Science publications are written in the language [Marginson 2021, 25].)

Yet to avoid perpetuating the neo-colonial hegemony of Western knowledge and its publishing models it's not enough to *merely* open up the theory and philosophy of the North Atlantic: literally, in our case, by making it available open access, albeit still in English or, at best, Spanish, French and Portuguese. Such accessibility may of course be needed and welcome at times. (To this end Open Humanities Press published *Magia realista* in 2020, a Spanish translation of Timothy Morton's *Realist Magic* [2013].) Still, remaining at the level of this gesture would risk implying that the supposedly universal theory of the 'Global North' (which, like the 'Global South', is not an unproblematic term – see Toshkov 2018), would stay as it is and would just be translated, exported and made accessible to readers in places such as Argentina, Brazil and the Democratic Republic of Congo. Expansion of this nature would once again not really alter the research forms, perspectives and frameworks, the questions raised or their underlying assumptions. In fact, by making the research of the Global North available open access such expansion may actually increase the neo-colonial hegemony of Western knowledge.

Nor is it adequate to merely add the 'south-to-south and south-to-north (equity model)' to this 'north-to-south access to knowledge (charity model)' (Morrison and Rahman 2020, 2-3; Chan *et al.* 2011). Once again, adopting such an approach as an expression of transnational solidarity and linguistic diversity may be a perfectly understandable and important thing to do. (The 2022 issue of *Culture Machine*, co-edited from Chile, was published in Spanish and Portuguese, for instance, and was the first edition of the journal to appear entirely in a language other than English [Celis Bueno and freire 2022].) To help bring about epistemic and cognitive justice, however, it's insufficient to cite and quote 'directly, unambiguously and generously' more Indigenous scholars as 'thinkers in their own right, not just disembodied representatives of an amorphous Indigeneity ... and not just as research subjects or vaguely defined "collaborators"'" (Todd 2016, 7). Nor is it enough for scholars in Africa, Asia and Latin America to join their UK and US counterparts in being frequent contributors to the world's production of *universal knowledge*. (AI generation systems can now of course assist authors with writing in English, Spanish and French when they are not their first languages.) Such an approach is unsatisfactory even if these scholars should do so using their own naming and referencing styles and in their own languages, for all those languages may be formerly subaltern. As Leanne Betasamosake Simpson asserts, there is the prospect here of 'meeting the overwhelming needs of the Western academic industrial complex or attempting to "Indigenize the academy" by bringing Indigenous Knowledges into the academy on the terms of the academy itself' (2014, 13). It is equally inadequate to 'replace the epistemologies of the North' with those of the South (de Sousa Santos 2018, 7). Rather than being seen as something that can be simply universalised or imported to the North from the South, the undoing of the Euro-Western culture/nature dualism, like ideas of decolonisation, intersectionality and pluriversal politics, must be politico-ethically situated in specific knowledge contexts that are invariably complicated and messy (Hall 2021b; Tuck and Yang 2012).

Other approaches to be wary of include treating the Global South as a laboratory for exploring alternatives to the 'failures' of modern, western-centric thinking (Cavalcante Silva 2023), or as being incapable of producing more general knowledge. It's extremely limiting for the Global South to be portrayed as generating primarily materialist, activist theory that is historically and politically rooted in specific places and local contexts: in terms of the interdependent relations of individuals with family, community, the land (Giraldo 2016, 161). There is a danger in the latter position especially that those in the Global South will *only* be permitted to engage with their situations and ways of life; that attempts on their part to participate in the production of other kinds of ('non-situated') knowledge will be dismissed as uninteresting at best. (This is why we need to think of commons in terms of neither public nor private, neither global nor local, neither modern nor traditional.) What is required instead is 'an-other thinking, an-other logic': a thinking and logic that works to create the conditions for the radical diversity, pluriversality or indeed multi-polarity – rather than universality – of knowledges, cultures, worlds.[134]

. . . . .

Such an-other thinking should include a messy, co-constitutive and aporetic opening to those knowledges that are 'other' in the sense of what might be called 'standard' forms of knowledge. (It is aporetic because, as Samuel Weber observes when writing about the future of the humanities and of theory, 'this opening to the other can never be free of a degree of closure'. Once again, it is not just the other that is difficult; the relation to the other is also difficult, with the potential to take heterogenous forms [Hall 2008, 99; Weber 2000].) This includes peer-reviewed academic books and articles published in conventional formats with recognised presses and journals that are written by professional researchers who are considered 'other' in geographical terms, because they are living in 'less-advantaged' countries in the Global South and East. It also includes those who are considered other because they belong to marginalised and silenced communities in the Global North and West. These are communities that have historically been excluded from publishing their own legitimate knowledges (say, because their members have been regarded as less-than-human or as lacking in reason, and thus incapable of contributing to scholarship), and who have often gone unrecognised or uncited, even when they have managed to publish: working-class, Black, Global Majority, LGBTQIAP2S+ and GTRSB (Gypsy, Traveller, Roma, Showmen and Boater) professional researchers, for instance. Neither the West nor the Global North is unified and self-identical, then. Just as one can be Black and Global Majority and still think very much in white terms, so the epistemological Global South 'also exists in the geographic North', as de Sousa Santos notes when discussing the epistemologies of both the Global South and the future (2016, 19).[135]

An-other logic of this kind should also include an aporetic welcoming to those knowledges that are not, or not yet, regarded as legitimate if judged by the prevailing rules and conventions of the Euro-Western world. Included in this category are those non-conforming knowledges that issue from presses, journals and languages that are outside the so-called mainstream of the academic industrial complex. After all, publishing practices can vary significantly from country to country and field to field. Take some of the many small-scale, local and community-driven presses and journals in the epistemological, nongeographic Global South. These entities may be *ethical*, in that they do not resort to having fake editors, or demanding authors pay APCs only to then publish their articles without peer review or editorial quality control in order to generate a profit. Yet they can still find themselves labelled 'low quality' or even 'predatory' (i.e., dishonest, fraudulent, illegitimate, exploitative, questionable) according to the evaluation criteria of what counts as 'proper', 'valid' knowledge and research. These criteria are established by the most powerful institutions in the Global North; institutions that are able to reproduce their (neo-colonial) dominance by imposing these criteria and the associated notions of quality and prestige on the rest of the academic world with the help of league tables, rankings, checklists, indexes, metrics and impact factors such as those provided by Elsevier's Scopus citation database and its CiteScore journal evaluation metric.[136] (The development of LLM AI has compounded the situation. AI-detection software has been found to 'consistently misclassify non-native English writing samples as AI-generated, whereas native writing samples are accurately identified' [Liang *et al.* 2023)].) In short, these knowledges – and these knowers – are not naturally non-conforming. They are culturally and politically constructed as such by the dominant ways of knowing and treated accordingly.[137]

That the kind of non-exhaustive, plurilingual bibliodiversity we are looking towards features these different, unauthorised knowledges is important, then. Such knowledges constitute alternative, underrepresented ways of understanding and perhaps even transforming the world. As de Sousa Santos makes clear, however, they remain 'unacceptable today in our curriculums, in our canons of social studies in Europe or in the United States' and their prescriptive and colonial modalities of enquiry, because they 'are not rigorous, they are not monumental' (2016, 21-22, 20). As far as he is concerned, we need to 'give credit' to a range of 'other knowledges … other conceptions of productivity … other conceptions of spatial scale' (22), other 'ways of conceiving of time and the relations among human beings and between humans and nonhumans' (20).

It's this emphasis on diversity that makes de Sousa Santos's work on the epistemologies of the Global South so compelling (even if it's not without its problems and critics).[138] I'm therefore going to call on de Sousa Santos's help to offer something of a loose collection of 'alternative thinking of alternatives' that takes shape 'in ways not foreseen by Western thinking, including critical Western thinking', with its emphasis on written, Latin-alphabetic approaches presented in a rigorous, ordered, disciplined fashion according to certain legal-political systems and notions of intellectual property and capital (2016, 20). Contained in this collection are other modes of knowledge that have academic researchers involved in their production. (A variety of less authoritative practices, formats and media can be gathered under this category as well, even if they go unmentioned by de Sousa Santos. They include grey literature and self-published works; material that scholars make available informally via emails, websites, blogs, wikis, archives, databases, podcasts, newsletters, social networks and video-sharing platforms; and experimental work that is published in non-standard book and journal formats with non-professional print and binding: artists' books, zines, samizdat texts and so forth.) What we might call non-academic ways of knowing such as those associated with social and political struggle, where knowledge is 'lived performatively' and tends not to have an 'individualizable subject', are also important (de Sousa Santos 2018, 3). So are what de Sousa Santos refers to as 'popular vernacular knowledge', 'artistic knowledge', 'performative knowledge' (2016, 22), lay knowledge, religious knowledge and the knowledge of native, aboriginal, First Nation and Indigenous peoples (e.g., regarding how to assimilate humans with fragile ecosystems), along with the new possibilities they all carry. To this list of non-academic knowledges I would add: the hybrid knowledge of citizen science, fab labs and maker-spaces; the kind of popular vernacular knowledge found in memes and text messages that often takes the form of image-word hybrids; the hyper-emotional knowledge characteristic of big social media in an age of populist nationalism; as well as orature (the oral equivalent of literature) and other 'non-industrial' ways of knowing, many of which have no written version. Significantly, a link can be established here between the negative perception of such non-academic knowledges and the antipolitical moralism inherent in 'dark side' critiques of digital humanities (Chapter 2). For certain obscure, hidden, masked ways of being political that are difficult to comprehend and even detect according to the terms in which political struggle is usually understood can be appended to this list too. They 'are very different from what we think they are', de Sousa Santos remarks, precisely because they are involved in challenging the preconceived, preauthorised knowledge of what it is to be political (2016, 25). He provides as an example the 'struggle of the social movements and the daily struggles of the people that have to survive in hostile contexts in an exclusionary society. They are the silent struggles', he emphasises. 'This is very clear for migrant communities in our societies when they know that open confrontation with the legal powers will mean deportation, so they cannot afford active resistance. They prefer passive resistance' (25).

· · · · ·

Knowledge thus has a colonial and class system, with some ways of knowing (and some knowers) being valued over others. In this context, scaling small has the potential to create the conditions for a radical diversity, pluriversality or multi-polarity of knowledges, none of which are complete and all of which are contestable. What scaling small offers is an-other logic for developing a dynamic ecology of epistemologies about the human and nonhuman that has a highly complex, decentred, antagonistic structure.[139] It is antagonistic because, among other things – and to build on the work of de Sousa Santos one last time – we need to question 'both the reified dichotomies among alternative knowledges (e.g., Indigenous knowledge versus scientific knowledge), and the unequal abstract status of different knowledges (e.g., Indigenous knowledge as a valid claim of identity versus scientific knowledge as the only valid claim of truth)' (2016, 22). Yet what is so promising about developing in terms of scaling small – rather than in terms of the diversity-flattening philosophy of infinite growth and expansion – is that the emphasis on forming transformative relationships that might change the project as elements are added contains the possibility of opening initiatives such as Open Humanities Press and the Radical Open Access Collective to something more radical still. This something more radical is what, in *Digitize This Book!*, I termed 'non-knowledge': 'the apparently useless, unimportant, irrelevant, obsolete, worthless, senseless, trivial, or mistaken' (Hall 2008, 100). We can mention here the note found in Friedrich Nietzsche's papers after his death stating 'I have forgotten my umbrella'; and the content of dreams as described by Hélène Cixous in her notebooks, now archived in the *Bibliothèque nationale de France* (Hall 2008, 163-164). There is also the role of hypnosis in Freudian psychoanalysis, phantomism in the thought of Jacques Derrida, and naffness in mine (Borch-Jacobsen 1993; Derrida 1994; Hall 2002a). And, of course, when it comes to non-knowledge, there is care work. After all, there can be no finished products or outcomes, no books, journals or presses, without large numbers of human and nonhuman actors operating in the background to provide the kind of affective labour (involving inspiring, encouraging, building, developing, maintaining, supporting, repairing) that is needed at all stages of the workflow and supply chain. The most valid and legitimate of knowledges depends on this non-knowledge even as it tries to mask or erase it.

To spiral back to the discussion of understanding in relation to media from the first part of this book: consider how misunderstanding should not be eliminated from the cognitive process in an effort to render the act of conception, interpretation or judgement more authoritative and legitimate. This is because:

> Any attempt to know and understand an object ... must by necessity proceed by means of two 'distinct, if interdependent operations': the one involving a

> certain closure whereby that which has already been *re*-cognized is incorporated into our already existing systems of knowledge and understanding; the other involving an openness to that which, in its very newness, alterity, difference, and heterogeneity, requires an alteration and transformation of these systems in order for it to be capable of being understood. (Hall 2008, 92; quoting Weber 1978, 2)

It follows that misunderstanding should not be positioned as the other of understanding because misunderstanding is actually part of what makes understanding possible. We cannot place limits on the cognitive process if we want to know something. Yet, at the same time, we must do so. We cannot be certain of where to bring the process of cognition to an end. But if we really want to *know* then we must end it somewhere (Hall 2008, 93). If we want to understand, we have to make a decision, a cut, in the undecidable terrain between openness and closure. The question is not whether to do so, but how and where.

Despite their apparent eccentricity, the above examples concerning hypnosis, phantomism and so forth are already considered a legitimate part of the Eurocentric critical theory of the North Atlantic. Nevertheless, they raise questions even for the legitimacy and authority of what is deemed by the Global North to be the most proper, accredited and acceptable forms of academic scholarship. For what are the implications for that knowledge by which those that are 'other' are to be understood – those knowledges that are not, or not yet, regarded as legitimate, those discounted knowledges, those non-knowledges of both other human and nonhuman actors – if 'misrecognition, error, projection, hallucination, and illusion cannot be denied or excluded from the analysis, but are all terms for that which makes it possible in the first place' (Hall 2008, 94)?

More radically still, scaling small contains the potential for a messy, co-constitutive and aporetic opening toward that which refuses to fit into the category of knowledge, even *as non-knowledge*. This is a reference to that which is neither knowledge of the other nor the other of knowledge; that which rather resists knowledge as misrecognition, error, projection, hallucination, illusion; and that which, by resisting it, pushes knowledge to adopt new forms and inhabit new spaces where it may no longer recognise itself *as knowledge*:

> For there is a paradox or contradiction or, indeed, *aporia* in the relation to the 'other' or the 'outside' of knowledge. Identifying and naming these non-knowledges (even as misunderstanding, misrecognition, error, illusion, projection, hallucination, hypnosis, transference, naffness, death, or whatever) is what makes this relation possible. It is only by identifying and naming them that we can have any such relation to these non-knowledges. At the same time it is also that which renders this relation impossible, because this relation is in effect only being extended to that which *can* be named and identified; whereas the difference between non-knowledge and the other of knowledge is that the latter cannot be named or identified – it is rather that which knowledge cannot or does not know, and which is therefore indeed the other of knowledge. The aporetic relation to non-knowledge thus involves a break with knowledge, with what can be known. It requires that we open knowledge up, not only to that which can be named and identified as the other of knowledge (as non-knowledge, or *not yet* knowledge, or knowledge-to-come), but also that which cannot. (Hall 2008, 100-101)

Isn't the latter the truly transformative relation, in that it eludes translating the difference of the other of knowledge back into the same, into knowledge (albeit non-knowledge), and thus cancelling its very difference? Certainly, it takes us further even than the Radical Open Access Collective, which responds to inquiries from prospective members that it has no joining fees or entry criteria other than an 'affinity with our philosophy' and a readiness to 'share with the other members of the collective in a horizontal, non-competitive manner'. For when it comes to the scaling-small of a community of communities such as the Radical Open Access Collective or Open Humanities Press, such an aporetic relation requires that we open them 'to the absolute, unknown other; that we be prepared to let it in, to receive it without necessarily asking it to respond reciprocally, by identifying or naming itself, not just as legitimate or not-yet-legitimate, but even as non-knowledge or the unknown' (Hall 2008, 101). Without doubt, there is a risk – which is also an opportunity – that as a result the contents and form of any such community of publishing communities will not look too much like knowledge as it is most commonly understood according to the inherited modernist and liberal humanist conventions of the West. Be that as it may, this questioning of knowledge is still the most responsible thing to do, at least according to Derrida's notion of responsibility. There can be no responsibility in this sense – and no ethics or politics for that matter – without the 'experience of the undecidable' which, in this case, involves the constant taking of the decision as to what knowledge is (Hall 2008, 101).

· · · · ·

Perhaps due to the cocreative relationship with generative media, this particular theory-performance of artificial creative intelligence has come to entangle itself closely with others in the meshwork of texts published under the name-cum-mask 'Gary Hall'. Rather than reiterate any more from this corpus of text I'm therefore going to end this chapter here. To prepare the ground for the slight change of direction that follows I simply want to emphasise an earlier point: that it's important our theory-performances constitute a multiplicity of forms of intervention that are engaging with particular issues across a number of different sites. With this in mind, my collaborators and I are now turning our attention to the following question: can the de-liberalising, inhumanist, scaling-small approach we have adopted with projects such as Open Humanities Press and the Radical Open Access Collective be translated to cities in order to help transform them?

Chapter 9

The Commons as Coming Together of Those with Nothing in Common: or, How to Redesign a City

I

Imagining societies differently requires imaging the places they inhabit differently, which is why cities are so important to progressive politics. It's also in cities where political forces for change frequently emerge these days (the bed as public platform and site of protest of Chapter 2 notwithstanding). Over the last few decades numerous events have testified to the significance of cities in this respect: from the roundabout revolutions of Bahrain, South Korea and Egypt, through Occupy Wall Street and the movements of the squares in Spain and Greece, to the pro-democracy street protests of Hong Kong's 'umbrella revolution' and beyond.

Additionally, cities operate at a scale that makes progressive change in a leftist sense a realistic possibility, further emphasising their political importance. Being smaller than nations – and, in the case of the UK, less subject to the attentions of the Tory press and its satellites – it's often far easier for towns and cities, and, within them, local governments, council leaders and mayors, to take a more radical and experimental approach. It's a state of affairs borne out by the celebrated community wealth-building model, dubbed 'guerrilla localism', which has been pioneered by Preston

City Council in the UK, and which is based on the collective economic and social power of the city's public institutions (Brown and Jones 2021). Many of those responsible for the initial impetus behind the Arab Spring, *Indignados*, Occupy and YoSoy132 protests subsequently went into municipalism for just this reason. Ada Colau, the housing activist who served as Barcelona's mayor between 2015 and 2023, is only one of the most prominent and oft referred to examples of the transition from protestor to politician.[140] Similarly, in the UK, much of the energy and ideas generated by the left prior to and during Jeremy Corbyn's leadership of the Labour party were relocated to the nation's town and city halls (even if the more centrist Keir Starmer and his followers worked hard over subsequent years to ensure no actual Corbynistas remained in power by the middle of 2023). Political leaders, such as Andy Burnham, Mayor of Greater Manchester, and Tracey Brabin, Mayor of West Yorkshire, don't necessarily try to engage in large-scale national politics. Their main focus is on providing smaller-scale localised government at a regional-city level. This means that, in order to offer something different to England's prevailing status quo, they don't have to wait for a sympathetic government to be elected to Westminster that is prepared to enact a programme of radical transformation; nor even for a like-minded opposition party to appear, as they would with the 'state capture' approach. Their attitude is more independent, involving taking action without always asking 'for permission or guidance from above' or the centre (Brown and Jones 2021, 20). (Evidence Burnham's role in removing private operators from the running of Greater Manchester's bus system in 2023 and placing it under public control.) Some go so far as to say that the city is to the twenty-first century what the nation state was to the twentieth century and the empire was to the nineteenth.

Yet cities are facing numerous problems of course. They include poverty, unemployment, population density, political polarisation, war, massive displacements of peoples, racist state violence, segregation, social and economic inequality, housing shortage, labour exploitation, violence against women (or female-identifying, female-presenting people), climate breakdown and the threats to public health posed by novel viruses. Given the funding cuts that were imposed by numerous governments in the name of austerity to defend the neoliberal order in the Global North and West after the financial crisis of 2008, many cash-strapped cities have been forced to respond by reducing that proportion of their budgets dedicated to providing infrastructure and offering alternatives to the market. In the UK public spending was shrunk from 42% of GDP in 2009-10 to 35% in 2018-19, with that allotted to local government declining by 40% in real terms in the decade leading to 2020. Inflation-adjusted per capita spending on British public libraries decreased by 53% between 2009-10 and 2020-21 (Campaign for the Arts & University of Warwick 2024). As a result, Britain has closed approximately 800 of its public libraries since 2010 – that's almost one fifth of the total amount – with the loss of over 8,000 jobs. Nearly 130 libraries shut in 2018 alone. And that is despite the value libraries offer to their communities (in terms of helping to address issues such as literacy, disability, social isolation, health and wellbeing and digital inclusion) being worth six times what it takes to run them (Gordon *et al.* 2023). More closures are expected to follow in the wake of Brexit, the Covid-19 pandemic and the cost of living crisis. Shrinking budgets and income, combined with the growing price of goods, utilities and services such as public housing and health care, mean numerous councils have a substantial gap in their funding, with many in England facing deep cuts. Birmingham city council, the largest local authority in the UK, declared itself effectively bankrupt in September 2023. Nottingham city council announced it was in the same position shortly afterwards. Over twenty more are in danger of doing likewise in the coming years according to a collective of forty-seven urban councils known as the Special Interest Group of Municipal Authorities (Sigoma 2023).

Nor is this state of affairs confined to the UK. Public libraries in the US are facing catastrophic budgets cuts as well. On top of that they are having to cope with book bans driven by right-wing activists, violations of which could result in the withdrawal of public funding. So much so that the production of lists of prohibited texts has reached an unprecedented level in the US, mainly impacting works with themes relating to race, racism or LGBTQIAP2S+ issues. American Library Association figures for 2023 identify 1,247 censorship demands involving 4,240 unique book titles, representing a 65% increase on the previous year (ALA 2024).

2

The widespread policy of reducing spending on local civic infrastructure and amenities has cleared a path for private providers to enter spaces long considered the domain of the public sector. In 2017 Innisfil in Ontario, Canada, infamously gave Uber complete responsibility for the provision of public transport in the town. It did so with the goal of saving money, as Uber seemed a cheaper option than the bus system Innisfil was originally planning to build. Unfortunately, it did not quite turn out like that. The town financially supported rides, so the more the system was used the more it paid out to Uber. It quickly reached the point where Innisfil was spending a larger amount of money on what was effectively a subsidised taxi service than it would have cost to construct a public transit system from the outset.

Many towns and cities are nonetheless planning for their future by deliberately turning to for-profit businesses to provide investment and help improve their infrastructure, often partnering with, or outsourcing to, multinational surveillance capitalist companies in the process. As Morozov observes, when it comes to turning to the Big Tech of Silicon Valley, towns and cities 'do so in the hope' that the 'superior ability to gather, analyse and act on data' of these companies will 'yield tremendous savings for the public sector while stimulating innovation and entrepreneurship' (2016, 26). Such neoliberal thinking is apparent at a national level, too. In 2021 it led the UK government, under cover of the Covid outbreak, to look to scrape all GP (general practitioner) data from patients' medical records and make it available for sale to private companies. (This was a replay of a similar initiative called Care.data that was announced in 2013 and cancelled not long afterwards due to fears about the security and confidentiality of the extracted data, particularly when it came to corporate access.) Plans of this kind appear all the more surprising post-Covid, given the virus clearly exposed the danger of relying on the private sector. Doing so led to vaccines for diseases with pandemic potential not being developed in advance as businesses regarded them as having insufficient capacity to generate profits for their owners, shareholders and investors. Companies preferred to let their priorities be set instead by the desires of the rich: for makeup, skincare, dietary products and the like. Yet as the emergence of coronavirus variants in different places around world showed, the fight against a pandemic requires *everyone everywhere* to be safely vaccinated, not just those people and countries that can afford to pay for the privilege.

The same can be said of other aspects of municipal welfare. Cities are only really fit to live in if they provide all of their human and nonhuman inhabitants, including people, animals and plants, with a decent quality of life. The climate crisis makes this quite clear. When it comes to humans, the environment is shared by everyone, not just a select few who are able to ensure their own wellbeing by displacing threats to the ecosystem onto the vulnerable members of society in an effort to maintain the status quo. Among the dangers are the spread of plastics, the erosion of soils and increasing carbon dioxide emissions, 8% of which come from that basic building material of cities, concrete. (The latter is the planet's second most used resource. The most used is water. Its scarcity now impacts 3 billion globally. Approximately 1.5 billion people have experienced acute water shortages in the twenty-first century – to the point some are predicting drought will be the next pandemic. That's if food and energy shortages exacerbated by 'global boiling' don't get there first.)

Faced by these threats to the elemental commons, we should all be communists, Michael Marder suggests (2016, 34). And, to be sure, sooner or later even the wealthiest of city occupants are likely to feel the impact of climate breakdown, not to mention population density, racist state violence and the growing gap between labour and capital. Indeed, it could be argued that we already have evidence of the most comfortable in society experiencing something of this kind, most visibly at the hands of twenty-first century mobilisations such as the *gilets jaunes* and Just Stop Oil. These protest groups are demanding change in ways that the well-off are finding difficult to ignore as it rapidly becomes clear just how vulnerable they, too, are to the world around them. Even so, the development of municipal infrastructure, as with vaccines, has often been driven more by the profit motive and the needs and desires of the rich than by, say, social goals based on the values of justice, equality and solidarity.

3

There has been a lot of criticism of the direction in which cites are headed as a result of various 'smart' city initiatives. In May 2020 Naomi Klein reported that the former CEO of Google, Eric Schmidt, was due to head up a 'blue-ribbon commission to reimagine New York state's post-Covid reality, with an emphasis on permanently integrating technology into every aspect of civic life' (Klein 2020). Schmidt joined New York Governor Andrew Cuomo's daily coronavirus briefing on May 6th to declare that the initial focus would be on telehealth, remote learning and broadband. Viewing the coronavirus outbreak as providing New York with an opportunity to create '"a smarter education system"', Cuomo had made public a similar partnership the previous day with the Bill and Melinda Gates Foundation (Klein 2020; quoting Cuomo from Strauss 2020). Klein identifies in such arrangements the beginnings of an extremely profitable, 'no-touch', 'pandemic-proof' vision of the future: what she refers to as both a 'Screen New Deal' and a 'Pandemic Shock Doctrine'. At its heart lies a 'seamless integration of government with a handful of Silicon Valley giants – with public schools, hospitals, doctor's offices, police, and military all outsourcing (at a high cost) many of their core functions to private tech companies' (Klein 2020). How much this vision of a screen new deal remains intact post-pandemic is open to question. Be that as it may, Amazon's 2021 launch of Sidewalk in the US – which turns its Echo speaker and Ring security camera into a shared wireless network, with a view to creating city-wide 'mesh networks' in the name of providing a better, more convenient and connected service for citizen-customers, and which covered 90% of the US population by 2023 – is presumably paving the way for similar arrangements over the longer term. So is the 2023 decision to base the new 'federated data platform' (FDP) for England's National Health Service on technology from Palantir, despite opposition from the BMA (British Medical Association) and Doctors' Association UK. Along with a contract worth £480m, this decision provides the US data-analytics software company with access to the personal health records of millions of citizens. (Founded in 2004 by Peter Thiel, Palantir Technologies has been backed by the CIA's venture capital arm, In-Q-Tel. It has assisted the digital spy agencies of the United States [NSA], United Kingdom [GCHQ] and elsewhere in overseeing mass surveillance initiatives such as the XKeyscore data retrieval system, which is designed to monitor the online activities of millions of individuals throughout the world. If the latter sounds familiar, it's because XKeyscore is one of the global surveillance programmes whose purpose and use were revealed by the Snowdon leaks.)

Meanwhile, in their book *How to Run a City Like Amazon and Other Fables*, Mark Graham, Rob Kitchin, Shannon Mattern, Joe Shaw and their fellow authors imagine just how bad it would be to actually live and work in a city run by, or in conjunction with, hyper-capitalist, algorithm-led companies such as Uber and Deliveroo, with their emphasis on precarity, mass surveillance and behavioural control (Graham *et al.* 2019). Here, the seamless interconnectivity and 'coherence' of 'wishful Uber-like thinking', whereby municipal systems and infrastructures, with their ubiquitous sensing and real time data flows, are amalgamated into an effective whole, thus making them *smart*, is presented as being 'possible only when we ignore the realities of platform urbanism, foregoing conceiving of the urban realm as a shared public good, and fail to understand cities as complex, democratic, multiscale entities full of competing interests and wicked problems' (Leszczynski and Kitchin 2019).

It is a critical perspective on smart cities that very much resonates with that of the architects Parsons & Charlesworth. For the 2021 Venice Architecture Biennale, which took as its organising theme 'How We Live Together', they created a satirical *Catalog for the Post-Human* that uses tactics of defamiliarisation and estrangement to speculate on what the future is likely to be for precarious labour, including those who provide city services (2021; 2020). Success in such a forthcoming society rests on the ability to be 'permanently cognitively sharp'. Workers are thus forced to augment themselves, physically and mentally, just to keep their jobs (Parsons & Charlesworth n.d.). Along with smart drugs that enable people to adjust their circadian rhythms to their work schedules the catalogue features memory implants and data tattoo monitoring systems (Parsons & Charlesworth 2014). Other products enhance an employee's ability to recover from their labour by enhancing their short-term napping, or by matching their arcadian rhythm to their economic rhythm (Parsons & Charlesworth 2021).

Yet while satirising the stupidity of such apparent smartness can be extremely satisfying and cathartic, my collaborators and I want to go further than some of the critical infrastructure studies and infrastructural turn-type approaches just mentioned.[141] Taking our inspiration, in part, from municipal socialism and Transition Town Initiatives such as the Preston model and Frome's Flatpack Democracy – not forgetting the self-organised networks of mutual care that emerged in the early days of the pandemic in many locations around the world, without waiting for permission from central government – our concern is to focus on what we *do* want when it comes to the future of cities as much as, if not more than, what we don't. The idea is to offer a speculative provocation designed to promote the radical reimagining of our cities, towns, neighbourhoods, streets, even our homes, along more non-modernist-liberal (i.e., *entangled, relational, processual*) lines. Furthermore, it aims to achieve this by viewing the disruption generated by deindustrialisation, the coronavirus and the conflicts in Ukraine and Gaza – together with the emergence of small-scale, decentralised computing practices such as permacomputing and salvage computing (de Valk 2021) – as an opportunity to challenge both the public and private paradigms as they currently exist.

Extending such a challenge may seem ambitious, utopian even. As the UK Conservative Party's response to the Covid-19 outbreaks demonstrates, however, if the will is there we can make radical changes of a kind that would once have been thought unimaginable, not to mention unaffordable. (The UK

Government allocated £370bn to address the pandemic and its associated economic repercussions – and that was just to cover the period from February 2020 to July 2021.) Not to do so is therefore a political decision rather than an economic one. We can fund such changes by defunding other parts of culture and society (Hall 2022b; 2024). We have the money. The environmental activist George Monbiot insists that:

> For the price of one or two contracts issued to ministers' friends through the dodgy Covid 'VIP channel', the current government could have reversed all the losses to the Arts Council's budget, or brought national spending on libraries back to its 2010 level. ...
>
> The budget for the test-and-trace scheme – £37bn – which, according to the public accounts committee, has achieved none of its aims and failed to make 'a measurable difference to the progress of the pandemic', equates to more than twice the entire cut across 10 years in the central government grant to local authorities. (Monbiot 2022)

The government's Covid business support program in England alone lost £1.1bn to fraud and error, the National Audit Office reveals (2023), only £11.4m, or 1%, of which has been recuperated. (£1.1bn is a little less than 5% of the overall amount spent on the scheme.)

4

My collaborators and I are looking to challenge the public and private paradigms by drawing on the de-liberalising, inhumanist, scaling-small approach we have developed with some of our projects. We want to examine the extent to which this approach can be adapted to provide inspiring – but also relatively flexible and affordable – possibilities for radically reconceiving cities, their infrastructure and the ways in which their inhabitants operate within them, so that these urban environments are 'fit for purpose' in the age of artificial creative intelligence. We want to do so not least by exploring how offering a diverse range of more horizontal, collaborative and commons-oriented alternatives to those galleries, libraries, archives and museums (GLAM) currently being provided by the state and corporate realms can help to redesign cities – not just conceptually, but practically and concretely too. GLAM is singled out here because this is where much of our immediate expertise lies. But also because galleries, libraries and museums are some of our most 'public' entities, being encountered (if not actually used) by many city dwellers on a relatively regular basis. Yet other aspects of municipal provision could also be addressed and even invented, since there would be no need to mimic those (often 'universal', Enlightenment, liberal) institutions that, historically, have gone to make up a city, especially in the Global North. If the city helps to create *us*, we also help to create *the city* by acting on, within and as part of the urban setting. Here, too, the relationship between our minds, bodies, technologies and environments is intra-active and co-constitutive. Excitingly, new – and very different – kinds of post-Gutenberg, de-liberalising entities could therefore be designed; entities that do not adhere to traditional models and that function both online and offline as well as in hybrid combinations thereof. (It's a process of invention that could be extended to the design of new institutions for dealing with the issues of law enforcement, public safety and security I discuss elsewhere in relation to the defunding of white, male, middle-class culture [Hall 2022a; 2024]).

A starting point would be to use our experience of working with scholar-led publishers, shadow libraries, DIY pop-up exhibitions and similar ventures to assess the potential for providing such a range of alternatives that is offered by the advocates of open access, open GLAM, FLOSS, p2p filesharing, copyfair, copyleft, copyfarleft, copyfarAI, piracy and the anti-privatised knowledge commons. The various hardware and software, tools and collections that have been made available by these advocates should be included in this assessment as well. The question we want to consider is: can we make it possible for the inhabitants of cities to be able to select from these resources to create not only their own ways and means of knowing the city, different from the algorithmic and data imaginaries of Big Tech and the state, but also their own bespoke anticapitalist, antiracist and antiheteropatriarchal cultural institutions? The idea would be for a diverse multiplicity of actors to be able to do so according to the needs and requirements of their specific situations: either by copying them more or less as they are, if that what's they wish to do and have the necessary time and means for; or by developing, modifying and repurposing those elements they want and discarding the rest. All this could be fed into an informal, flexible, latent commons, or a more formal distributed union or federation of open city infrastructure – or, indeed, an uncommons. It would then be made available to be critically and creatively reused by others. (The weight placed on open tools and resources is deliberate. Not only does such openness enable creative cross-pollination, it also counteracts the current tendency for technology to become concentrated around a small number of extremely large companies. The latter is due in part to these businesses minimising the degree to which their products – laptops, phones, earbuds – are interoperable with those of their competitors.)

In keeping with the philosophy of Open Humanities Press and the Radical Open Access Collective, the building of such bespoke institutions would be undertaken in a non-rivalrous, non-competitive (but not necessarily non-antagonistic or friction-free) fashion, to collaboratively proliferate experiments with renegotiating and reimagining the city. Again, the emphasis would not be on scaling up or scaling out any one model for the conception, commission, creation, ownership and management of civic resources and social infrastructure – a model in which who is included is all too often decided on the basis of everyone having similar characteristics and worldviews. Rather, the scaling small approach detailed earlier would be used to develop dynamic and potentially transformative inter-group relationships with a diversity of human and nonhuman others operating at different levels: internationally, nationally, locally. (That is assuming such distinctions still hold at a time of remote working and online consumption from home, which is far from certain). It would thus be an ontologically heterogenous, relational commonism that includes the nonhuman as actors and not just objects.

The city in this conception would not be concerned with growth or expansion in the conventional sense. To encourage diversity it would promote neither homogenisation nor universal sets of unified standards, be they ethical or technical. Nor would the city be arranged hierarchically on a centre/periphery or inside/outside model, whether the latter be the suburbs, the countryside or nature. Instead, by allowing tools and resources, systems and infrastructure to be appropriately copied, shared and reiterated free of charge on a mutually non-exclusive basis, it would scale small through the establishment of collaborative relations of cocreation and custodianship between a variety of distributed initiatives. These could be global or international, but they could also be regional and local (so much as these terms, too, still apply). There is no reason why scaling small has to connect to other scaling small initiatives at a macro level. It could be conducted at a micro, neighbourhood, even street level, and remain that way.

With regard to humans, a list of those involved could include (but would not be limited to) academics, architects, artists, activists, builders, craftspeople, designers, engineers, journalists and technologists as well as trade unionists, voluntary organisations, citizens groups, community campaigners and everyday city folx. An extended multi-polarity of *disparate* projects could thus be cultivated, involving people beyond the white, middle-aged and middle-class, who tend to be both the main participants in art and culture and the main audience for galleries and museums (in the UK at least). They could also engage people beyond the usual suspects of professional politicians, councillors and retired middle-class professionals with experience in local or third sector politics, who too often make up their boards and steering committees.

5

The reason for the emphasis on the potentially *disparate* nature of these activities is because there are many kinds of city. The appropriate combination and mixture of principles and protocols, tools and infrastructure, priorities and resources, roles and responsibilities would need to be negotiated. It would differ from location to location and municipality to municipality, and would be highly situated and site-sensitive – materially, ecologically, culturally, aesthetically and politically. It would also need to constitute an extended multipolarity of disparate initiatives for the simple reason that there is not one commons nor one model of commons. As was observed earlier, commons can be understood as shared, non-proprietary resources and spaces, along with the collective social processes that are necessary for commoners to produce, manage and maintain them and themselves as a community. There are many different kinds of commons, however, some of which have little or nothing in common with one another. Liberal approaches to commons, such as those of Elinor Ostrom and Yochai Benkler, concentrate on the normative frameworks and principles of governance that best enable the management and maintenance of a shared pool of spaces and resources: common goods. Within this, neoliberal free marketeers see commons as representing an alternative to state regulation and centralised bureaucracy. More radical approaches, such as those of Michael Hardt and Antonio Negri, or Fred Moten and Stefano Harney, focus on the social relations *of* commoning – common good rather than common goods – and on constructing commons on the basis of shared political practices and principles. They are less concerned with associating commons with resources like rivers, seas and forests, or media such as music files and digital books (Hall 2020, 153, 154 n2). From this perspective, commons offer an alternative to capitalism's privatisation, commodification and corporate trade. Meanwhile, as we have seen, Blaser and de la Cadena propose the concept of the uncommons:

> as counterpoint to the common good and to enclosures, and, as important, to slow down the commons (including its progressive versions.) ... all three concepts converge in that they require a common form of relation, one that (like labor or property) connects humans and nature conceived as ontologically distinct and detached from each other. (2018, 18)

Hence the argument I referred to previously when discussing the connection of Open Humanities Press to the Radical Open Access Collective and COPIM: that those who go to make up commons might have certain elements they do not have in common, and that this can include the common relation between them.

In line with what we might call a stance of *responsible openness* (to build on Derrida's notion of the responsible decision referred to in Chapter 8), such diversity would include the possibility of some communities addressing different forms of epistemic and cognitive injustice with different kinds and degrees of openness. Others might refuse to make their tools and infrastructure openly available at all, insisting instead on keeping them closed, masked, even secret. Rather than sharing their knowledge and technologies with any larger community of communities, some migrant, LGBTQIAP2S+, GTRSB, neuroatypical, differently abled or vulnerable people may prefer to keep working by themselves in their own specific contexts and languages. I:ts are making this point under the influence of Silvia Rivera Cusicanqui and the feminist group Feminismo Comunitario. Both see the refusal of translation – and with it the kind of decontextualised connection that can be achieved when their writings are not accessed in their original Spanish – as a way of denying extractivist power relations, and of keeping English-only speaking actors at the margins (see Francke, in Cisneros and Francke 2020, 227; and Simpson's concept of 'Indigenous refusal – refusal to struggle simply for better or more inclusion and recognition within the academic industrial complex' [2014, 22]).[142] Likewise, I:ts are aware some marginalised subjects and communities have neither the time nor the financial means to get involved in building or moderating their own open source DIY digital tools, resources and environments. They prefer to operate on ready-made (and privately-owned and corporately controlled) platforms such as Facebook and X (previously Twitter). Johnathan Flowers presents just such an argument in defence of the continuation of the Black Twitter community despite Musk's takeover of the platform. He contrasts this stance on the part of Black Twitter (which made up 24% of its userbase in 2018 [Smith and Anderson 2018]) favourably with the obvious alternative, which would see Black users of Twitter migrating to the 'very white space' that constitutes the Mastodon network (Hendrix and Flowers 2022].)

The speculative proposal outlined here is not trying to provide a uniform, interoperable, 'one-size-fits-all' model, then; nor a 'blueprint for "universalisable localism' (Brown and Jones 2021, 2). If anything, it is closer to a 'pluriversalisable localism' (Hall 2021b). Even within any 'one' city there would likely arise a messy plurality of actors and groups, organisations and institutions, epistemologies and worldviews, methods and modes of collaborating and negotiating differences, all of them rooted in specific places with their different histories, experiences and expectations. (I'm saying it is only *closer to*, but not the *same as*, a pluriversalisable localism, for two reasons. Firstly, because as already mentioned, there is no reason why scaling small has to connect to other scaling small initiatives at a macro level, even as a pluriversalisable localism. It can do. But it can also remain at a local, micro level. Secondly, it is only closer to a pluriversalisable localism because, as Esposito points out:

> coming prior to adequate legislation, we currently lack even a vocabulary to talk about something – the common – that was effectively excluded first from the process of modernization and then from the process of globalization. The common is neither the public – which is dialectically opposed to the private – nor the global, to which the local corresponds. It is something largely unknown, and even refractory, to our conceptual categories ... (2013, 89)

In other words, we need to think of commons in terms of neither public nor private, neither global nor local, as Chapter 8 has it.)

6

To be clear and to put this in context: we're adopting this pluralistic philosophy because it does not seem to be either realistic or desirable to believe meaningful change is going to be achieved through the adoption of a single unified strategy that can be applied everywhere. (It is certainly not going to be brought about by the simple act of making open-source tools and infrastructure available to communities. As we have seen over the course of *Masked Media*, more *situated* forms of intervention are what is required.) In *How to Be an Anti-Capitalist,*

Erik Olin Wright argues that political change requires a combination of at least four strategic logics: resisting, escaping, taming and dismantling capitalism. Let me explain these logics in terms of the issues this book has been engaging with. If, post-Covid, the war in Ukraine and the cost of living crisis – not to overlook the multiple protests against planetary destruction and violence toward women and people of colour – we want to produce a very different future for cities to those currently offered by the state and corporate realms, then:

A We need some actors to build reimagined trade unions and social movements capable of eroding neoliberal capitalism by resisting the constant surveillance, performance monitoring and behavioural control that is being normalised by Silicon Valley and its gig economy companies – practices satirised both by Parsons & Charlesworth, and by Graham, Kitchin, Mattern, Shaw *et al*.

B We need others to experiment with means of escaping capitalism: through 'community activism anchored in the social and solidarity economy', such as those campaigning to abolish the police or those self-organising groups that responded to the pandemic by plugging the gaps in care left by the market and state (Olin Wright 2019, 120-121); and through the development of a range of cooperative, collaborative and commons-oriented initiatives of the kind outlined in this book.

But we also need some actors to go through the traditional democratic channels of political parties and government legislation:

c We need them to do so in order to tame the excesses of neoliberalism: by restoring to gig economy workers the rights to sick pay and maternity leave they have lost, for instance; or, by establishing new twenty-first century institutions such as the 'data trust for digital workers' proposed by innovation economist Francesca Bria (2023). The idea is to provide employees and unions with increased access to, and control over, their data and the otherwise black-boxed AI systems that generate it. This can be achieved by defining the appropriate ways and situations in which information can be gathered by Big Tech, including academic-publishers-turned-data-analytics-businesses such as Elsevier, and specifying the intended purposes to which it can be put.

D   We also need them to do so with a view to dismantling capitalism and helping transition society into something more socially, epistemologically and cognitively *just*. This could involve lobbying for the monopolies of Amazon, Alphabet and Meta to be broken up, and for communities to be able to generate, capture, control, store and share their own information and data on a self-managed (and other-managed) social and ecological basis.

The importance of making a decision in an undecidable terrain notwithstanding, it is possible to imagine the process of radically recomposing our cities and their infrastructures incorporating all four of these strategic logics.

7

Ours is thus a very different approach to the city than is traditionally offered by architecture and urban design. And this is so regardless of whether the approach in question is focused on fostering bottom-up incremental changes at a local level, or top-down master-planning ('omnipotence' being the 'distilled goal of high modernism', for Carlo Ratti in his own rather humanist and liberal take on an 'open source architecture', conceived as it is 'by humanity, for humanity' [2015, 12-13, 102]). Despite our emphasis on the media-technological environment, we're certainly not talking about an equivalent to the smooth Smart City here. As far as we are concerned, without a non-dualistic, aporetic opening to the 'stupid', the rough, dirty, humble, impure, disordered, disorientating and dysfunctional, cities are boring and antiseptic at best.

To take a case in point: for all the weight placed on digital technologies (and on thinking beyond the public/private binary), none of this is to suggest that cities should no longer make room for old-style public libraries; that in the age of Amazon, Academia.edu and OpenAI these physical institutions are universally outmoded. For one thing, public libraries are enclosed, safe, well-lit spaces in which people can remain for long periods of time to think and study for free: they are 'the universities of the streets', as the poet Benjamin Zephaniah calls them (quoted in Andersson 2019). For another, public libraries can serve an important role as alternative community centres: for the very young, the very old, the disabled, the unemployed and the socially marginalised. This is the case no matter how underfunded and run down many of these institutions may currently be. At the same time, for the 'working poor' and those in precarious employment, public libraries can offer various forms of care, advice and support, including email and internet access.

The public library as warm bank, and as 'work-close-to-home-space' or 'third place' for those continuing to practice remote and hybrid working following the pandemic, exemplifies how the inhabitants of a city frequently engage with infrastructure and utilities in ways that diverge significantly from the original visions of experts in architecture, planning and urban design.[143] Learning from this lesson regarding overdetermination and overspecification, the sketch for how to build an uncommons, latent commons or perhaps federated community of 'open' cities provided here has been deliberately left loose and unfinished. It needs to remain adaptable enough for others to be able to do their own thing and 'complete' it by mutating it in dynamic, unpredictable and surprising ways, according to their particular needs and circumstances – although of course this proposal (like the cities it reconceives) will never actually be *completed*. Besides, not everything needs to be designed or modelled, nor should it be. Escobar goes so far as to insist that such transitions are not actually designed at all: they are emergent. One of the key features of emergence is that it 'takes place on the basis of a multiplicity of local actions that, through their (largely unplanned) interaction, give rise to what appears to an observer to be a new structure or integrated whole ... without the need for any central planning or intelligence guiding the process' (2018, 152).

It is also vital for cities to remain hospitable to the 'useless' and 'unproductive', including the marginalised, disadvantaged, disempowered and disaffected. Equally important is being open to the strange, the monstrous and the unsettling. The latter encompasses the idea that nonhuman species and other agents and elements (technologies, infrastructure, the built and natural environment) actively participate in both culture and cities. Let me offer some illustrations of how this idea is gradually coming to be appreciated to differing degrees and extents even within the mainstream. A study published in 2011 showed that, while the 41,247 trees in Lisbon cost the city around $1.9m annually to maintain, the services they provide – which include improving air quality, mental health and real estate values, and reducing CO_2 and stormwater runoff – were worth $8.4m (Soares 2011, 69). (This point is worth emphasizing, especially since numerous city councils, including those in Madrid and Malta, have plans to remove trees in favour of big business interests and are only being prevented from carrying them out by the actions of protestors.) A more recent demonstration of the manner in which nonhuman entities can participate in the co-constitution of cities, this time relating to AI, is provided by *The Heart*. This is a project of the interactive media artist Robert Walton working with a team of architects, builders, lighting designers and data scientists. It consists of an artwork embedded into the Melbourne Connect building and linked to its 'nervous system of sensors and its respiratory system of heating, ventilation and air conditioning' (Melbourne Connect 2022). *The Heart* is thus going much further than using AI to augment or extend the intelligence of human architects by automating certain tasks: from generating initial ideas during the concept phase and reducing the time spent on calculation, predictive modelling and managing drawing sets, through simulating how people will move around and use buildings, to summarising local planning policy and simplifying the permissions process. For Walton, 'Modern "smart" buildings are life support systems on the verge of becoming beings in their own right at the dawn of the AI age: sensitive to activities within and around them. ... When we think of AI we often think of horror films and scary robots, but actually, lots of these kinds of systems are about supporting life and creating optimum experiences for us to live in work. They nurture us' – much like trees, in fact (Walton *et al*. 2020; see also Walton n.d.). Yet buildings today don't *have* to be equipped with AI to be perceived as having a certain agency. Evidence the Reggio school in the Madrid suburb of Encinar de los Reyes. Conceived by Andrés Jaque's Office for Political Innovation and completed in 2022, this six-story structure is regarded as 'the third teacher', in keeping with the Reggio Emilia educational approach pioneered in northern Italy. 'The design, construction and use of this building is intended to ... engage with ecology as an approach where environmental impact, more-than-human alliances, material mobilization, collective governance and pedagogies intersect through architecture'

(Jaque/Office for Political Innovation n.d.; North American Reggio Emilia Alliance n.d.). (For the Heidegger of 'Building, Dwelling, Thinking' [1971] buildings are able to propose new worlds to people, so this is not an altogether new idea.)

In this respect, we need to recognise that – for all our mention above of academics, artists, architects and so on – the diverse multiplicity of actors we want to help to cocreate their own bespoke cultural institutions does not already exist: either as a civic population or as a public. Rather these, too, are missing communities. What my collaborators and I are endeavouring to do is invent the contexts out which such multiplicities can emerge and develop through the process of radically rethinking cities and their infrastructure. The architect Stavros Stavrides comes close to capturing something of this approach to commons when he writes that:

> Orienting the building of communities towards the production of the common, makes those communities a work in progress, since neither the common is a reality to be grasped and to hold on to, nor the commoners can be identified by an identity that preexists their participation in the commoning process. In other words, commoning communities develop themselves through commoning, and so their members. This has at least two implications:
>
> First, a shared identity considered as a defining characteristic of the community's membership loses its centrality: since commoning shapes subjects, identities develop in relation to the practices of sharing that shape them.
>
> Second, belonging is related not to origin but to practice: those who act as commoners belong to an acting community that comes to existence exactly due to such acts. (Stavrides 2022, 26-27)

This is why we are interested in cities: because they enable us to invent the contexts out of which such missing communities can emerge. Although the same goes for cities themselves: there are no blueprints for the urban environments my collaborators and I are looking towards. (Le Corbusier's 'Plan Voisin' for 1920s Paris is often cited as the classic modernist example.) Like the common for Stavrides, these cities and their infrastructure do not pre-exist this process, not even in our imaginations. (Which is why I have not furnished any examples of such city-interventions already in existence; and why the strong temptation to present the city itself, in all its complexity and pluriversality, as an intelligent inhuman actor to rank alongside buildings such as Melbourne Connect, has also been resisted.) They are *missing cities*; cities that need to be called forth in different ways, at different times and places: theoretically, practically, concretely. In short, we need to keep the question of the city and its inhabitants (aporetically) open as well.

The proposal for radically redesigning cities and municipal infrastructure along more non-modernist-liberal lines that is provided here should therefore be seen less as a model and more as an aspiration or horizon of possibility. Here again, the idea is to cultivate the kind of meaningful diversity when it comes to the development of self-governing, collectively-managed and controlled, community-owned initiatives that might actually change things. Such a scaling small approach would thus add to those experiments with transforming existing cultural, economic and social relations that are being undertaken in places as different as North Ayrshire in the UK, Cleveland in the US, São Paulo in Brazil, Rosario in Argentina, Cape Town in South Africa and the Basque region of Spain. In *Paint Your Town Red*, their book on the infamous Preston community wealth building model, Matthew Brown and Rhian E. Jones emphasise that 'the UK already has over 7,000 cooperative enterprises, while around the world approximately one billion people in 96 counties have become members of at least one cooperative', with 140 million of them in Europe (2021, 99; Cooperatives Europe n.d.). Taken together such experiments constitute a 'living' repertoire of transformative ideas that is not confined to Transition Town Initiatives, worker-owned cooperatives or commons creation. Far from it. This repertoire also takes in 'sanctuary' and 'solidarity' cities, Murray Bookchin-influenced (2014) communalism with its direct democracy and popular assemblies (as practiced in the Rojava region of north-eastern Syria), the Right to Repair movement, mutual care networks, mutually owned businesses, social (and socially conscious) enterprises, credit unions, people's banks and community land trusts, to name but a few.

8

Of course, there is still a great deal to be worked out, including how the above relates to theories of the 'algorithmic', 'sentient' and 'brain' city. Suffice it to say this is where universities come in. Universities are particularly important when it comes to thinking about the future of cities. Along with councils, hospitals, trade unions, housing associations and football clubs, they can act as 'anchor' institutions. These are institutions that have a crucial stable presence in a place: they tend to have long historical associations with and ties to it; they employ a great many people, buy large amounts of goods and services, and own vast amounts of buildings and land. As pointed out by Neil Garenflo, co-founder of Shareable, a non-profit connection hub for bringing about cultural transformation for the common good, alternative organisations and entities such as platform cooperatives frequently require the kind of long-term support that a reliable anchor institution can provide if they are to 'work out the interrelated legal, financial, and organizational challenges' associated with providing a situated alternative to Big Tech and its service providers. They need this support to enable them to tackle this change of culture together; and what's more, not just survive financially without getting bogged down in business-as-usual issues of how to be economically resilient – important though these may be – but also have space and time for sustained risk-taking and experimentation (Gorenflo 2015; CLES n.d.). In Preston, an institution that plays this anchoring role is the University of Central Lancashire (UCLan):

> As an educational institution, UCLan has the capacity to use its resources and facilities to bring together international knowledge and expertise and to make it publicly available to benefit the local area. ... Preston City Council has funded the university's academic research into the development of cooperatives, and UCLan has in turn taken the lead in securing financial support for start-up collectives, all of which is done with an eye to the collective economic and social benefit that cooperatives can impart to the city as a whole. (Brown and Jones 2021, 55)

I'm therefore going to bring this site-specific performance of *Masked Media* to a close by returning to the institution of the university which, as well as being the sphere of society most readily associated with theory, is itself another example of information media, as Foucault makes clear. I want to return to the university in order to provide a brief sketch of two of the more recent initiatives of my collaborators and I, by way of loosely recapping some of the main themes and arguments of this book.

Chapter 10

Post Office

Going postal ... means becoming extremely... angry ... usually in a workplace environment.
– *Wikipedia*

The post office has brought us luck ... a message from the world. A message of hope.
– *Ngũgĩ wa Thiong'o*

The First of the Final Two Initiatives

The Centre for Postdigital Cultures (CPC) was launched at Coventry University in 2017. A disruptive iteration of our earlier Centre for Disruptive Media, for the first five years of its operation it was located in the Faculty of Arts and Humanities. It then became part of the University's Institute of Creative Cultures, before coming to stand alone in 2023.

The Centre brings together people and projects from a range of backgrounds, including art, activism, design, film, feminism, philosophy and 'piracy'. To focus on some of those who are most closely related to the themes of this book, there is Janneke Adema (Open Humanities Press, Radical Open Access Collective, ScholarLed, COPIM, Open Book Collective), Mel Jordan (Partisan Social Club), Rebekka Kiesewetter (COPIM), Samuel Moore (Radical Open Access Collective, COPIM), Marcell Mars (Public Library: Memory of the World,

COPIM), and Toby Steiner and Judith Fathallah (COPIM, Open Book Collective). All are, or have been at one point, members of the Centre.

The CPC has gathered these people and their projects together with a view to reimagining twenty-first century societies and their cultural institutions (galleries, libraries, archives, museums) at a local, national and 'planetary' level. There is an ongoing discussion among us as to how best to describe the Centre. On the university's website, it says: 'the CPC has as its collective vision working toward the establishment of a more socially and environmentally just postcapitalist society. It is doing so by means of an interdisciplinary research agenda that extends from computing science, through the social sciences and humanities, to open education, political activism and art practice to explore how intellectual, community and civic engagement can prefigure different ways of being together. The Centre therefore does not only comment on the world; it endeavours to actively intervene in it'. As befits an entity concerned with networked digital cultures, however, the CPC has a somewhat fluid, decentred organisational structure. At the time of writing it consists of five quasi-autonomous collaboratories: AI and Algorithmic Cultures; ArtSpaceCity; Ludic Design; Postdigital Intimacies; and Post-Publishing. But the intellectual identity of the CPC is better understood in terms of what happens in-between and across its different collaboratories as much as within them.

It is an experimental, decentred approach that is continued in many of our external relationships. Far from being fixated on growth and expansion, we are proudly antigrowth. Our preference is to scale small by establishing collaborative networks with a diverse ecology of groups and organisations distributed in various places around the world, including the epistemological Global South.

· · · · ·

Within this a number of us in the Centre do identify as theorists. We therefore have a particular interest in examining the opportunities that the transition from analogue to digital media technology provides for reinventing our ways of being and knowing, whether we think of ourselves as feminists, Marxists, neo-Marxists, post-colonialists or new materialists. Yet, despite the reference to new materialism, the theory-performances of myself and various colleagues and collaborators shouldn't be framed in terms of concrete, *material practices* – as opposed to *immaterial theory*. In articulations of this nature it's often overlooked that the practices that go to create and disseminate theory are *always already* concrete, while theory that privileges the concrete and the material can end up being quite weak, precisely because its materiality is left invisible, masked, black boxed.[144] (Hence the arguments that feature throughout *Masked Media* concerning the immateriality of new materialism's supposed rematerialisation of scientific research: environmental destruction, digital rubbish and so forth.)

In our identification as theorists, the reading and writing of texts is of course incredibly important to us. Yet if we are to engage in the inhumanist de-liberalisation of our institutions, our culture, and ways of living, we cannot continue to practice our disciplines in Euro-Western, modernist terms, according to the narrow worldview of privileged white men and their regulative norms and codes of conduct. Instead, we need to experiment with different behaviours and gestures as theorist-mediums; different modes of creating and sharing knowledge; different forms of the relation between us and our media information technologies: pens, books, journals, computers, phones, GenAI systems. It's this we're working towards with our norm-critical projects.

Doing so requires us to reimagine the accepted ideas about how we compose, publish and 'protect' our work. Once again, this reimagining extends beyond the printed paper codex book or journal article. It takes in the named individual author as modernist genius; the sovereign, proprietorial subject; the long-form argument; the immutable text; originality; copyright; right down to the very concept of the human. Hence our interest in what we've called radical open access, pirate philosophy and post-publishing.

Publishing is particularly important to us because of the crucial role it plays not only in shaping how we, as theorists, produce and disseminate our work, but also in shaping us *as theorists*. As my Centre for Postdigital Cultures colleague Janneke Adema argues, publishing and research do not exist in a dualistic relation. Publishing is not something we become involved with only once the process of research is complete. It's an inherent part of (the various stages of) the research process (Adema 2021) – and has been the case since the Royal Society in London published the first edition of the world's first periodical in 1665. Or, as Chapter 1 showed, taking the idea of the non-dualistic relation between publishing and research still further, our books and journal articles are not *just* information media: they also help to form the conditions of possibility that govern our ways of being and thinking and doing as theorists. And that's the case even if we never actually publish our research.

One definition of publishing, as noted in Chapter 1, is 'making public', which we understand as both making available *to* the public (for want of a better term), and as actually making *the* public. The latter means that what the public is cannot be taken-for-granted as something already known and decided upon. Instead, the public has to be 'called forth', as another of my CPC colleagues, Mel Jordan, emphasises in her work on art and the public sphere. Common-sense notions of the public are therefore something else we interrogate in the Centre. As part of this, we are interested in how the distinction between public and private is changing in the context of the shift explored in *Masked Media*: from the Gutenberg galaxy of the print book to a post-Gutenberg universe of computational data flows. As we have seen, Alphabet, Amazon and Apple have all been using human contractors to analyse recordings from home voice assistants. Is what has been recorded and scrutinised here public or private? Meanwhile, a poll of American adults revealed 90% regularly use their phone while *on the toilet*, Elon Musk admitting on Twitter that he is one of them (Musk 2021). Again, are these people communicating in public or in private?

Similarly, our Postdigital Intimacies collaboratory, under the leadership of Ady Evans and Lindsay Balfour, is interested in the manner in which surveillance capitalist companies are collecting data about the most intimate parts of our lives: our closest relationships, our sexual desires, our bodily health, even our borrowing of a book on personal healthcare from the local library after having travelled for an abortion. These companies are then selling this data to brokers for potential use by employment services, insurers, law enforcement agencies and those training AI machine-learning systems. Does all this mean the private is becoming increasingly public today? Or are our very concepts of public and private no longer useful or appropriate? Is the latter what is in fact being revealed to us by reality TV shows such as *Big Brother* and *Love Island*, in which contestants surrender their private selves to the public gaze? Can these programmes acquire both contestants who are prepared to submit themselves to such an experience and an audience who are prepared to watch and participate in them doing so, because the separation between public and private has already been eroded? In which case, do we need to rethink these modernist, liberal concepts, as Jane Bennett does with her theory of the ontologically heterogenous public (2010)? Or do we need to go ever further than this and invent entirely new concepts to replace them?

There is a connection here to what the point of a university, the humanities, indeed a research centre, is for us. It's to:

- provide spaces where society's common-sense beliefs can be examined and interrogated – and where, as one of the Centre's visiting professors, Angela McRobbie, has emphasised, this can be done in order to make connections between what's happening in different parts of society and so produce a better understanding of it.

- act as a test site for imagining and developing new subjectivities, new knowledges, new practices, new ways of life of the kind that are often hard to explore elsewhere, but which we are going to need if we *do* want to reconstruct a better world after the coronavirus crisis, cost of living emergency and wars in Ukraine and Gaza/Israel. (It should be stressed that a research centre or university is not the only such test site. Art, activism and architecture are all capable of providing others.)

- help actualise such new practices and subjectivities.

We see the Centre as being able to do so in places traditionally associated with the white, male, modernist-liberal space that is the Euro-Western university. Accordingly, some of our projects use collaborative documents and wikis to experiment with de-liberalising the material forms and practices of research. The collaborative disappropriation of COPIM's *Ecological Rewriting* project is a recent example of this approach. Others are concerned with building and developing a wide variety of counter-organisations and communities – the Open Book Collective and so on – that help us to perform our subjectivities and ways of being together as theorists and researchers along more anti-surveillance, anti-monopolist, commons-oriented lines. But a research centre such as the CPC can also help to actualise new subjectivities and social relations in places associated with the city. Hence our concern to collaborate on reconceiving elements of municipal infrastructure including universities, art galleries, public libraries, archives and museums. In sum, we could say that the Centre for Postdigital Cultures is interested in using the shift from analogue to digital, Dalí to DALL-E, as an opportunity to explore some of the alternative, non-oppositionally different, inhumanist ways of being-in and being-with the world that Chapter 1 referred to: pluriversality, collectivity, processuality, performativity, responsible openness and so forth. The idea with this aspect of the Centre's work is to actually assume some of the implications of radical thought, including ontologically relational thought, to the point where we do indeed live, act and work differently.

The Second of the Final Two Initiatives

The CPC is more than just a research centre, though, which is the real reason I:ts are mentioning it here. The CPC is also a project that is endeavouring to make a performative intervention in its own right. One way it is doing so is through the establishment of a postdigital arts and humanities 'practice' or 'studio'. The inspiration for this initiative was 'The Masked Philosopher' interview by Foucault, with which I:ts began this book. Our Centre, too, is concerned to engage with and create not so much mass media as *masked media,* in the sense of media that are not easy to read. The first mask donned by the studio is that of the name itself, Post Office.[145]

As was shown earlier, commercial social media and social networks are contributing to a process of academic subjectivation whereby we act as highly visible microentrepreneurs of ourselves. Some researchers have responded to this situation by moving offline and not using the likes of LinkedIn and Slack at all. Doing so can be an art practice in itself, as Mark Amerika acknowledges (2019). And, to be sure, there's a certain thrill to be had in going against the prevailing ideas of participation and connectivity in this fashion and just saying 'no, enough'. We cannot simply *become* anonymous, however. Disconnecting from such networks, or subverting their real-name policies by refusing to write under a proper name, or engaging only with those service providers where the system administrators explicitly state that no data will be shared with corporate or government actors, doesn't provide a means of escaping surveillance capitalism's existential system of capture and control. We are all on Facebook and X, whether we've set up an account with these data harvesting platforms or not (and regardless of whether we've reacted to their decline by migrating to the decentralised fediverse and Mastodon). Facebook can still predict the behaviour of people who don't have an account with them with a 95% degree of accuracy, as they nonetheless have a presence – a 'shadow Facebook account' – on that of their family and friends. Being aware of this puts into perspective software such as Ben Grosser's Go Rando web browser, which obfuscates your feelings on Facebook by randomly selecting one of seven reactions for you every time you click 'like' (2021). In fact, for all the tactical use we may make of certain browsers, plug-ins and VPNs, it's not clear to what extent privacy from these networks is actually possible in the post-Snowdown era. It was reported in 2019 that even by then Amazon had assumed control of more than 23 million IP addresses, Microsoft 21 million, Apple 17 million, Google just under 9 million, with Facebook operating *only* 122,880 (Hill 2019). Nor is this situation at all new. When the UK Post Office was first set up as a state monopoly by Oliver Cromwell in 1657, it was as a means of surveillance: the opening of mail was thought to be 'the best means to discover and prevent any dangerous and wicked designs against the Commonwealth' (*Monthly Supplement of The Penny Magazine* 1834, 35; see Jeffreys-Jones 2017).

Instead, 'anonymity must be actively constructed', as Nicholas Thoburn emphasises with reference to the radical activist, multiple name project Luther Blissett (2011, 127). (Blisset was an English footballer who played for AC Milan in the 1980s. Beginning in Italy in the following decade, his name was adopted by a collective movement of anonymous actors as a pseudonym for an imaginary author.) In the Centre for Postdigital Cultures a number of us have therefore on occasion taken to responding to data capitalism by using a mask to hide ourselves in plain sight.[146] The mask we have chosen for this is not some cool, artist-designed, anti-surveillance device such as Zach Blas's *Fag Face Mask*, tempting though the idea is. Part of Blas's *Facial Weaponization Suite*, the *Fag Face Mask* has been generated to protest computer networks that use biometric data to search for, identify and mark individuals across huge populations (n.d.). A survey of countries between 2012 and 2020 found that seventy-seven now use AI-driven surveillance of some kind, with facial recognition technology the most common, being employed in sixty-one of them (Johnson 2023). Our mask is not something we wear to conceal or deface our faces, however, in an effort to restore a degree of individual privacy. For one thing, like legal defences of the right to privacy or attempts to go off-grid (such as the fantasy of escaping social collapse by relocating to places such as New Zealand and Mars that is shared by many of the hyper-rich), or establishing 'free-face' spaces in which the use of live biometric surveillance technologies in public is prohibited, there would be too much of a risk in doing so of maintaining, rather than breaking, the public and the private as conceptual categories. For another, as was made clear during the pandemic, facial detection and verification technologies have, with the aid of networked artificial intelligence and multimodal biometrics, developed to such an extent that today they can function even when people are wearing masks. The artist Adam Harvey observes that: 'At a high enough resolution, everything becomes unique' (2021); and that includes lips and ears, right down to vein patterns. It's also the case that while a particular design may block one recognition algorithm, it might not necessarily block another, and it is unlikely to block them all. Besides, even taking biometric failure into account – including the tendency of these automatic surveillance systems to misidentify those who do not fit the normative, cis, white, heterosexual, male templates for measuring features and body parts, with the result that already marginalised populations are subject to further discrimination (Buolamwini 2023; Najibi 2020) – it's difficult, if not impossible, to achieve total anonymity these days given all the other technologies there are for controlling humans. The list is an extensive one and includes GPS data, automatic vehicle number plate recognition (APNR), biometric passports, location tracking apps and home-based sensors in smart TVs, washing machines, even toothbrushes, to name but a few. Moreover, such cybernetic prostheses themselves function as digital masks, as we saw Preciado indicate in Chapter 2.

In fact, our mask in the Centre for Postdigital Cultures is not something we wear to hide our faces (or biometric identities) at all. Instead, we have chosen to operate in the tradition of anonymous authors such Tiqqun and the Invisible Committee, to take a couple of theory-related examples, in that our mask concerns the collective pseudonym we have given the studio: Post Office. As a name it serves a number of functions:

1. Post Office acts as a protective shield – albeit an imperfect and temporary one – behind which we can both retain energy and enthusiasm and put some of our more radical theory-performances to the test. At the time of writing a Google search for 'post office' turns up 5,590,000,000 results. Even 'Coventry post office' has around 22,300,000 results. Calling ourselves Post Office thus means we are not so easy to find, hidden as our post office is among the millions of others. (Where do you hide a leaf? In a forest!) Full anonymity is therefore unnecessary; nor is it the aim.

2. Post Office operates as a military-derived camouflage strategy of the kind described by Harvey with reference to his CV Dazzle designs, which experiment with utilising fashion to evade face-detection technology. As with Harvey's bold patterning, our camouflage strategy is one 'that works within the limits of appearance to minimize or downgrade the useful information received by the observer' or otherwise control it. 'If there is no means to disappear, the next best strategy is to appear less vulnerable' (Harvey 2018; n.d.). Even though our identities are not necessarily always secret, Post Office gives our studio a disguised or obfuscated identity that offers a form of limited liability.

Another, albeit related, way in which we endeavour to obfuscate its identity and bestow it with a limited degree of protection and liability is by making the Post Office a *ghost office* replete with its own ghost press, Post Office Press (POP). What this means is that the name of both the studio and the press can be used by anyone, not just members of the Centre for Postdigital Cultures. Like Luther Blissett or Karen Eliot, to provide another example of the active construction of anonymity through a multiple-name project, the names 'Post Office' and 'Post Office Press' may be fixed, but who adopts them is not. Anyone can be (in) the Post Office and use it to provide their work with a certain institutional presence and authority. They just have to be willing to associate themselves with the theory-performances of those who have also adopted it. Membership being open and indeterminate, who exactly is responsible for what goes on under the shared name Post Office is thus uncertain.[147]

3 Post Office avoids the trap of trying to circumvent attaching a proper name to a work by leaving the author field blank, making the author 'anonymous', or by providing the author with a pseudonym. Doing so is a trap because, as the fate of enigmatic figures as different as Banksy and Elena Ferrante bears witness, it comes with the risk that (unless we're talking about a form of 4chan-like 'per-message anonymity') the work of a missing author will remain prone to much the same processes of individuation, subjectification and commodification as one with a conventional name (Fathallah 2021).[148] Post Office enables us to avoid this situation by instead using a pseudonym for a collective whose membership is neither finite nor stable.[149] But we also try to elude this trap by differing from the likes of Tiqqun and the Guerrilla Girls group of anonymous feminist artists by *not* writing or creating with a single voice. Instead, the idea behind our adoption of Post Office as a pseudonym is to create an opportunity for the distinctions between the individual, the communal and the collective to be rendered less stable here, too, and for novel forms of togetherness to be again generated by a mode of theory-performance that comprises neither simply singularities nor pluralities. Last but not least, it is hoped that by not identifying ourselves with individual authorship – either in terms of an imaginary identity such as Luther Blissett or a collective that writes with a single voice such as the Invisible Committee – we will encourage others to copy, remix, build upon and re-use any work published under the aegis of the Post Office even more than a project such as Living Books About Life does with its named initial authors and editors.

4 Post Office serves as a cloaking device that – similar to the balaclavas of the Zapatista Army of National Liberation in Chiapas, Mexico, and the feminist protestors of Pussy Riot in Russia – can be left unused when we want to be visible as 'individuals', and adopted only when we want to make ourselves visible as a 'collective' entity (although, unlike the Zapatistas and Pussy Riot, we are not endevouring to be hypervisible).[150] Post Office therefore acts much as a mask does for the curator Bogomir Doringer: it enables the performance of 'the impossible, something one alone could not do that easily' (2018, 41).

For many state, military and commercial actors there is something dangerous about the performance of this *impossible* aspect of masks. Their adoption by pro-democracy protestors in Hong Kong, for example – some of whom actively dismantled surveillance apparatus – led the island's then chief executive, Carrie Lam, to activate an Emergency Regulations Ordinance in September 2019 not used since the colonial era. This law made the wearing of masks and other kinds of face covering at public gatherings punishable by a HK$25,000 fine and a maximum of one year in prison. (The use of Guy Fawkes masks by Anonymous to identify themselves as members of the hacktivist group while simultaneously hiding their individual identities saw the introduction of similar laws restricting facial concealment in Canada and Spain in 2013.) Such legislation takes us back to the etymological origins of the word 'mask' in the Latin *persona*, which means 'character in a play'. To take off a person's theatrical mask is thus to de*persona*lise them. Except in the case of the Hong Kong protestors: it could be said that they can only perform democratic personhood and exercise the liberal humanist rights that come with it – including the right to gather and demonstrate – by wearing masks that render them anonymous and collective. To strip these protestors of the opportunity to conceal their faces, to de-anonymise them, is to de-personalise them. It's a means of removing their rights as liberal democratic human personages – ironically by making their identities biometrically visible, and so bringing them back into play as far as state surveillance and control is concerned.[151] By contrast, for my collaborators and I, the more-or-less playful adoption of various masks and alternative and affirmative personas – including the collective pseudonym Post Office – is what makes performing the impossible de-liberalisation of the human that little bit more possible.

Repurposed from a commonly available public service, Post Office is also a decidedly unglamorous name that is almost the antithesis of individualistic celebrity, conjuring up for most people as it does associations of queuing in drab surroundings. Its sheer ubiquity has the advantage of making it tricky to mobilise as a capitalist resource in terms of marketing and promotion, not least because in the UK the Post Office is already a registered trademark of Post Office Ltd, which is owned by the government.[152] (With its 11,500 branches, the Post Office claimed to be the UK's 'most trusted brand' until as recently as 2019. It is now trusted rather less after it wrongly prosecuted hundreds of the self-employed workers running many of those branches for theft, fraud and false accounting, resulting in what has been described as the widest miscarriage of justice in UK history.)

We realise that this active construction of a (limited) degree of pseudo-anonymity on our part – or at least refusal to simply play the game of self-promotion in a straightforward fashion – may appear somewhat counterintuitive, given we live in a society that has long been based on pervasive monitoring and the celebration of runaway individualism.[153] As I:ts have been demonstrating throughout *Masked Media*, however, these are the kinds of actions we need to take if we want to give our work a chance of landing in unexpected places and forming shapes that we had never thought of.

Author's bio

Born in Iceland, Gary Hall is an architect of ideas living in Wimbledon, London.[154]
He studied from 1989-95 in Berlin at the Hochschule der Künste (Academy of Fine Arts). During these years he extended his studies towards experimental writing and site-specific conceptual art.

He is currently co-director of the postdigital arts and humanities research centre/studio The Post Office at Coventry University, where he experiments with alternatives spaces for knowing and doing.

His ongoing projects include:

1. street art: series of urban installations and performances; applying adhesive bandages on the surface of urban objects, blank walls or pavements.

2. street writing – prose on the sides of building and sidewalks.

Notes

I believe that bibliographies and endnotes and references and sources are alternative stories that can, in the most generous sense, centralize the practice of sharing ideas about liberation and resistance and writing against racial and sexual violence. *Alternative outcomes.*
– *Katherine McKittrick*

[W]as it possible to be many things at once? To derive from a plurality of abandoned pasts?
– *Stanisław Lem*

1. This is not to deny that I have, on occasion, overtly written collectively, just as I have resorted to the use of the first-person plural 'we' to refer to the hybridised community of human/nonhuman readers that is in the process of being created by this book and the performative projects featured within it.

2. For more, see Chapter 3's account of the 'dark side' critique of digital humanities and its collaborative, openly shared, lab-based research and project-based learning over the kind of critical reading and writing that is carried out by lone scholars in private studies and offices.

3. My thanks to Jurij Smrke for reminding me of Wittig's use of *j/e* and *t/u* in *The Lesbian Body*.

4. It might have been more expected to collaborate with classic figures from the twentieth-century modernist theoretical canon: Friedrich Nietzsche, Henri Bergson, Hannah Arendt, Frantz Fanon, Vilém Flusser, Paul Virilio and so forth. Contemporary authors have been chosen for the most part, however, because doing so is another way of making my work less monumental. The fact that the majority of these thinkers were living at the time of writing also makes the

collaboration even more 'real' in many ways. Moreover, it is more ethico-political, as it affords them an opportunity to respond should they so wish.

5   K Allado-McDowell's pioneering experimental novel *Amor Cringe*, for instance, is 'half traditionally-written and half AI-generated' (2022), and is published accordingly on an all-rights-reserved basis by Deluge Books. The same applies to Allado-McDowell's collection of essays, poems and stories, *Pharmako-AI*, which bills itself as the 'first book to be co-written with the language AI GPT-3' (2020). It is published all rights reserved by Ignota Books, with serif being used to identify those parts of the book written by Allado-McDowell, and sans serif for the text written by GPT-3, the two co-authors – human and machine – thus remaining conceptually distinct.

6   Even one of the main ideas on which *Masked Media* is based, that of remixing the work of Mark Amerika on remix, is not an original one. It has been done before: not least by Janneke Adema (2011) with regard to Amerika's *remixthebook* (2011b), on the companion website to that volume, *remixthebook.com*. *Masked Media* is not even the first time I:ts have remixed the work of Amerika on remix. *remixthebook.com* contains an essay called 'Force of Binding: On Liquid, Living Books (Version 2.0: Mark Amerika Mix)', in which I:ts remix Amerika's 'Sentences on Remixology 1.0' from *remixthebook* (Hall 2011).

7   Wark characterises low theory in terms of 'the organic conceptual apparatus a milieu composes for itself, at least partly outside of formal academic situations. ... It's useful to have some perspective outside of the criteria of success of academia itself. After all, many of the "greats" of low theory – Spinoza, Marx, Darwin, Freud – they were not philosophers. ... You could think of low theory as what organic intellectuals do. It's defined by who does it and why, rather than by any particular cognitive style' (2017a).

8   This part of the argument of *Masked Media* is derived from Hall (2023). More on revolutionising theory can be found in Hall (2021b).

9   Even this comment on plagiarism is plagiarised: from the appendix to Shields (2011, 209).

10 'Collective Conditions for Re-Use' (CC4r) 'articulates conditions for re-using authored materials'. Developed by Constant, the association for arts and media in Brussels, it is inspired by the principles of Free Culture and focuses on conveying 'conditions for re-using authored materials'. However, CC4r aims to steer Free Culture towards a viewpoint where authorship and creativity are seen as inherently collective, collaborative and situated. This perspective includes collaborations between humans and machines as well as being open to 'other-than-human contributions', rather than attributing creativity solely to the unique, inspired individual human 'genius', as

traditional copyright practices do (Constant 2023). Yet even CC4r has to acknowledge that it is 'reluctantly formulated within the framework of both the Belgian law and the Berne Convention for the Protection of Literary and Artistic Works'; and that 'work licenced under the CC4r is reluctantly subject to copyright law' (Constant 2023).

Moreover, while the CC4r licence is far better in spirit than Creative Commons, does it not suffer (at this time of writing at least) from one of the same problems as CC licences? Is the decision-making happening too much at the level of the specific actors concerned – be they individuals or collectives in CC4r's case – and on what *they* are persuaded is the right thing to do? Does CC4r not rely heavily on the good faith of these actors? Take the section of the CC4r document on Conditions. This runs that: 'The invitation to (re-)use the work licenced under CC4r applies as long as the FUTURE AUTHOR is convinced that this does not contribute to oppressive arrangements of power, privilege and difference' (Constant 2023). But what if – as in the case of certain companies, who have been putting new covers on books from Open Humanities Press and other open access publishers and selling them online as theirs, often at inflated prices – such a future author is convinced that what they are doing is perfectly acceptable, and does not contribute to 'oppressive arrangements of power, privilege and difference', even though for others it does?

Constant's *Authors of The Future: Re-Imaging Copyleft* (2019) booklet identifies a number of other licences that address some of the lacunae and limitations of open access and Free Culture Licences, especially the emphasis on 'openness and freedom as universal principles' (Constant 2023). They include the Decolonial Free Media Licence 0.1, the Non-White Heterosexual Male Licence, the Climate Strike Software Licence and the Feminist Peer Production Licence. But, again, is there not a danger of this being somewhat liberal on Constant's part, to the extent that – as with Creative Commons – what is being presented to authors is a range of different licences from which they are *free to choose as individuals*, rather than any of this being the result of a collective philosophy, policy or decision-making?

11 The Open Humanities Notebook took as one of its initial models the Open Notebook Science philosophy of the organic chemist, Jean-Claude Bradley (2007). The idea of making research openly available for free as it emerges has been further built upon and developed both by what's called 'living documents' or 'living notebooks', often created using Jupyter notebooks (https://github.com/a-paxton/living-documents), and by the Octopus platform. The latter has created a method of recording research that divides it into smaller sections than the standard journal article. The platform breaks research down into the eight component parts it sees as being 'most closely aligned with the scientific research process'. These are problem,

hypothesis/rationale, methods/protocol, data/results, analysis, interpretation, real-world implementation, and peer review. These elements can then be connected to form a 'chain' of collaboration that allows for faster feedback, sharing and recognition of 'individual work at all stages of the research, including peer review' (Octopus n.d.).

12 The Open Humanities Notebook is not being used to make my work openly available with the goal of generating a personal online presence designed to build an audience. If that were the primary concern, there are newsletter platforms like Ghost and Substack that, for many, have superseded blogs in terms of personal audience-building. Nevertheless, as Amerika writes: 'As far as I'm concerned, there is no way for you to self-consciously rid yourself of any affiliation with the idea of aura. No one would ever buy that or maybe I should say no one would ever BUY that' (*rtc*, 178).

13 Turning to novelist and theorist Gabriel Josipovici on the world of the ancient Greeks can be illuminating here. That the hero of Greek tragedy was not an autonomous individual is why 'Greek drama is essentially a masked drama', according to Josipovici. 'To us moderns a mask hides something, to the Greeks it revealed. "Masking"', he writes, drawing this time on a book by John Jones from 1962 titled *On Aristotle and Greek Tragedy*, '"shows forth the psychophysical and institutional solidarity of the descent group". And masked drama implies that what we see enacted before us is not a fiction or a reconstruction, but in some sense a re-enactment: "What was done by the man in the story is done again by the mask". For "the actor-mask is not a portrait; it presents, it does not represent, it gives us King Oedipus"' (Josipovici 2010; quoting Jones 1962).

14 Not everyone working in these domains identifies with the posthumanist label. Some remain humanists even while criticising humanism; some distance themselves from one of the main traditions of continental antihumanism – that associated with critique and a dualistic philosophy of the other – despite rejecting such binaries in favour of a more affirmative and monistic approach; some regard the historical moment of posthumanism as representing the end of the opposition between humanism and antihumanism; and some are a hybrid combination of all three.

15 Posthumanism has been chosen as one of the examples of radical humanities research in this book, rather than the work of 'neo-rationalist' legacy theorists such as Benjamin Bratton, Luciana Parisi and Reza Negarestani, which would have been another option, because of the latter's emphasis on rationality and humanism – albeit an 'enlightened humanism' in Negarestani's case (2014). The close association of liberalism with both means there is a danger that *unmasking* the manner in which such so-called neo-rationalists continue to operate as liberal humanists would be perceived as almost too

straightforward. In contrast, posthumanism is frequently held up as one of the most critical responses to liberal humanism we have. But the decision not to concentrate on the neo-rationalists has also been taken to avoid simply submitting to the constant (Euro-Western) academic desire for the 'new', the 'up-to-date', the 'latest thing'; and because, for all they have a certain popularity, among graduate students especially, their language and ideas are not nearly so prevalent within the humanities as those of posthumanism, even if explicitly identifying as a 'posthumanist' has perhaps now passed its peak of fashionability in many places. Adam Nocek provides an incisive analysis of the neo-rationalist thought of Bratton *et al.* in a paper titled 'On the Ecological Complexity of Algorithmic Media', presented to the Creative AI Lab and Computational Humanities Research Group at King's College London on March 14, 2023.

16   The reference is of course to Bruno Latour's *We Have Never Been Modern* (1993). In this passage, and in several others, *Masked Media* is – in its own playful, teasing fashion – echoing the provocativeness and lack of sympathy toward other schools of thought characteristic of much of Bruno Latour's writing and that of many of those who have followed in his footsteps. Other posthumanist thinkers have a less 'scorched earth', more humble and hospitable attitude of the kind adopted elsewhere in *Masked Media's* polyphony of voices, tones and moods.

For a more detailed engagement with materialism, including the posthumanist materialism of Karen Barad and Rosi Braidotti, the performative materiality of Johanna Drucker, and the materialist ontology of Tim Ingold, see my *Pirate Philosophy* (Hall 2016a, 85-125). Chapter 3 of the present volume contains more about new materialism. Meanwhile, in *Pandora's Hope*, Latour explains blackboxing as 'the way scientific and technical work is made invisible by its own success. When a machine runs efficiently, when a matter of fact is settled, one need focus only on its inputs and outputs and not on its internal complexity. Thus, paradoxically, the more science and technology succeed, the more opaque and obscure they become' (1999, 304).

17   See Chapter 2 for an engagement with digital humanities; on third generation electronic literature, see Flores (2021); on the future of reading in the age of AI, see Riely (2023).

18   *Masked Media* doesn't deal extensively with the work of Simondon, Stiegler or Hayles. One such engagement with that of Stiegler is provided in Hall (2016a, 57-83).

19   If *Masked Media* frequently references brand-name legacy theorists from the epistemological Global North, it is partly because it is the very liberal humanist ways of being and knowing they represent that the book is attempting to disarticulate and transform. It should be stressed, nonetheless, that there are many others, both inside and

Notes

outside of the epistemological Global North, who are also experimenting with de-liberalising theory and research. A good number of them are included in *Masked Media*'s pluriverse of thinkers and works in a practice that exists in an uneasy tension with those alternative approaches discussed in Chapters 8 and 9. For instance, Leanne Betasamosake Simpson's concept of 'Indigenous refusal' – understood as a refusal to strive for more acceptance and recognition within the 'academic industrial complex' and its particular naming and referencing styles (2014, 22) – warns of the risk of meeting that complex's needs or endeavouring to '"Indigenize the academy" by integrating Indigenous Knowledges on the academy's own terms (2014, 13).

20 *remixthecontext* is hereafter abbreviated as *rtc*. All further references to Amerika are to this book unless indicated otherwise. At the time of the *GRAMMATRON: 20 Years into the Future* symposium I was working from a review copy, as *remixthecontext* was yet to be published.

21 It should be noted that, while 'foundational' AI models that are capable of a wide variety of general tasks may be trained on data scraped from large corpora of text, like the people and organisations behind them, these technologies do not actually keep or share the original texts themselves. The latter are held for just a brief period of analysis before being dispensed with. This makes the nature of any copyright infringement legally uncertain in many jurisdictions. Further legal uncertainty arises around the question as to whether the process involves copying the text or just reading it.

22 A survey of 10,000 academics found that articles and the prestige of the journal they are published in continue to be the main measure by which academics judge one another – although it is slightly different in the humanities, where monographs published with esteemed presses tend to be the gold standard (Grove 2022, 9).

23 As the editors of Open Humanities Press's Technographies series observe, originally the word 'technolog' was used to refer to a type of writing that was about a 'practical art or craft'. Over time, it began to be used in reference to the things that were produced by those arts or crafts. Eventually, the word came to be associated with the 'machinery or equipment used in production'. Nowadays it is typically assumed that technology refers to a 'machine, a system, a piece of kit'. This shift has occurred over the centuries, changing the word's meaning from a form of discourse or way of thinking to a term for a physical 'object, or set of objects' (Connor *et al.* n.d.).

24 Thanks are due to my fellow member of the Centre for Postdigital Cultures, Rebekka Kiesewetter, for pointing out that even open collaborative publishing tools such as PubPub and Manifold are designed for linearity and for translating static books to the web, rather than for facilitating more experimental publications.

Notes

25 For more on artists' books, see Adema and Hall (2013).

26 Earlier examples of such experimentation on the part of theorists include Jacques Derrida's *Glas* (1974/1990) and Avital Ronell's *The Telephone Book* (1991).

27 Since Amerika brings up intellectual property (IP), it's worth pointing out that a similar question can be raised for the conventional distinction between plagiarism, in which someone immorally presents the creative work of someone else as their own, and IP theft and copyright infringement. The latter is where someone uses IP and copyrighted work without the permission of its rights holder. I mention this because, for some, while the extraction and appropriation of copyrighted material by companies such as OpenAI and Microsoft to train their large language model (LLM) AI may be 'theft', it is not plagiarism. This is because DALL-E and Bing do not attempt to present the work of others as either their own or that of the people and organisations behind them. They may reproduce the 1928 Steamboat Willie version of Mickey Mouse – and since its ninety-five year period of copyright expired on January 1, 2024 and it passed into the public domain, doing so without permission from the Walt Disney Company is not a legal case of infringement. But they do not claim that they, rather than Walt Disney, are to be recognised as its original author. If they did, they would continue to be morally culpable of plagiarism. The same would apply if they reproduced other, later versions of Disney's Mickey Mouse before they too enter the public domain. All of which is further complicated by the fact that, as noted earlier, foundational and LLM AI models do not keep or share the original creative materials themselves, rendering the nature of any copyright infringement and thus *theft* uncertain in many legal systems. Moreover, if in 2015 Google's scanning of millions of published books without permission was deemed by the US courts not to be an infringement of copyright under the principle of fair use and on the basis that the company's Google Books project had a 'transformative purpose', it's easy to imagine a similar verdict being reached in relation to LLM AI.

28 remixthebook.com, accessed December 13, 2022.

29 Mark Amerika, personal email, October 2021.

30 These words are taken from the back cover blurb of *My Life as an Artificial Creative Intelligence* to emphasise that even the unnumbered parts of the text count, and that there is indeed nothing outside the book, especially not what's on its cover.

31 There is no shortage of legacy thinkers providing such monumental histories. They include Jeff Jarvis with *The Gutenberg Parenthesis: The Age of Print and Its Lessons for the Age of the Internet* (2023), and Matteo Pasquinelli with *The Eye of the Master: A Social History of Artificial*

Intelligence (2023), to cite just two recent examples relating to print and AI respectively.

32 According to McLuhan: '"Authorship" – in the sense we know it today, individual intellectual effort related to the book as an economic commodity – was practically unknown before the advent of print technology. Medieval scholars were indifferent to the precise identity of the "books" they studied' (McLuhan and Fiore 1967/2008, 122). Similarly, the reworking of existing source material, free from concerns about plagiarism and extractivism, has often been presented as the socially accepted means by which the creation of literary works of good quality was held to be achieved in the premodern period. In his memoir *The Future Lasts a Long Time*, however, Louis Althusser complicates this historical narrative concerning original, autonomous authorship. Althusser writes about how it has been challenged by some medievalists. He refers specifically to how, in the European Middle Ages:

> in a violent controversy with the Averroists Saint Thomas declared his opposition to the impersonality (in other words, the 'anonymity') of the individual thinker, arguing very much as follows: all thought is impersonal since it is a product of the intellect as agent. But since all impersonal thought must be thought by a 'thinking being', it necessarily becomes the property of an individual. In law, it should therefore bear this person's name. (Althusser 1994, 210)

Althusser continues by pointing out in his memoir: 'It had not even crossed my mind that, in the Middle Ages, when, as Foucault told us at Soisy, the law of literary impersonality reigned, Saint Thomas should have established under philosophical law the need for authorship, albeit in the context of his controversy with the Averroists' (210).

33 For some of the bodily gestures involved in reading other material forms of media, see Rosa and Strauven (2020).

34 As *A Stubborn Fury* (2021a) shows, it is a relationship that Derrida and Stiegler explore using ideas of *originary technicity* and *originary prostheticity*. Karen Barad, meanwhile, makes the link between performativity and intra-action in *Meeting the Universe Halfway*. Barad proposes what she calls an 'agential realist approach' that steers clear of 'representationalism' and proposes instead a performative appreciation of 'technoscientific and other naturalcultural practices', including various 'knowledge-making practices'. From an agential realist perspective, activities such as 'knowing, thinking, measuring, theorizing, and observing are material practices of intra-acting within and as part of the world' (Barad 2007, 90-91). For this reason, Barad favours the term 'intra-action' over interaction, as the latter assumes that entities exist prior to and independent of their relation (Barad 2003, 815). She thus regards intra-action as constituting 'a profound

conceptual shift' (815). What's more, the emphasis on 'performative alternatives to representationalism' has the effect of directing attention away from 'questions of correspondence between descriptions and reality (e.g., do they mirror nature or culture?)' and placing it on 'matters of practices/doings/actions' (802).

More recently, Arturo Escobar has described such 'relationality' as follows:

> Relationality signals that life is interrelationship and interdependence, always and at every level. Everything exists because everything else exists, as the Southern African principle of Ubuntu tells us. There are no intrinsically existing objects, subjects, or actions, as modernity has taught us to presume at least since the time of Descartes. In other words, the real is not made of isolated objects that interact with one another; the observer does not preexist what she observes (Maturana and Varela 1987); there is no external world for us to cling to. ... What we call 'experience' is always coemerging with the experiences of many other beings. (2020, 92)

35 Despite any impression that may be given by the reference to the posthumanities here, this messy, processual, co-constitutive relationship between our minds, bodies and media did not come into being only with the development of 'cyber-authorship'. In other words, it is not beholden to the emergence of new era technologies such as computer- and AI-generated prose, or before that, digital hypertext. On the contrary, this extended, generative relation is what makes the human *possible* in the first place. There is no human without it. Still, there is something about the contemporary conjuncture (the sheer volume, speed and intensity of communication) that forces our attention in the epistemological Global North onto this co-constitutive relationship perhaps more than has been the case in many other periods of history. As to why the concept of inhumanities is ultimately preferred to posthumanities in *Masked Media* – or to Donna Haraway's notion of *humusities* for that matter – see Chapter 5 as well as Hall (2017).

36 More facts about the environmental impact of paper, as provided by The World Counts:

> In the USA, Japan, and Europe an average person uses between 200 and 250 kilos of paper every year. Producing 1 kilo of paper requires 2-3 times its weight in trees. If everyone used 200 kilos of paper per year there would be no trees left. It takes between 2 and 13 liters of water to produce a single A4-sheet of paper, depending on the mill. The pulp and paper industry is the single largest industrial consumer of water in Western countries. (The World Counts n.d.-a)

37 Nor were libraries generally quiet until only relatively recently. The ancient Greeks and Romans often read scrolls aloud. See also McLuhan (1962, 43).

38 Hall (2016b) provides more on the microentrepreneur of the self. There is one particularly notable feature of the shift from the world of privacy and the book to the new (dis)connectedness of social media, as Felix Stalder shows. This is that the latter retains much of the former's emphasis on the individual human subject – albeit in the form of a subjectivity that is generated through an individual's interactive social relations within multiple communicative networks and collectivities:

> In order to create sociability in networked, communicative environments people first have to make themselves visible, that is, they have to create their (re)presentation through expressive acts of communication. Simply being present, passively, is not enough. In order to connect to such networks, a person also has to be suitably different, that is creative in some recognisable fashion. ... This creates a particular type of subjectivity that sociologists have come to call 'networked individualism'. ... There are two important points here. First, people construct their individuality through sociability rather than through privacy, that is, through positioning themselves within communicative networks. Second, they do so in multiple networks and shift their allegiances over time across these networks and from old to new ones. Thus, individuality arises from the unique concurrences of collectivities within a particular person. (Stalder 2014, 22-23)

Interestingly, as far as the argument I am making here is concerned, Stalder goes on to note how the requirement 'to express one's desires and passions in order to enter into a sociability that creates one's identity slowly erodes the distinction between the inner and outer world, so central to the modern (liberal) notion of subjectivity, forged in the Gutenberg Galaxy' (24). The result is that forms of subjectivity today are progressively based less on introspection and more on interaction.

39 Uber called a halt to its trials of driverless vehicles after a pedestrian was killed in 2018. Nevertheless, such automation, while ambitious – and frequently the subject of hyperbolic predictions – may not be so very far off. Some are calculating that actuators (autonomous cars, drones) and sensors (cameras, thermostats) will soon be connected to large language model AI and from there to the larger world in order to 'increasingly control our environment' (Schneier 2023).

40 The library without walls is of course a play on André Malraux's museum without walls (1953).

41 It has been suggested that we respond to this state of affairs by expanding the language with which we talk about privacy to take in different concepts such as 'ambient privacy'. The latter refers to realising the importance of keeping our day-to-day interactions beyond the range of surveillance, and of not having every aspect of lives documented and remembered. We should not have to worry about what we do in our homes, jobs, educational institutions or spare time being filed away and made part of the 'permanent record' (Cegłowski 2019). Yet even a shift in perspective such as this continues to make use of a distinction between public and private that may no longer be appropriate or fit for purpose.

42 For example – and to continue with the theme of masked media – Judith Fathallah notes how on 4chan:

> In place of a username, posters may be assigned a 'tripcode' (a unique number generated from their password) to identify themselves across multiple postings. Most users, however, do not even use this, and post with a new anonymous identity each time. Auerbach calls this 'per-message anonymity' or 'near-total anonymity' as opposed to the partial anonymity provided by using a tripcode. It is possible to enter a username in the posting field, but there is nothing to stop the next poster from entering the same name.

Echoing the shift from the concept of the author to the concept of the work that Foucault traces in 'What is an Author', Fathallah points out that 4chan

> users may not have a distinct or stable identity, but the group certainly does. The identity of the group itself is both more distinct and more important than the identity of individual users. This is why mastery of in-group profane discourse is so important. ... This accords with Knuttila's observation that 'focusing then not on the person, but the act, becomes one way to articulate the [4chan] community: not the troll, but the act of trolling; not the joker, but the act of joking'. (Fathallah 2021)

43 See Janneke Adema's 'Performative Publications' for one instance of a text produced in multiple versions and formats. Itself an iteration of 'The Political Nature of The Book: On Artists' Books and Radical Open Access', written by Adema and myself and originally published in the journal *New Formations* (Adema and Hall 2013), 'Performative Publications' comes in at least three different versions:

1) an online interactive version with accompanying posters designed by Nabaa Baqir, Mila Spasova and Serhan Curti (Adema 2017);

2) a specially designed postprint platform version (Adema 2018b);

3) a Taylor & Francis published version (Adema 2018).

Another instance is provided by *Masked Media* itself, a much shorter version of which was published as a pamphlet to accompany THE HOUSE THAT HEALS THE SOUL, an exhibition at The Tetley Centre for Contemporary Art and Learning, Leeds, February 9 – April 22, 2018.

44 Examples of projects – early adopters – that use AI to move us in this direction include those mentioned earlier: K Allado-McDowell's collection *Pharmako-AI* (2020) and novel *Amor Cringe* (2022); Mark Amerika's own experimental novel *Planet Corona*, which he co-authored with OpenAI's large GPT-2 text generation model and brought out in 2020, the same year as Allado-McDowell's *Pharmako-AI*; and Amerika's book of media theory, *My Life as an Artificial Creative Intelligence*, also co-authored using AI text generation (2022c). Another particularly interesting example worth mentioning is Karen ann Donnachie and Andy Simionato's publishing experiment, The Library of Nonhuman Books (2019).

45 Compare Franzen's rule to Amerika's insistence that 'I can't write without the Internet on. If I don't have a connection, I'm catatonic' (*rtc*, 65). Staying with the novel for a moment, is this one way of reading the celebrated multi-volume *My Struggle* by Karl Ove Knausgaard? Has Knausgaard reacted against the intense connectedness of the post-Gutenberg world and its impact on the public/private distinction by using auto-fiction – a combination of the novel form with autobiography in which the author reflects on the conditions of their writing – to shore up the boundary around the personal and the self all the more? For one interpretation of *My Struggle* along these lines, see Dames (2016). Does this also provide a way of understanding the memorification of culture explored in *A Stubborn Fury* (Hall 2021a)?

Nathan Jones, meanwhile, offers a somewhat different reading of auto-fiction: in this case that of Tao Lin, Ben Lerner, Sheila Heti, Lauren Oyler and Sally Rooney. For Jones, the firm Gutenbergian boundaries between subject and object, self and other, non-fiction and fiction are glitching in the 'internet age'. Authors of auto-fiction 'emphasise the emergent ideas of data malleability to produce narrative "errors" as deviations from established modes of realism. The characters in these books seem to flicker in and out of existence like flocks of data points' (2022, 197). In this way, the authors of auto-fiction Jones looks at distort – or glitch – 'the self with its fictionalised form' (197-198).

46 For an example of how digital humanists associate critique with negation, interrogation, antagonism, refusal and rejection, as opposed to constructive building, see Fitzpatrick (2019). Although it has been something of a humanities trope of late, one can't help wonder just how *generous*, how open and receptive to others, is this kind of reading of critique and critical thinking. Is that of the theorists Michel Foucault and Judith Butler not rather more generous? After all,

Notes   293

for them critique is very much a constructive art, a practice, a doing. There is more on Foucault and Butler's understanding of critique in Hall (2016a).

47 The latter has been the case with regard to theory since at least the publication of Jean-François Lyotard's *The Postmodern Condition: A Report on* Knowledge in 1979, as I showed in *Pirate Philosophy* when arguing that, strictly speaking, *there are no digital humanities* (Hall 2016a). That 2016 book analyses several specific, 'actually existing', digital humanities projects: most closely and extensively the Cultural Analytics of Lev Manovich and the Software Studies Initiative.

48 Another way of characterising this creatively transformed humanities is in terms of what Goldberg refers to as the 'afterlife of the humanities'. He takes the word 'afterlife' from Walter Benjamin. According to Goldberg, the value of translation for Benjamin is to be located in 'extending the life of the work translated, in liberating its "afterlife"' (Goldberg 2014, 29, 27). Intriguingly, however, Benjamin never actually uses the German equivalent of 'afterlife' (*Nachleben*) – not in the 'The Task of the Translator', at any rate – preferring '*Überleben*' (survival) and especially '*Fortleben*'. In a fascinating essay on the difficult concept of *Fortleben* and how it has been understood by Blanchot, Derrida, de Man and others, Caroline Disler shows how Benjamin employs it in 'The Task of The Translator' to mean 'metamorphosis, evolution, transformation, renewal, renovation, supplementation' (Disler 2011, 193); that the 'original is not a fixed, stable text' (194). In other words, as far as Benjamin is concerned: '*Fortleben* implies constant, dynamic change of the original' (194). Yet 'afterlife' is how *Fortleben* has often appeared in English and French translations of Benjamin's essay. This means that 'afterlife' is itself an issue of translation, transformation and indeed afterlife, of 'constant calling forth' (Disler 2011, 209). Liberating the afterlife of digital humanities and new materialism is nevertheless one way of describing what I am trying to do in this chapter – and in *Masked Media* overall.

49 Ron Broglio provides a brief telling of the story in *Animal Revolution* (2022, 34-35). Anna Munster also offers an interesting reading of Naruto's case in a paper given at Goldsmiths, University of London, on June 16, 2016, under the title of 'Techno-Animalities – The Case of The Monkey Selfie'. Neither Broglio nor Munster focus specifically on its implications for theorists of the posthuman, though.

50 In *Staying with The Trouble*, Donna Haraway writes: 'My partner Rusten Hogness suggested compost instead of posthuman(ism), as well as humusities instead of humanities, and I jumped into that wormy pile. Human as humus has potential, if we could chop and shred human as homo, the detumescing project of a self-making and planet-destroying CEO. Imagine a conference not on the Future of the Humanities in the Capitalist Restructuring University, but

instead on the Power of the Humusities for a Habitable Multispecies Muddle!' (2016, 32).

51 For more on Déborah Danowski and Eduardo Viveiros de Castro in relation to the Anthropocene and Latour, Meillassoux, Brassier and Shaviro, see Wark (2017b).

52 The work of Bruno Latour has been taken as the focus here: because it provides an opportunity to briefly situate the human-centeredness of Harman, Meillassoux and Brassier, too; and because other variants of posthumanist thought, including new materialism, media archaeology and, indeed the object-oriented philosophy of Graham Harman, have already been engaged with at some length in Hall (2016a). *Masked Media's* fragmented analysis of Latour continues below.

53 In an article critiquing Latour's critique of critique, Eva Haifa Giraud and Sarah-Nicole Aghassi-Isfahani draw on the work of Angela Wiley to trace one version of this argument as it is played out in the context of feminist theory:

> New materialism, Willey argues, often self-narrativizes the origins of the field by telling a story of a gradual evolution: from theoretical work that is simply deconstructive and critical of scientific knowledge, to work that is reconciliatory, interdisciplinary, and actively builds on the insights of the natural sciences in developing its own conceptual stance. This story, however, relies on reasserting lineages with feminist figures who lend themselves more readily to a reconciliatory position (such as Karen Barad and later Donna Haraway) while cutting away others whose postcolonial feminist position fits less neatly with contemporary new materialist aspirations (notably Sandra Harding).
>
> [T]his positioning of new materialisms as somehow overcoming the critical excesses of poststructuralism, by reconciling with recent work in the natural sciences, is a pervasive narrative. The danger of this narrative is that it valorises particular ways of knowing as being productive of 'truth' in a manner that makes it difficult to open space to ask the questions about *how* these knowledges are implemented (as called for by Raman), or create space to include divergent perspectives when exploring these questions (in line with Puig de la Bellacasa), let alone recognize that alternative ways of knowing might exist (as central to Harding's standpoint epistemology). (Haifa Giraud and Aghassi-Isfahani 2020)

54 Like others in the preamble and indeed throughout *Masked Media*, this comment is intended to recognise the difficulty of operating in a non-modernist-liberal fashion, even as one strives to do so. In its attempt to take *account of* and *assume* some of the implications of

ontologically relational thought, it is certainly not the aim of *Masked Media* to present itself as being completely and consistently inhuman, as if it were somehow able to simultaneously enact all those alternative concepts and values regarding the composition, production and distribution of theory itemised in Chapter 1 (pluriverality, co-constitution, collectivity, polyphony and so on). Instead, *Masked Media* is operating according to Derrida's notion of the quasi-transcendental, whereby the process of disarticulating and transforming some aspects of our liberal humanist, Euro-Western ways of being and doing by necessity requires others are left relatively untouched, at least temporarily. It's a question of deciding which datum points to focus on and radically reconfigure, and when. An incomplete list of such blind spots is provided in Hall (2024). It includes: the autonomous and proprietorial human subject; the self-identical rational liberal individual as ultimate point of reference; linear thought; coherent, single-voiced, narrative truth; the unified, homogeneous, fixed and finished autograph text; monumentality; originality; creativity; self-expression.

55 See Hall (2021b) for a thinking of such a performance and transformation in terms of the relation of pluriversal to the universal, the ontological to the hegemonic/counterhegemonic, the radically relational to the modernist liberal developed by English-speaking Latin Americanist theorists such as Arturo Escobar and Gareth Williams.

56 In *What Ever Happened To Modernism?*, Josipovici is able to draw on Søren Kierkegaard to find evidence of what some might read as a form of posthumanist relationality in the pre-modern world of the ancient Greeks, a world which is for many the very foundation of the humanities:

> today each person is deemed to be entirely responsible for his actions while 'the peculiarity of ancient tragedy is that ... the action does not find its sufficient explanation in subjective reflection and decision'. ...
>
> The hero of Greek tragedy was not an autonomous individual. He was caught in and made by a whole web of different interpenetrating elements. (Josipovici 2010; quoting Kierkegaard 1959, 141)

57 The phrase 'so-called dark side critiques' is Kirschenbaum's (2014, 59). Meanwhile, in an intriguing defence of digital humanities against such critiques, Brian Greenspan puts the appeal of the latter down to the fact they tap into 'a large undercurrent of *ressentiment* within academia that blames the digital humanities and neoliberalism alike for sapping both prestige and resources from the "pure" scholarly pursuits of merely thinking and writing, which allegedly require only books, pens, and paper; and need not involve any newer technologies' (2019).

58 Kirschenbaum identifies as a major influence on dark side critiques and their 'rhetoric of contempt', Evgeny Morozov, 'the caustic technology critic whose first book was titled *The Net Delusion: The Dark Side of Internet Freedom* (2011). Morozov, as much as the dark sides of Star Wars or Pink Floyd, furnishes the referential framing for the current debate' (Kirschenbaum 2014, 52). Yet when it comes to the humanities' 'material turn', the dark side argument can be seen to have other precursors. Among them is *The Spam Book: On Viruses, Porn and Other Anomalies from the Dark Side of Digital Culture*, edited by Jussi Parikka and Tony Sampson, which appeared in 2009, two years before Morozov's *The Net Delusion*.

59 At the time Grusin was Director of C21 at the University of Wisconsin-Milwaukee, where *The Dark Side of the Digital* conference was held. Both Grusin's essay and the 'In the Shadows of the Digital Humanities' issue of the journal *differences*, in which the text was published (alongside Kirschenbaum's 'What Is "Digital Humanities"'), emerged out of the roundtable Grusin organized at the 2013 Modern Language Association Convention in Boston under the same title of 'The Dark Side of the Digital Humanities'. That roundtable was in turn published as Chun *et al.*, 'The Dark Side of Digital Humanities' (2016).

60 Grusin, Koh and Risam were writing before the appearance of a number of books that have endeavoured to address precisely such issues. They include Risam (2019); Risam and Baker (2021); and Fiormonte, Chaudhuri and Ricaurte (2022).

61 Lest it is thought I am not interested in working conditions and the precarity of labour, see my *The Uberfication of the University* (2016b).

62 A similar argument could be developed with regard to Kirschenbaum's defence of those who 'do' digital humanities as having 'been educated in the same critical traditions (indeed, sometimes in the same graduate programs) as their opponents', and as also being 'politically committed and politically engaged' (Kirschenbaum 2014, 53).

63 Orwell is here responding to an entirely docile outlook regarding fighting fascism and defending democracy he attributes to Henry Miller, whom the English writer met in Paris in 1936 on his way to take part in the Spanish civil war (1940, 174-175). For Orwell, both *laissez-faire* capitalism and liberal-Christian culture are in the process of breaking up, World War Two or not, and we are 'moving into an age of totalitarian dictatorships' (185). But if for Miller it does not matter that Western civilisation is 'destined to be swept away and replaced by something so different that we should scarcely regard it as human', it does for Orwell (175). He thus places the future writer of a hardly conceivable totalitarian literature in a position of contrast

to the sovereign, liberal, Euro-Western, modernist human author of the past and present:

> literature, in the form in which we know it, must suffer at least a temporary death. The literature of liberalism is coming to an end and the literature of totalitarianism has not yet appeared and is barely imaginable. As for the writer, he is sitting on a melting iceberg; he is merely an anachronism, a hangover from the bourgeois age, as surely doomed as the hippopotamus. ... But from now onwards the all-important fact for the creative writer is going to be that this is not a writer's world. That does not mean that he cannot help to bring the new society into being, but he can take no part in the process *as a writer*. For *as a writer* he is a liberal, and what is happening is the destruction of liberalism. (1940, 185)

64   If they do so at all, it is often only when they write their acknowledgments that radical authors go some distance toward showing an appreciation of the relational nature of their work and identities. The following, rather knowing, variation on this theme is offered by Stalder in the acknowledgments to *Digital Solidarity*: 'Ideas and thoughts flow within and across networks, driven by the desire of people to appropriate and propagate them. The fact that I claim authorship is not to interrupt this process, but to speed it along' (2014, 59-60).

65   This analysis is based in part on the talk given by Michael Hardt during the book launch held for *Assembly* on October 12, 2017, at the University of Westminster in London. The points made here were also raised with Hardt in conversation and by email directly after this event. Hardt and Negri have been selected to illustrate this part of *Masked Media's* argument because, as the authors of influential works such as *Empire* (2001), *Multitude* (2004) and *Commonwealth* (2009), these two autonomist Marxists are among the most radical political theorists of recent years. But they have also been chosen because, like *Masked Media*, Hardt and Negri are interested in the generation of new forms of human and nonhuman cooperation, collaboration and the commons.

66   Newfield emphasises that 'humanism has always seen the liberal arts and sciences as central to higher education. They are "liberal" because all of their disciplines, from linguistics to history to sociology to biology to astrophysics, focus simultaneously on subject expertise and the formation of the self that is acquiring the expertise. Vocational training cannot be separated from self-development. The training is only as good as the self that grasps it. Every liberal arts and sciences course in a university is in principle about intellectual development and self-development at the same time' (2016, 328-329).

67 According to the sociologist Colin Crouch, this is how 'actually existing, as opposed to ideologically pure', neoliberalism can be understood (2011, viii).

68 Substack apparently now no longer offers such Pro deals.

69 In Zuboff's case this should come as no surprise, given the subtitle of the book for which she is best known, *The Age of Surveillance Capitalism: The Fight for A Human Future at The New Frontier of Power* (2019).

70 Roberto Esposito goes so far as to find a certain symmetry between liberalism and Nazism; although he is careful to acknowledge their fundamental difference and radical distance from each other too (2012, 12-13).

71 To show I am not alone in thinking like this, let me refer to the argument of John Milbank and Adrian Pabst: that, while the struggle between left and right that has dominated Western politics for the past half-century has often been presented in terms of opposing positions, they are in fact just two faces of the same liberalism. For Milbank and Pabst, too, far from representing alternatives to one another, these two liberalisms are 'mutually reinforcing' (2017, 23).

72 This is also one of the criticisms that have been raised against the development – largely within the US academy – of what is called Critical University Studies (CUS). For some of those in favour of an Abolitionist University Studies, 'CUS is haunted by its allegiance to a "crisis consensus" fuelled by nostalgia for the apogee of the postwar public mass university' (Boggs *et al.* 2019, 5).

73 An example relating to masked media: Nightshade v1.0 is a free tool made available by computer scientists at the University of Chicago that enables artists to protect their creative works from being used without their consent for training diffusion AI models (https://nightshade.cs.uchicago.edu/). It does so by 'poisoning' images at the pixel level (hence the name), obfuscating them from the perspective of AI, but not the human viewer.

74 To be clear, none of this is suggest posthumanist theory has up until now neglected to raise questions for notions of the author, the book and so forth, nor indeed for its own status. Wark's *General Intellectuals: Twenty-One Thinkers for The Twenty-First Century*, which this chapter proceeds to build upon in part, does just this. In the introduction, Wark acknowledges that today it would be nigh on impossible to 'write intellectually challenging books and make a living from it' (2017c, 3). As with those independent artists mentioned earlier, unless you have existing wealth you need 'a day job, and usually in the university' (3). She proceeds to explain what she means by general intellects – among whose number she includes Haraway, Morton and Meillassoux – as follows:

> I mean people who are mostly employed as academics, and mostly pretty successful at that, but who try through their work to address more general problems about the state of the world today.
>
> They are, on the one hand, part of the general intellect, in that they are workers who think and speak and write, whose work is commodified and sold. But they are, on the other hand, general intellects, in that they try to find ways to write and think and even act in and against this very system of commodification that has now found ways to incorporate even them. (2017c, 3)

This is so even though these general intellects continue to be 'rather bourgeois thinkers' for Wark (13).

Nor is any of this to overlook that some posthumanists have on occasion experimented with different ways of working and making. See, for instance, the accounts of the online interactive research platform Feral Atlas (2021), edited and curated by Anna Tsing, Jennifer Deger, Alder Keleman Saxena and Feifei Zhou, and Bruno Latour's AIME: An Inquiry into Modes of Existence platform (2013), that are provided below. Other examples include the multiply-authored *New Materialism: How Matter Comes to Matter Almanac*, edited by David Gauthier and Sam Skinner, and published iteratively and online in the first instance between 2016-2018 (newmaterialism.eu). (My thanks to the anonymous reviewers of *Masked Media* for this reference, and for those other suggestions now incorporated into the text.) And that's without even mentioning the way posthumanist theorists have been involved in the creation of films, art exhibitions, even theatre productions. Nevertheless, it remains the case that the most well-known and influential of these theorists have almost invariably continued to act, for the most part, as if they were still living in the Gutenberg galaxy of writing and the self-identical autonomous authorial subject: a galaxy in which, as we've seen, the linearly organised and commercially copyrighted codex book is in effect a proxy for liberal humanism.

The issue I raised in *Pirate Philosophy* with regard to another legacy posthumanist theorist, Bernard Stiegler, continues to apply today, then. There I showed how Stiegler may have worked, in his conceptual language, to 'develop a new, enlarged organology for the contemporary era that includes digital technology, networks, and software' (Hall 2016a, 65). Stiegler may even have done so by operating at times in less conventional academic terms: as part of the Ars Industrialis association of cultural activists and other collective groups and projects, for instance. But if he is correct in suggesting that we are now living in an era where the web and digital reproducibility mean subjects are created with a transformed awareness of time, then the question arises as to the extent this 'episteme and the associated changes in the media ecology that are shaping our memories and consciousness be understood, analyzed, rethought, and reinflected by subjectivities' such as Stiegler's (Hall 2016a, 65)? Subjectivities that, to a very large degree, 'continue to live, work, and think on the basis of knowledge instruments originating in a very different epistemic environment?' (Hall 2016a, 65). Evidence Stiegler's writing of over fifty single-authored books in the twenty-six-year period between the publication of his first in 1994 and his death in 2020. That's an average of almost one every six months – before we even get to all those volumes he co-authored and edited.

75 The understanding of the inhuman in *Masked Media* is somewhat different not only from that of Negarestani, for whom it is 'the extended practical elaboration of humanism' (2014), but from that of Wark, too. For Wark, the *inhuman* is 'an apparatus of labor and technology. Indeed, the inhuman is the zone where the partition between the human and nonhuman is negotiated, at the expense of rendering the inhuman labor in between invisible. There is no such thing as a "history of ideas", only of the labor and technics of producing them' (2017d).

The approach to the inhuman and the inhumanities in this book also differs from that of Wendy Chun. She ends her contribution to the debate over the dark side of digital humanities by arguing, along with Natalia Cecire, that 'DH is best when it takes on the humanities, as well as the digital' (Chun in Chun *et al.* 2016). For her, 'maybe, by taking on the inhumanities' – by which Chun means 'anonymity, the ways in which the Internet vexes the relationship between public and private, the ways it compromises our autonomy and involves us with others and other machines in ways we don't entirely know and control' (Chun in Chun *et al.* 2016), all of which has been discarded or decried as a result of the promise made by DH's bright side 'to save the humanities by making them and their graduates relevant, by giving their graduates technical skills that will allow them to thrive in a difficult and precarious job market' – we'll be able to 'transform the digital as well'. Nevertheless, Chun is careful to stress that her 'sympathetic critique is not aimed at the humanities, but at the general euphoria surrounding technology and education' (Chun in Chun *et al.* 2016). For more on some of the problems with such dark side critiques of digital humanities, however, and especially their emphasis on what Chun brackets under 'critical theory' and 'race studies', see Chapter 3.

76 The situation has changed somewhat even in the relatively short space of time that has elapsed since Ghosh and Wark first published their texts. A number of literary novels have since been written on the Anthropocene. They include *Gun Island*, Ghosh's 2019 response to the critique he made of fiction in *The Great Derangement*. Yet Ghosh identifies the year 2018 as the 'inflection point': 'It was partly because there were so many extreme climate events that year – the California wildfires, flooding in India, a succession of brutal

hurricanes – but partly also because of the publication of Richard Powers' *The Overstory*. ... It wasn't hived off into the usual silos of climate change or speculative fiction, but was treated as a mainstream novel. I do think that was a very major thing. Since then, there's been an outpouring of work in this area' (Ghosh, quoted in Armitstead 2021). The question remains, though: to what extent is this new literary fiction actually reinventing the bourgeois novel enough to overcome its formal limitations?

77 This seems to be something that the commercially-minded, liberal humanist professional in Wark prevents her from recognising, in this essay on Ghosh at least. Wark comes a little closer to doing so in 'The Engine Room of Literature', an earlier text on Franco Moretti and the bourgeois novel (2013). Here she suggests that the evolutionary model Moretti adopts for thinking about the novel, in which the 'tree of literature is constantly sprouting new branches, but some die off, taking their place in the fossil record of "the great unread" ... makes many of Moretti's colleagues particularly squeamish'. This is because it implies that culture is determined by the market. Whereas of course critics of literature '(even Marxist ones) like to think we have in the literary work some relatively autonomous object not completely subsumed within the system of capitalism'. Yet what Moretti's theory makes clear is 'how the market feedback loop exaggerates differences in success between the more and less fit kinds of literary form'. It is a complex web of bourgeois culture in which the whole of literary criticism takes part, according to Wark, regardless of whether it does so consciously or not. In the upper echelons 'it may be all high-minded talk of resistant readings and counter-canons, but down in the engine room the business of literature is all about making variants on products for a panoply of markets' (2013).

It would be interesting to pursue this line of thought in the context of Isabel Waidner's argument about how white, bourgeois and patriarchal most experimental literature is, certainly in the UK – for more see *A Stubborn Fury* (Hall 2021a). Suffice it to say for now that it leads Wark to conclude that: 'It must surely pass through the minds of many professional readers of Moretti that our works, too, are just variations of forms, thrown on the market, where a fickle readership – mostly of grad students – decides for itself whether the form addresses the actual tensions they experience in everyday life' (2013).

78 To extend this reading of Wark's text with and against itself, it can be argued that the last things Wark in fact pays attention to with *General Intellects* are the very things she herself sees as requiring 'more attention than they usually get'. Of these, the first is the 'development of new *forces of production*', by which she means information technology, which Wark perceives as 'transforming the whole social formation' (2017c, 4) The second is 'an unexpected effect of how information technology has also found its way into the sciences. ... Climate change is just the most pressing of what are now often grouped

together as signs of the *Anthropocene*' (4). The result, according to Wark, is that one can longer 'bracket off the question of *techne* from questions about the social, the historical, the political and the cultural and so on' (4). Nor can one 'treat social phenomena as if there is a stable background of natural phenomena that can be bracketed off and ignored' (4). Yet this is precisely what I am arguing bourgeois theorists do – and Wark herself can be included in this. She may well ask elsewhere in *General Intellects*: 'how can we even write books in the era of Snapchat and Twitter? ... books are a problem for the era of communicative capitalism, which resists recombination into longer threads of argument' (145). Consider, though, the fact that *General Intellects* is itself ultimately rooted in the old Gutenbergian information technologies of the codex book and mass printing, and with them the singular author and copyright. Is this not indeed a case of endeavouring to continue to do 'today's job with yesterday's tools – with yesterday's concepts', as McLuhan has it (McLuhan and Fiore 1967/2008, 8-9). Wark does not consider, at least in the introduction to *General Intellects* (the specific text being read against itself here), how the media technologies she uses are both 'virtual and actual and could have other forms' (11). Such other forms *might* enable her to cooperate with 'different kinds of knowledge of different parts of the metabolism' in ways 'other than via the commodification of knowledge as intellectual property' that is achieved by publishing on an all-rights-reserved basis with the aggressively proprietorial, for-profit independent press that is Verso (12). For further engagement with Wark's *General Intellects*, see Chapter 2 of Hall (2021a).

79 Wark here seems to come close to positioning digital humanities as an example of post-bourgeois theory. At any rate she suggests the work of Moretti 'might be profitably used to advance the critical project onto the post-bourgeois terrain'; and the latter's quantitative distant reading approach to the study of literature has of course been an influence on much of the computational turn toward data mining in digital humanities (2013). For Wark, Moretti is:

> a practitioner of the characteristic arts of post-bourgeois life. What, after all, does the post-bourgeois reverence above graphs, maps, trees, algorithms, infographics, and other examples of so-called 'big data'? The delight we once took in the skill of the novelist, or the literary critic, is today elicited by the extraction of patterns from vast swaths of texts and other sources, via the kind of perceptive operations that machines perform much better than people.
>
> The difference, of course, is that Moretti's project is a critical one ... (2013)

Indeed, while for Wark the data mining method of Morreti 'is of a kind more common and accepted in media studies – such as in the work of Henry Jenkins and Lev Manovich – than in literary scholarship', it has the 'added virtue of retaining some link, however

Notes 303

attenuated, to the critical project of his Italian Marxist ancestors' (2013). Since I've already engaged with the uncritical humanism prevalent in much of digital humanities – and also the lack of political critique from those 'dark side' theorists who chastise digital humanities for not being political or critical enough – I won't rehearse these arguments again here.

80 Like *General Intellects*, Wark's 2015 book on the Anthropocene, *Molecular Red*, is published by Verso, as is *Sensoria: Thinkers for The Twenty-First Century*, her 2020 follow-up to *General Intellects*. A critique of Verso's politics in relation to publishing and copyright going back at least as far as 2016 is available from Joy and van Gerven Oei (2022).

81 These examples show that, whereas for so long it was apes that were seen as occupying the 'blurry and murky border both between animals and humans and nature and culture' (Weizman 2016), or at least quadrupeds, as in Jeremy Bentham's *An Introduction to the Principles of Morals and Legislation* of 1780 and John Oswald's *The Cry of Nature, or An Appeal To Mercy And Justice On Behalf Of The Persecuted Animals* of 1791, it is now increasingly other entities too. Yet this brings with it other problems. How exactly do you define a river, the writer Patrick Barkham asks. Although many people consider a river to consist of the water that flows through it, he quotes Erin O'Donnell, a researcher specialising in water law, as pointing out that no river that has been granted legal recognition as a living entity or legal personage in fact possesses any entitlement to its water. 'There is increasingly an attempt to give rivers a right to flow and so the Magpie River in Canada has got the right to flow, but how you enforce that right is very unclear', according to O'Donnell. 'And if that's not actually embedded within water law, which it isn't yet, then it's probably not worth the paper it's written on' (O'Donnell, quoted in Barkham 2021). Barkham proceeds to show how this is demonstrated by the Whanganui treaty in New Zealand, where a water company is still using 80% of the river's flow for hydropower and will continue to do so until 2039, which is when its licence runs out. Despite this, Barkham and O'Donnell maintain that the concept of rights for rivers still contains real potential for change, as it encourages a move away from a Lockean extractive model in which rivers are seen as resources that are freely available for humans to exploit (Barkham 2021).

82 See the Tree That Owns Itself, the original of which is thought to date back to somewhere between mid-sixteenth and late eighteenth century (https://en.wikipedia.org/wiki/Tree_That_Owns_Itself). My thanks to Jurij Smrke for this reference. Intriguingly, the very concept of the Rights of Nature was first introduced with regard to trees by law professor Christopher Stone, in a 1972 article titled 'Should Trees Have Standing? – Toward Legal Rights for Natural Objects' (Stone 1972).

83 Thanks to George Ttoouli for pointing me in the direction of *Decomp*.

84 Artist Maggie Roberts' Becoming Octopus, part of a 2020 online group show called *THIS IS A NOT-ME*, curated by Mark Jackson (https://imagemusictext.com/exhibition-this-is-a-not-me/), also moves us in this direction. Becoming Octopus is a 'guided' meditative experience. Consisting of a total of eight sessions, it conveys participants into the decentred, resonating body, sensations and watery habitat of a Common Octopus. Live-streamed once a week from September 8 to October 27, 2020, Becoming Octopus involves letting go of the vision-led perspective of humans. Instead, it prioritises 'the senses of touch and taste; processing reality with 8 arms and a central brain simultaneously; flowing the outside through the insides and camouflaging the body to become the ground using an array of colour effects and protean skin textures' (Roberts 2020). Scott, Collis, Roberts and Berck thus all appear to be going a step further than works that convey the world from the point of view of nature. (One of the central protagonists of Richard Power's novel *Overstory*, for example, is a chestnut tree, while theatre director Katie Mitchell has created a version of Anton Chekhov's *The Cherry Orchard* from the perspective of the trees.)

85 An interesting variation on such questions is offered by Regine Debatty in an interview with the artist Marija Bozinovska Jones (2018). Debatty's questions are provoked by 'Treebour', Jones' contribution to a 2018 exhibition at Furtherfield Gallery in London called *Playbour – Work, Pleasure, Survival*: https://www.furtherfield.org/playbour-work-pleasure-survival/.

86 Do we need to mention here that Wark's *General Intellects* is itself ostensibly concerned with twenty-one proper, unique, named, individual human thinkers, rather than nonhuman actors or even nonindividualistic human groups and communities? This is so despite the fact that, for Wark, the writing of these individual thinkers can explain our times when read collectively as the result of collaborative practices of knowledge production.

Of course, Wark can be understood as trying to work against such separation and individualism in *General Intellects* by bringing all these writers from different disciplines together and drawing attention to some of the 'comradely' affinities and points of connection between them. It is noticeable, however, that she does so by focusing on an individual published text by each individual thinker. She gives each their own separate chapter too. This approach can be interpreted as Wark showing how the work and ideas of these general intellects (along with her own) can be reorganised, recombined – remixed even – into different forms; forms that are perhaps a little more appropriate to the post-Gutenberg galaxy of WhatsApp and Twitter/X. Although *General Intellects* is a codex print book, for instance, it does not have a linear argument or structure. It is more of a network or mesh in that respect. Still, while appreciating decisions need to be taken and cuts made, the question occurs: what would it mean for Wark to privilege theory that has been expressly and explicitly produced co-constitutively by heterogeneous assemblages of humans and technologies, as well as a host of other nonhuman actors and material elements? The work of Mattering Press (https://www.matteringpress.org) would be an example, in addition to those already featured in *Masked Media*. See Abrahamsson and DeVille (2013). For more on Mattering Press, see McHardy (2014) and Adema (2018a).

87   There can be said to be something humanist about theories of the Anthropocene even in their content. As Eyal Weizman writes: the 'exclusion of the orangutan from humanity' by the anatomist Petrus Camper 'took place at an important fold in history: the destruction of the *Ancien Regime*, a period bracketed by two important markers by which the ideology of humanism was ratified – the American *Declaration of Independence* and France's revolutionary assembly's *Declaration of the Rights of Man and of the Citizen* – and the beginning of the geological era of the anthropocene. (The era of human could seemingly only begin once the question of what is a human was decided.)' Weizman goes on to note that: 'One can also look at the same issue differently: The idea of "human exceptionalism" that saw humans uniquely distinct from animals, is echoed in the idea of the anthropocene, with exceptionalism this time articulated not as heroes but as villain-gods, alone in their ability to transform the material composition of the planet' (Weizman 2016). This is why some prefer the term Capitalocene to Wark's use of Anthropocene – because the former shifts responsibility even more from human exceptionalism to capitalism. Wark in turn comments elsewhere that Capitalocene 'leaves out much of what is really challenging about thinking the Anthropocene'. She also makes the point that 'even were capitalism to end tomorrow, the problems of the Anthropocene are not then magically solved' (2017b). Further criticism of the humanism of the Anthropocene narrative, this time in terms of its relation to differences of race and gender, can be found in Yusoff (2019) and Zylinska (2018).

88   Much like Didier Eribon and Édouard Louis, then – albeit for different reasons – there is not a ready-made audience I:ts are writing for (Hall 2021a).

89   It's worth emphasising once more that with *Masked Media* I'm not attempting to invent an entirely new inhuman way of writing *ex nihilo*. And this is the case regardless of any impression that may be given to the contrary, both in the identity-focused opening sections of this chapter, with their playful, almost excessive, use of the authorial first-person 'I', and elsewhere. I'm rather building on formal and conceptual innovations taken from a diverse multiplicity of sources. Hence the inclusion of numerous quotations and endnotes in a book

in which I'm also trying to make it difficult to determine where the *voices* of others end and mine begins. (Although an intriguing option, it seems to me that eliminating citations altogether – common in trade books – would have risked foregrounding the individualistic liberal humanist voice all the more.) As the preamble acknowledges, these references are designed to locate the book-cum-assemblage in a mesh of other thinkers, works and media technologies. But such bibliodiversity is also intended as a further means of reducing my own status as the original human author of *Masked Media*. Missing communities, for example, is a riff on a number of concepts, including Giorgio Agamben's 'coming community' (1993), Jacques Derrida's 'democracy to come' (2005), and Gilles Deleuze's 'missing people' (1997).

90 To be clear, *performative* is being used in the John L. Austin/Jacques Derrida/Judith Butler sense. For these authors performative language is language that does something in the world. This is distinct from the more popular, contemporary use of *performative* in the sense of wanting to overtly signal allyship – say, with the Movement for Black Lives – out of a desire for attention rather than a genuine wish to help.

91 None of this is to dismiss the long history of important feminist work on the autobiographical read as a collective, if intimate, experience. The latter is very different from neoliberal individualisation of the personal, as Jackie Stacey insists in 'Personal Value, Impersonal Subjects' (2022), her contribution to the Coventry Cultural Theory series.

92 A politico-ethical decision also has to be taken in each case as to whether to make knowledge open or not. As Cath Traynor and Laura Foster observe when writing on what they refer to as 'situated openness':

> Scientific commitments to openness and sharing were misused to justify the exploitation of Indigenous San and Khoi peoples' lands, bodies, and knowledge(s). European colonial scientists treated the lands, animals, and plants they found as in the public domain, thus available for taking and transporting to Western Europe. In encountering and learning from Indigenous San and Khoi peoples about the natural world of South African lands, colonial scientists regarded San and Khoi knowledge as freely shared information that could be scientifically validated, disclosed, and published to support the production of knowledge about nature and the development of technological innovations. Through these practices of colonial science, colonial scientists reinforced regimes of expertise and hierarchies of knowledge production that positioned Indigenous peoples as suppliers of raw material, rather than producers of knowledge. (Traynor and Foster n.d.)

Notes 307

> For Traynor and Foster, situated openness, although a process that necessitates a perpetual cycle of involvement, analysis and adjustment, still presupposes that the creation of knowledge is situated in specific 'historical, political, legal and social-cultural relations that are continually interacting with each other and changing overtime' (n.d.). As far as I am concerned, however, a politico-ethical decision has to be taken as to whether to situate knowledge in terms of particular historical, political, legal, and socio-cultural relations like this or not. Rather than situated openness, I'm therefore interested in what I term *responsible* or *undecidable openness*. See Chapter 9 for more.

93 Does this emphasis on the law of the subject also help to explain why the ideas of Latin American decolonial theorists, Mignolo included, have been taken up by far-right thinkers in Europe who see colonialism as ruling the world by stripping people of their identities (Davidson 2024)?

94 What's being engaged here are books on how to write well, such as Joe Moran's *First You Write a Sentence* (2018). For further examples of making the objects of information media weird, see Are Not Books (2017) and Hemmings (2011). Hemmings, for instance, cites the context of publication rather than the author. She does so in order to emphasise the important role citation practices play in 'securing the dominant narratives of Western feminist storytelling' (180), and to intervene in those narratives, not least by privileging 'conditions of production and collective practices over individual argument, success, or failure' (176).

95 For one version of this history concerning the intellectual life of the working classes, see Rose (2001). The historian Steven Mintz, meanwhile, has provided a helpful list of examples of the impact of theory on society. Although written in a North American context, it applies to Britain too. There's:

> the Foucaultesque notion that power and hierarchy can be found everywhere: for example, in language, in cultural categories and narratives and in representations as well as in economics or politics.
> There's the concept of performativity and the cultural, social and political dimensions of performance.
> There's postcolonialism – the study of the cultural, political and economic legacies of colonialism and imperialism. ...
> Especially influential is critical identity studies ... how gender, race, ethnicity, socioeconomic class, sexuality, dis/ability, nation, non-/religiosity and region influence identities; and how identities are shaped by structures of inequality and systems and practices of power. (Mintz 2023)

96 There have been a number of collections published of late arguing for the 'institutionalised bias and prejudices' against those from certain

backgrounds and communities to be rectified; for the elitism, classism, sexism and racism that fastens itself to writing to be kicked back against and smashed. Yet isn't struggling for 'fairer representation and greater equality' in order to 'give each other the freedom to achieve all that we can', also to risk continuing to operate within the liberal tradition and its belief that individual human rights and liberties are sacrosanct? (The above quotes are from what is just one of many interesting possible examples: Sabrina Mahfouz's introduction to her edited collection, *Smashing It: Working Class Artists on Life, Art & Making It Happen* [2019, 6].)

97 For both Olúfémi O. Táíwò and Kevin Ochieng Okoth the deferential version of standpoint epistemology they associate with identity politics and decolonial studies respectively is contradictory even on its own terms. It actually works to prevent '"centering"' or hearing from those marginalised and 'most affected' identities whose exclusion it is supposed to be struggling against. This is because, as Táíwò emphasises, it concentrates our attention 'on the interactions inside the rooms we occupy'. These are rooms that have been constructed in advance, but not by us. Nor have we had much input into their design. 'From a structural perspective, the rooms we *don't* enter, the experiences we *don't* have (and the reasons we are able to avoid them) might have more to teach us about the world and our place in it than anything said inside' (Táíwò 2022, 80; see also Ochieng Okoth 2021).

98 It's at this point that the idea of acting *something like* pirate philosophers also comes into play. Doing so might be a transformative gesture that has the potential to lead to new, nonhumanist and nonliberal ways of creating, publishing and circulating knowledge and ideas – ways that *are* more appropriate to the post-Gutenberg world than books and journal articles, written by *named* authors, and then turned into market commodities by for-profit publishers using a copyright licence. For more on pirate philosophy, see Hall (2016a).

99 This is why some modernist formal innovations are still drawn upon in *Masked Media*; and why experimental modernist writers such as Virginia Woolf, Henri Michaux and B. S. Johnson are included in its bibliodiverse mesh of thinkers and works.

100 It's also why – despite their inclusion in the title – I am reluctant to overtly push the concepts of masked media and artificial creative intelligence too heavily when it comes to framing such theory-performances; or to position the portfolio of projects that feature in the second part of *Masked Media* as an application of the theory set out in the first (or, indeed, to wrap its interest in capitalist surveillance, networked infrastructure and facial recognition technology into some grand theory of planetary sensing). I say this despite knowing doing so would help bring the book together into a more conventional unified whole.

Notes

101 See Chapter 8 for a more detailed explanation of scaling small; and Adema and Moore (2018; 2021) for more on scaling small in relation to open access specifically.

102 A desire to know-with rather than know-about is another reason even more thinkers from the epistemological Global South have not been added to the polyphony of voices that make up *Masked Media*. As noted above, some *have* been included as it is of course an important thing to do, not least as an expression of transnational solidarity. But as far as I am concerned it's even more important to create opportunities for knowing-with such thinkers: by helping to develop opportunities for those in the epistemological Global South to publish for themselves, if they so wish, by setting up their own journals and presses, for instance.

103 These descriptions have been adapted in part from the Open Humanities Press website, and in part from the responses provided by David Ottina and Sigi Jöttkandt on behalf of OHP to a 2019 *American Book Review* 'Scenes' Questionnaire.

104 It should be noted that, starting in August 2021, Cambridge University Press (CUP) first piloted and then adopted a new model for publishing at least some of its books open access. Called Flip It Open, this programme 'aims to fund the open access publication of 100 titles through typical purchasing habits. Once titles meet a set amount of revenue, [CUP] have committed to make them freely available as open access books … and also as an affordable paperback (Cambridge University Press n.d.-c; see also Cambridge University Press n.d.-a).

105 Something similar has been said of the August 25, 2022 memorandum from the US Office of Science and Technology Policy (OSTP), recommending that the public should be given immediate access, without an embargo, to all publications resulting from federally funded research 'as soon as possible, and no later than December 31st 2025' (Nelson 2022, 1). Green open access was endorsed by what has come to be known as the Nelson Memo, after its author, Alondra Nelson, Deputy Director for Science and Society. There was even explicit mention of a desire to 'reduce inequities in publishing of, and access to, federally funded research and data, especially among individuals from underserved backgrounds and those who are early in their careers' (Nelson 2022, 7). Yet the only model of paying for open access identified was that involving 'reasonable publication costs and costs associated with submission, curation, management of data, and special handling instructions'. Federal agencies were to permit researchers to include these costs 'as allowable expenses in all research budgets' (Nelson 2022, 5). As Peter Suber and Heather Joseph (2023) insisted, this didn't mean APCs *had* to be paid to comply with the OSTP's policy. Nevertheless, it did lead some to argue

that the OSTP's plan for bringing about open access to federally funded research depended heavily on APCs.

OASPA (Open Access Scholarly Publishing Association) made much the same criticism of the Public Access Plan released by NASA on May 18, 2023 (National Aeronautics and Space Administration 2023). OASPA observed that, with its 'emphasis on repository-enabled OA of any version (often likely to involve the authors' accepted manuscript) taken together with the draft policy's overtly stated willingness to allow for research grants to be used (against reasonable costs) for OA of the Version of Record (VoR)', NASA's Public Access Plan 'could heighten prevailing inequities in publication opportunities' (Redhead 2023).

106 See n10 for some of the problems with Creative Commons licences, including CC BY.

107 In November 2023 UKRI announced a maximum level of funding of £10,000 for supporting the open access publication of a monograph or edited collection by means of a BPC (UKRI 2024). Meanwhile, for more on COPIM's Opening the Future revenue model, see Opening the Future (n.d.).

108 Morrison and Rahman are here referring to a feedback letter with 1800 signatories from researchers reacting to Plan S (Research Community 2018). Similarly, Kowaltowski *et al.* note that in Brazil the maximum amount of funding available for federal two-year research grants ranges from $5,640 to $22,560, depending on the experience of the researcher in question. (To put this in context, some journals in the Global North have APCs of around half that top figure. *Nature's*, for instance, is $11,690.) Even the São Paulo State's FAPESP, which is the research funding agency that offers the most money, has a limit of slightly less than $30,000 a year. That figure is meant to cover all materials and services as well as APCs:

> When we mention these economic barriers to international colleagues, we are often told the solution is a waiver system for struggling economies. Indeed, Plan S, which spearheads the push for open access, stipulates that 'the journal/platform must provide APC waivers for authors from low-income economies and discounts for authors from lower-middle-income economies'. But most Latin American countries with significant scientific output, such as Brazil, Argentina and Mexico, as well as large countries such as China and the Russian Federation, are classified by the World Bank as upper-middle-income economies. Scientists in these nations must therefore ask for individual waivers (based on, as Plan S puts it, 'demonstrable needs') after manuscript acceptance. If the waiver is denied or the discount insufficient, the only

Notes

right an author has is to take the manuscript elsewhere, restarting the already lengthy revision process. (Kowaltowski et al. 2021)

It is a problem cOAlition S eventually recognised, at least to the extent of working with UNESCO, the International Science Council (ISC), the Open Access 2020 Initiative (OA2020), Electronic Information for Libraries (EIFL), the Association of African Universities, and Science Europe to coordinate a series of workshops on how a globally agreed pricing system for academic publishing services that is fair, equitable and transparent could be devised and implemented (cOAlition S 2023b).

109 Ellie Masterman, for example, warns that, even within the Global North, the APC model could result in the emergence of a two-tier system of open access academic publishing. Here, research in less economically valued areas such as literature and history would be deposited in green self-archiving OA repositories, while research that is held as having obvious commercial worth in terms of either economic or symbolic capital would be made available on a gold author-pays basis (Masterman 2020, 22).

110 As Adema and Moore acknowledge, there is a clear preference for non-profit publishing. At the same time the ROAC is aware there is a significant difference between a profit-maximising organisation and an initiative that is seeking to generate sufficient funds simply to be able to continue publishing.

111 For an example, see the Radical Open Access/ScholarLed collaborative, open-source book stand that members of both communities use to cross-promote one another's work at academic conferences and other events in a non-competitive manner. The book stand, first set up in during the *Radical Open Access II – The Ethics of Care* conference, held at Coventry University June 26-27, 2018, has both an online and offline version (https://radicaloa.disruptivemedia.org.uk/collaborative-open-source-bookstand-roac-flash-drives-and-postcards/).
It was subsequently reimagined during the pandemic as the Virtual Book Stand, which contains links to the books, journals, issues, articles, projects, catalogues and repositories of the various members of the ROAC (http://radicaloa.disruptivemedia.org.uk/latest-publications/). The aim is to eventually create a catalogue of all of the ROAC's publications.

112 There are other ways of achieving this, of course. One model is that offered by the book sprints with which the web artist and FLOSS Manuals founder Adam Hyde has been involved. Adopted from the open-source community, especially its use of hackathons, a book sprint is an instance of conducting this sort of collaborative activity with groups of people clustered together over a short period of time.

Notes

113 As many as three quarters of the papers published in literary theory go uncited (Baker 2018, 25). It could be that, because academics in the humanities attach more weight to monographs, they are citing any research that is initially published in a journal only when it appears in final book form. Yet it's hard to believe even taking this possibility into account would be enough to shift the percentage of work that goes uncited in literary theory significantly closer to 0%.

114 The 'About' page of *Living Books About History* explicitly states: 'This project was inspired by *Living Books About Life*, a digital publication series initiated at Coventry University in 2011 under the direction of Gary Hall'. On the main page of *The Living Bibliography of Animal Studies* project we find: 'LBAS is influenced by the JISC-funded 'Living Books About Life' series published by Open Humanities Press' (http://www.lbanimalstudies.org.uk/index4875.html?title=Main_Page). The 'About BOOC' page contains the following: 'This innovative new digital format presents subjects in the form of a "living book"' (https://ucldigitalpress.co.uk/BOOC/Article/1/55/).

115 Examples include Goldsmith's own 836-page *Day* (2003), in which he transcribes one 'day's *New York Times*, word for word, letter for letter, from the upper left hand corner to the lower right hand corner, page by page'; and Martin Howse's *Diff in June* (2013), a 740-page book that records and prints all the changes that were made to one computer's hard drive in a single day.

116 Making it possible for others to undertake experimental projects of this kind for themselves is extremely important to OHP. There are a number of bespoke publishing experiments that have been produced by posthumanist theorists, including Feral Atlas (2021), edited and curated by Anna Tsing, Jennifer Deger, Alder Keleman Saxena and Feifei Zhou. This work invites the user 'to explore the ecological worlds created when nonhuman entities become tangled up with human infrastructure projects' (https://feralatlas.org/). Another example is Bruno Latour's AIME: An Inquiry into Modes of Existence platform (2013), which describes itself as 'an investigation to learn how to compose the common world' (http://modesofexistence.org/). Yet, as Adema has emphasised to me in personal correspondence, Feral Atlas and AIME are very much one-off prestige publications. Highly advanced technically and beautiful to look at, they are difficult to produce unless you are a star theorist-cum-brand such as Tsing or Latour, able to attract large amounts of funding and institutional support. As many as thirteen people are named as having helped to design and build the Feral Atlas *online interactive research platform,* funded by the Danish National Research Foundation, James Cook University, Aarhus University, Aarhus Universitet Forskningsfond, University of California, Santa Cruz and the Royal College of Art, and which isn't available for others to use on an open source basis but is published and copyrighted by Stanford

Notes 313

University Press. (That's without mentioning all the others involved in creating Feral Atlas, including the six research assistants, three drawing assistants and more than twenty design and upload assistants.) Similarly, the AIME platform was funded by a research grant from the European Research Council (ERC) and is the property of the Fondation Nationale des Sciences Politiques. The site's section on IP explicitly states that: 'Any use or reproduction, total or partial, of the site, of the elements which compose it and/or of the information which appears there, by any means whatsoever, is strictly prohibited and constitutes an infringement punishable by the Intellectual Property Code'. (The PBworks wiki technology used to publish OHP's Liquid Books series isn't open source either. It was chosen because it is low-tech, extremely easy for anyone to use and available for free.) Actually, it could be argued that prestige projects such as Feral Atlas and AIME can have a detrimental effect – again, I'm drawing on correspondence with Adema in saying this. They may each have the advantage of having a high-quality design that is especially tailored to the respective projects and philosophies of Tsing and Latour. Nevertheless, they risk directing authors and publishers away from attempting experimental projects of their own, in the mistaken belief that doing so is a rather large-scale and expensive business that is only realistic if one has the means to engage numerous designers and developers. It would certainly be hard if not impossible for a non-profit scholar-led press or an early-career researcher to try to create a derivative of Feral Atlas or AIME according to their own singular situation and circumstances.

117 An attempt to move the design and building of institutions in this direction in relation to AI – albeit one that remains human-centred in that it is ultimately concerned to 'enhance human capabilities' and ensure AI is 'better-aligned with human values' – is offered by the Collective Intelligence Project (https://cip.org/) of the Cooperative AI Foundation (https://www.cooperativeai.com/). Especially interesting in this respect is its Project Card 'Conversational AI for Non-Human Representation in Decision-Making' by Shu Yang Lin (2023). The above quotations come from the Collective Intelligence Project (n.d.).

118 See Hall (2016a) for one earlier version of the history of Open Humanities Press, the Living Books About Life series, and also the development of the third volume of the Liquid Books series, *Technology and Cultural Form: A Liquid Theory Reader*.

119 COPIM's *Mutant Assembly* is another example of a publication whose fixed and final form is never arrived at. Instead, *Mutant Assembly* is 'designed as a mutating document that dynamically generates different versions or mutations of the book whenever a user exports content for download or print' (COPIM 2022).

120 OHP is not the only press to operate in this fashion. For other instances, see mediastudies.press, who portray themselves as publishing 'living works, with iterative updates stitched into our process' (mediastudies.press n.d.); and also the description of Are Not Books & Publications that is provided in their *The Sales Rep Will Be Right Back: Are Not Books & Publications as Performative Publishing, or Notes On Productive Non-Documentation* (2018). Writing, design, publishing, sales, marketing and distribution, for *Are Not Books & Publications*, too, can all be 'understood as part of the performance' (2018, 40). This includes the display of their books in 'conference, trade show, museum, gallery and online settings' (27). For an example of OHP's involvement with marketing as a form of theory-performance, see the Collaborative Marketing and Events of the Radical Open Access Collective (http://radicaloa.disruptivemedia.org.uk/resources/collaborative-marketing/), and its offshoot subgroup, the ScholarLed consortium (https://scholarled.org/).

121 *Filter* (https://linktr.ee/filterinstazine), a zine for electronic literature curated by founder Sarah Whitcomb Laiola and published entirely on Instagram, is an example of a more recent intervention in this space. *Filter* published its inaugural issue in summer 2021.

122 See the description of Coventry University's Open Media classes provided in van Mourik Broekman *et al.* (2014). These classes are also featured in McGill and Gray (2015), and to a lesser extent, Universities UK (2013).

123 An account of some of the additional projects pointed to here is provided in Hall (2020).

124 This speculation is not quite as eccentric as it may sound. It is a variation on an idea put forward in 2015 by Sir Mark Walport, who at the time was chief scientific adviser to the UK government. Speaking at the Royal Society's *Future of Scholarly Scientific Communication* conference, Walport suggested that in the future researchers might come to share the outcomes of their work in the form of just two or three 'evolving manuscripts' that are continually in the process of being updated over the span of a career. A report of Walport's speech is available in Else (2015).

125 If we did start Open Humanities Press now, we would do so very differently. In 2008 it seemed important to prove that it was perfectly possible for scholar-led, grassroots presses in the humanities to publish books open access and not just journals. Today, we might place more emphasis on publishing translations from, into and between languages other than those belonging to European colonisers (English, Spanish, French, German, Italian, Portuguese). When OHP launched we had plans for such a series. It was to be edited for us by Ngũgĩ wa Thiong'o, who is a member of our editorial board. Unfortunately, for one reason or another, it never happened.

Notes 315

To provide another quick example: more than ten years on from our first liquid book series, I'm not sure how much OHP would be interested in trying to break new ground with another series of liquid or living books.

126 As noted above, COPIM was funded by the Research England Development Fund and the Arcadia Fund from November 2019 to April 2023. As with many of the other initiatives described here, I'm continuing to refer to COPIM in the present tense because its life extends beyond that initial three-and-a-half-year period when Adema and I acted as principal co-investigators for the project. The three-year Open Book Futures project (https://copim.pubpub.org/open-book-futures-project) – also funded by the Research England Development Fund and the Arcadia Fund – which launched in May 2023 and which takes much of the earlier work of COPIM forward, is an obvious case in point. For more on COPIM, see the interview conducted with Adema and I by Paula Clemente Vega for the Open Library of the Humanities (Clemente Vega 2020); and the website of the COPIM community (an evolution of the COPIM project) that went live in February 2024: https://www.copim.ac.uk/.

127 Even the cOAlition S consortium that initiated Plan S has backed a diamond open access action plan: the DIAMAS (Developing Institutional Open Access Publishing Models to Advance Scholarly Communication) project designed to build capacity throughout Europe for institutional open access publishing – including journals and platforms – that charges fees to neither authors nor readers (cOAlition S 2022).

128 The GitLab repository is here: https://aesthetic-programming.gitlab.io/book/; the static site is here: https://www.aesthetic-programming.net/.

129 More on such computational publishing in relation to Soon and Cox's *Aesthetic Programming*, Open Humanities Press and COPIM, is provided in Bowie (2022).

130 For more on the Radical Open Access Collective, ScholarLed and COPIM in relation to scaling small, see Adema and Moore (2021).

131 Poynder makes the same point about ScholarLed. Yet at the time of this writing there are only two collections, that of Knowledge Unlatched (bought by Wiley in 2021) and that of the Swiss National Science Foundation, which have more books in the OAPEN online library and publishing platform than ScholarLed (OAPEN n.d.).

132 For one engagement on the part of ScholarLed with Knowledge Unlatched, see ScholarLed (2019). Elsewhere, COPIM colleagues have emphasised that 'the "scaling small" philosophy COPIM is following is explicitly and intentionally an alternative to large-scale, commercial approaches to academic publishing' (COPIM 2021).

133 This part of my argument is derived from Hall (2010, 42-43).

134 This is a riff on the work of Walter Mignolo (2002) and Arturo Escobar (2020), among others.

135 In *The End of The Cognitive Empire* de Sousa Santos defines the epistemologies of the South as concerning 'the production and validation of knowledges anchored in the experiences of resistance of all those social groups that have systematically suffered injustice, oppression, and destruction caused by capitalism, colonialism, and patriarchy. ... It is an epistemological, nongeographical South, composed of many epistemological souths having in common the fact that they are all knowledges born in struggles against capitalism, colonialism, and patriarchy. They are produced wherever such struggles occur, in both the geographical North and the geographical South' (2018, 1).

136 Boaventura de Sousa Santos defines the epistemologies of the North as follows: 'As in the case of the epistemologies of the South, rather than a single epistemology of the North there are several, though they all tend to share some basic assumptions: the absolute priority of science as rigorous knowledge; rigor, conceived of as determination; universalism, conceived of as a specificity of Western modernity, referring to any entity or condition the validity of which does not depend on any specific social, cultural, or political context; truth conceived of as the representation of reality; a distinction between subject and object, the knower and the known; nature as *res extensa*; linear time; the progress of science via the disciplines and specialization; and social and political neutrality as a condition of objectivity' (2018, 6).

137 Björn Brembs' insistence that Elsevier itself meets the criteria for being considered a predatory publisher acts as an interesting variation on this argument (Brembs 2022).

138 See Ochieng Okoth, 'Decolonisation and Its Discontents', for one example. He writes:

> On closer inspection, then, DS [Decolonial Studies] turns out not to be an emancipatory discourse at all. In fact, if one is inclined to take any perspective that holds on to even the smallest commitment to the idea of revolution, it is openly reactionary. In *The End of The Cognitive Empire*, de Sousa Santos goes so far as to proudly proclaim that the epistemological turn in DS is a reversal of Marx' famous statement ... that philosophers have interpreted the world, but that the point is to change it. (2021)

However, I have already shown some of the issues with this kind of antipolitical moralism – the deciding in advance of intellectual questioning what is political and what is not – albeit I did so with regard to the 'material turn' rather than critiques of the 'epistemological turn'. I have also shown how theory is not *just* theory: it is also a form of (material, political) practice, a way of being (political).

139 As two of my collaborators, Eva Weinmayr and Femke Snelting, have said, it is important such an-other logic includes more than viewing 'dissemination mainly from the perspective of the distributor, hence as a technical and controlled act of delivering from a central hub to known targets'. For them dissemination, coming as it does from the Latin 'semina', evokes rather the '"scattering" of seeds through wind, insects or birds. Once they've found the right environment, they germinate. Importantly, dissemination is perceived here as a relational act that needs both receptive ecologies as well as the seed in order to flourish. It is an act of reciprocity, response-ability and therefore relationality that comes much closer to *sharing*, which Linda Tuhiwai Smith (1999) has described as a decolonising methodology because of its focus on the relational' (Weinmayr and Snelting, 2022; citing Tuhiwai Smith 1999).

140 Michel Bauwens, Vasilis Kostakis and Alex Paziatis take Barcelona as a case study of radical municipalism in *Peer to Peer: The Commons Manifesto* (2019). More on the global municipalist movement is available in Barcelona en Comú (2019).

141 See Halpern and Mitchell (2023) for further criticism of smartness as it applies to cities (as well as to homes, phones and cars). Halpern and Mitchell present what they call the 'smartness mandate' as a new form of planetary scale computational governance.

142 Nontobeko Ntombela is another influence. She writes: 'It is important to leave certain things untranslated because some stories are embedded in the culture of the language, that is cultural codes and references that are sometimes not interpretable, and it is important to leave those nuances untampered with' (2018).

143 Over the winter of 2023/2024 nearly every library in England, Wales and Northern Ireland offered a warm, cost-free space for individuals who could not afford heating. Anyone was able to visit such a 'warm bank' without charge should their homes grow too cold and obtain free hot drinks, period products, even clothes.

144 Again, it's a little ungenerous to single anyone out. As was made clear earlier, it's about a system, a way of being-in and being-with the world. Consequently, there are any number of instances of legacy authors producing new theories of the politics of technology in old ways. When it comes to AI, however, Kate Crawford's *Atlas of AI: Power, Politics, and the Planetary Costs of Artificial Intelligence* (2021) is a classic example of a work that emphasizes how media is 'made from natural resources, fuel, human labor, infrastructures, logistics, histories, and classifications', while leaving its own media-materiality masked (2021, 8).

It may be the case that as Crawford points out in an article in *Nature*:

> Generative AI systems need enormous amounts of fresh water to cool their processors and generate electricity. In West Des Moines, Iowa, a giant data-centre cluster serves [what at the time was] OpenAI's most advanced model, GPT-4. A lawsuit by local residents revealed that in July 2022, the month before OpenAI finished training the model, the cluster used about 6% of the district's water. As Google and Microsoft prepared their Bard and Bing large language models, both had major spikes in water use – increases of 20% and 34%, respectively, in one year, according to the companies' environmental reports. (Crawford 2024)

But, as we have already seen, 'It takes between 2 and 13 litres of water to produce a single A4-sheet of paper, depending on the mill. The pulp and paper industry is the single largest industrial consumer of water in Western countries' (The World Counts n.d.-a). If we want to be more hospitable, though, we can follow Crawford's lead when she writes in her *Atlas of AI* about the importance of understanding 'how AI is fundamentally political' (9). Taking her ideas about a 'multitude of interlaced systems of power' to their logical conclusion, we can see Crawford as encouraging us to ask '*what* is being optimized, and *for whom*, and *who* gets to decide' with respect to the 'abstracting away' of the hegemonic, authoritative, 'material conditions' of the making of her own 336-page paperback book as well (12, 18).

145 The Post Office is not the first such mask at Coventry. The university has a building that has long born the name of one of the most famous pseudonyms in English literature: George Eliot. Nor was Foucault the first modern philosopher to have been attracted to the idea of adopting such a mask. Nietzsche originally wanted *Human, All Too Human* to be published pseudonymously so that readers who had already formed an opinion of him would not be prejudiced against the book one way or another. He even provided a fictitious name for the cover and an author biography for the accompanying publicity material. In the end his publisher refused to go along with the idea. See Prideaux (2018, 175-176).

146 I write 'on occasion' because, as *A Stubborn Fury* showed, in each situation it is necessary to take a contingent decision as to whether to wear a mask. Drawing on Foucault's 'What is an Author?', I argued there that the clearly identifiable author might be a means of responding to the politics of 'fake news' and 'alternative facts' epitomised by the regime of Donald Trump (2021a, 112, n30).

147 This aspect of *Masked Media's* account of how names such as Karen Eliot and Post Office work is based in part on Weinmayr (2020).

148 Minelle (2022) provides an example of Banksy asserting his economic and legal right to be recognised as the individual originator of his graffiti artworks, as is conventionally understood under UK and EU intellectual property law.

149 Uncertain commons are another theory-related example of such collective anonymity worth mentioning here. In the prologue to their book *Speculate This!*, uncertain commons describe themselves as 'a collective of academics, mediaphiles, activists, and dreamers who imagine ourselves as an open and nonfinite group. ... We perform anonymity as a challenge to the current norms of evaluating, commodifying, and institutionalizing intellectual labor' (uncertain commons 2013).

150 As indicated in Chapter 6, it is by *not* overtly masking our identities as individuals in particular situations, for example, that some of us are able to acquire positions in the Euro-Western (neo)liberal university. These positions provide us with time – time that we can then make the political decision to donate towards labouring to create certain experimental writing and publishing projects with a view to supporting others who lack such time and ultimately changing this situation. A further layer of complication and messiness is added by the fact that experimenting with masked media in order to unsettle and reinvent the authorial liberal-individual human 'I' can also be one of the means by which some of us are able to obtain and maintain such positions along with the associated networks of connections and influence: both as individual scholars and as part of inhuman forms of togetherness such as the Post Office. It is very much these kinds of tensions that *Masked Media* is wrestling with and endeavouring to help us to work through. And it is doing so in full knowledge of the fact that the book's questioning of the system that presents an assemblage of collective tasks as individual ones and results in prestige for a privileged few could also result in prestige being given more or less violently to the artificial creative intelligence that is 'Gary Hall' by the same system.

151 For the filmed interviews in the BBC Two two-part docu-series, *Hong Kong's Fight for Freedom* (first broadcast November 14 & 21, 2022), the faces of some of the protestors were again concealed, this time using AI technology, for fear of reprisals by the state. It happens in the other direction, too, with facial recognition software being used by the government in Iran to identify those refusing to comply with the country's dress code for women by wearing a hijab (Johnson 2023).

152 When it comes to the name of our postdigital arts and humanities studio, we have deliberately avoided using one of the 'original' concepts those working in the Centre are perhaps more readily associated with: pirate philosophy, radical open access and so forth. In actual fact, neither 'postdigital' nor 'Post Office' are new or *ours*: the former concept is associated with, among others, the work of Kim Cascone

(2000), Florian Cramer (2012) and Alessandro Ludovico (2012); while the latter name is also that of a design studio directed by Philippe Malouin (the latter Post-Office being distinguished by a hyphen).

153 As one more gift, this final paragraph samples and remixes both Foucault's 'The Masked Philosopher' and Gabriella Coleman's account of what makes the adoption of masks by Anonymous so radical politically (Coleman 2014, 399).

154 This biographical note was compiled from www.bioswop.net, a CV-exchange platform created by the artist Natascha Sadr Haghighian in 2004, almost two decades before the popularisation of AI-driven text generation tools such as ChatGPT. As part of her larger project of critiquing institutionalised regimes of knowledge, Haghighian rejects the totalising ideas of curriculum vitae, and insists that only biographies obtained from the bioswop project be used in printed material regarding her work. The idea is to provide curriculum vitae, bios and resumes for mutual utilisation and borrowing as well as basic elements of CVs for assembly.

Works Cited

Abrahamsson, Sebastian and Joe DeVille. 2013. 'New Forms of Care for STS Books'. *Mattering Press* (website), December 4, https://www.matteringpress.org/blog/new-forms-of-care-for-sts-books

Adams, Richard and Xavier Greenwood. 2018. 'Oxford and Cambridge University Colleges Hold £21bn In Riches'. *The Guardian*, May 28, https://www.theguardian.com/education/2018/may/28/oxford-and-cambridge-university-colleges-hold-21bn-in-riches

Adema, Janneke. 2011. 'CREATIVITY (Capital C) Has Been Hijacked by The Artists'. *remixthebook.com* (website): June 8, http://issuu.com/remixthebook/docs/remix_mark_amerika

Adema, Janneke. 2018a. 'The Ethics of Emergent Creativity: Can We Move Beyond Writing as Human Enterprise, Commodity and Innovation?'. In *Whose Book Is It Anyway? A View from Elsewhere on Publishing, Copyright and Creativity*. Eds. Sarah Kember and Janice Jefferies. Cambridge: Open Book Publishers.

Adema, Janneke. 2018b. 'Performative Publications'. *Journal of Media Practice*, Volume 19, Issue 1, 70-83, https://doi.org/10.17613/M6152X

Adema, Janneke. 2018c. 'Performative Publications'. *Media Practice and Education*, Volume 19, Issue 1, 68-81, https://doi.org/10.1080/14682753.2017.1362174

Adema, Janneke. 2021. 'Post-Publishing in Pandemic Times'. Paper presented as part of the Experimental Publishing programme, English Department, Maynooth University, March 25, https://www.youtube.com/watch?v=lc55wKpvGGE

Adema, Janneke (with accompanying posters designed by Nabaa Baqir, Mila Spasova and Serhan Curti). 2017. 'Performative Publications'. *Disruptive Media* (website), http://disruptivemedia.org.uk/thepoliticalnatureofthebook/index1.html

Adema, Janneke and Gary Hall. 2013. 'The Political Nature of The Book: On Artists' Books and Radical Open Access'. *New Formations*, Number 78, 138-156.

Adema, Janneke and Gary Hall. Eds. 2016a. *Journal of Electronic Publishing*, Volume 9, Number 2 (Fall), n. pag., https://quod.lib.umich.edu/j/jep/3336451.0019.2*?rgn=full+text

Adema, Janneke and Gary Hall. Eds. 2016b. *Really, We're Helping to Build This... Business: The Academia.edu Files.* London: Open Humanities Press, http://liquidbooks.pbworks.com/w/page/106236504/The%20Academia_edu%20Files

Adema, Janneke and Kamila Kuc. 2019. 'Unruly Gestures: Seven Cine-Paragraphs on Reading/Writing Practices in Our Post-Digital Condition'. *Culture Unbound: Journal of Current Cultural Research*, Volume 11, Number 1, 190-208, https://cultureunbound.ep.liu.se/article/view/255

Adema, Janneke and Pete Woodbridge. Eds. 2011. *Symbiosis: Ecologies, Assemblages and Evolution.* London: Open Humanities Press, http://www.livingbooksaboutlife.org/books/Symbiosis

Adema, Janneke and Samuel Moore. 2018. 'Collectivity and Collaboration: Imagining New Forms of Communality to Create Resilience in Scholar-led Publishing'. *Insights*, Volume 31, March 5, n. pag., https://insights.uksg.org/articles/10.1629/uksg.399/

Adema, Janneke and Samuel Moore. 2021. 'Scaling Small; Or How to Envision New Relationalities for Knowledge Production'. *Westminster Papers In Communication and Culture*, Volume 16, Issue 1, 27-45, https://www.westminsterpapers.org/article/id/918/

Agamben, Giorgio. 1993. *The Coming Community.* Minneapolis: University of Minnesota Press.

Aguado-López, Eduardo and Arianna Becerril-García. 2020. 'The Commercial Model of Academic Publishing Underscoring Plan S Weakens the Existing Open Access Ecosystem in Latin

America'. *LSE Impact Blog*, May 20, https://blogs.lse.ac.uk/impactofsocialsciences/2020/05/20/the-commercial-model-of-academic-publishing-underscoring-plan-s-weakens-the-existing-open-access-ecosystem-in-latin-america/

Ahmed, Sara. 2014. 'White Men'. *feministkilljoys* (blog), November 4, http://feministkilljoys.com/2014/11/04/white-men/

ALA. 2024. 'American Library Association Reports Record Number of Unique Book Titles Challenged in 2023'. *ALA American Library Association* (website), March 14, https://www.ala.org/news/press-releases/2024/03/american-library-association-reports-record-number-unique-book-titles

Allen. Rachael. 2023. 'Difficult and Bad'. *Too Little / Too Hard*, Issue 2 (Winter), n. pag., https://tlth.co.uk/difficultandbad

Allado-McDowell. K. 2020. *Pharmako-AI*. London: Ignota.

Allado-McDowell. K. 2022. *Amor Cringe*. Los Angeles: Deluge.

Allington, Daniel, Sarah Brouillette and David Golumbia. 2016. 'Neoliberal Tools (And Archives): A Political History of Digital Humanities'. *Los Angeles Review of Books*, May 1, n. pag., https://lareviewofbooks.org/article/neoliberal-tools-archives-political-history-digital-humanities/

Althusser, Louis. 1994. *The Future Lasts a Long Time*. London: Vintage.

American Alliance of Museums. 2023. *Annual National Snapshot of United States Museums*, March-April, https://www.aam-us.org/wp-content/uploads/2023/06/SnapshotReport_v3-portrait.pdf

Amerika, Mark. 2007. *META/DATA: A Digital Poetics*. Cambridge, MA: MIT Press.

Amerika, Mark. 2011a. 'Phon:E:Me'. *Mark Amerika* (website), March 6, http://markamerika.com/artworks/phoneme-by-mark-amerika

Amerika, Mark. 2011b. *remixthebook*. Minneapolis: University of Minnesota Press.

Amerika, Mark. 2018. *remixthecontext*. New York: Routledge.

Amerika, Mark. 2019. Speaking at the *Experimental Publishing II – Critique, Intervention, And Speculation* symposium. Centre for Postdigital Cultures, Coventry University, May 28.

Amerika, Mark. 2020. *Planet Corona: Words, Voices, Poems, Waves, Plague, Death, Breath and Starlight. Mark Amerika* (website), July, http://markamerika.com/news/planet-corona-words-voices-poems-waves-plague-death-breath-and-starlight

Amerika, Mark. 2022a. Speaking on the Education Beyond The (e) book: Experimental Post-Publishing and Performance Pedagogy panel, *Electronic Literature Organisation Conference*, Como, Italy, May 30.

Amerika, Mark. 2022b. *Everyone Has Their Price: An NFT Novel. markamerika.com*, first edition April 24, 2022, http://www.markamerika.com/nftnovel/

Amerika, Mark. 2022c. *My Life as an Artificial Creative Intelligence*. Stanford, CA: Stanford University Press.

Amerika, Mark and Laura Kim (MALK). 2019. *Remixing Persona: An Imaginary Digital Media Object from The Onto-Tales of The Digital Afterlife*. London: Open Humanities Press, 2019.

Andersson, Jasmine. 2019. '"Libraries Are the Universities of The Streets": Authors Call for Stop to Further Closures'. *iNews*, December 6, https://inews.co.uk/news/uk/libraries-800-shut-since-2010-austerity-benjamin-zephaniah-jacqueline-wilson-authors-371636

Are Not Books. 2017. 'The Goal Is to Weird the Object', *A Useless Guide to Book Design*. Texas: Are Not Books & Publications, http://arenotbooks.com/titles/useless.html

Are Not Books & Publications. 2018. *The Sales Rep Will Be Right Back: Are Not Books & Publications as Performative Publishing, or Notes on Productive Non-Documentation*. Texas: Are Not Books & Publications.

Armitstead, Claire. 2021. 'Stories to Save The World: The New Wave of Climate Fiction'. *The Observer*, June 26, https://www.theguardian.com/books/2021/jun/26/stories-to-save-the-world-the-new-wave-of-climate-fiction

Works Cited

Baker, Simon. 2018. 'Into the Ether: How Much Research Goes Completely Uncited?'. *Times Higher Education*, April 19, https://www.timeshighereducation.com/news/how-much-research-goes-completely-uncited

Baker, Steve *et al*. 2016. *Living Bibliography of Animal Studies*, https://www.britishanimalstudiesnetwork.org.uk/Home/Living Bibliography.aspx

Barad, Karen. 2003. 'Posthumanist Performativity: Toward an Understanding of How Matter Comes to Matter'. *Signs: Journal of Women in Culture and Society*, Volume 28, Number 3, 801-831.

Barad, Karen. 2007. *Meeting the Universe Halfway: Quantum Physics and The Entanglement of Matter and Meaning*. Durham, NC: Duke University Press.

Barber, Lionel, Henry Foy and Alex Barker. 2019. 'Vladimir Putin Says Liberalism Has "Become Obsolete"'. *Financial Times*, June 27, https://www.ft.com/content/670039ec-98f3-11e9-9573-ee5cbb98ed36

Barcelona en Comú. Eds. 2019. *Fearless Cities: A Guide to The Global Municipalist Movement*. Oxford: New Internationalist.

Barkham, Patrick. 2021. 'Go with The Flow'. *The Observer: Magazine*, July 25, https://www.theguardian.com/environment/2021/jul/25/rivers-around-the-world-rivers-are-gaining-the-same-legal-rights-as-people

Barth, John. 1984. 'The Literature of Exhaustion'. *The Friday Book: Essays and Other Non-Fiction*. Baltimore and London: The Johns Hopkins University Press.

Barthes, Roland. 1977. 'The Death of the Author'. *Image–Music–Text*. London: Fontana.

Bauwens, Michel, Vasilis Kostakis and Alex Paziatis. 2019. *Peer to Peer: The Commons Manifesto*. London: University of Westminster Press.

Beech, Dave, Andy Hewitt and Mel Jordan (Freee Art Collective). 2015. 'To Hell with Herbert Read'. *Anarchist Studies*, Volume 23, Number 2, 38-46.

Beech, Dave, Andy Hewitt and Mel Jordan (Freee Art Collective). 2017. 'The New Text Art of and Making Books A Difference by Ulises Carrión Freee'. In *The Idea of The Avant Garde – And What It Means*. Ed. Marc Leger. London: Black Dog Press.

Beech, Dave, Mark Hutchinson and John Timberlake. 2006. *Analysis v.8 (Transmission: The Rules of Engagement)*. London: Artwords Press.

Bell, Duncan. 2014. 'What Is Liberalism?'. *Political Theory*, Volume 42, Issue 6, 682-715.

Bender, Emily M., Timnit Gebru, Angelina McMillan-Major and Shmargaret Shmitchell. 2021. 'On the Dangers of Stochastic Parrots: Can Language Models Be Too Big?'. In *FAccT '21: Proceedings of the Conference on Fairness, Accountability, and Transparency*, March 3-10, 2021, Canada. *Association for Computing Machinery* (ACM), March 1, https://dl.acm.org/doi/pdf/10.1145/3442188.3445922

Bennett, Jane. 2010. *Vibrant Matter: A Political Ecology of Things*. Durham, NC: Duke University Press.

Berck, Anaïs. n.d.-a. 'About an Algoliterary Publishing House'. *Algoliterary Publishing* (website), accessed March 10, 2023, https://algoliterarypublishing.net/pages/about.html

Berck, Anaïs. n.d.-b. 'Paseo por arboles de madrid'. *Algoliterary Publishing* (website), accessed March 10, 2023, https://algoliterarypublishing.net/paseo-por-arboles-de-madrid.html

Berry, David M. and Anders Fagerjord. 2017. *Digital Humanities: Knowledge and Critique in A Digital Age*. Cambridge: Polity.

Birchall, Clare and Gary Hall. Eds. 2008. Liquid Books. London: Open Humanities Press, http://liquidbooks.pbwiki.com

Birchall, Clare, Gary Hall and Joanna Zylinska. Eds. 2016. Living Books About Life. London: Open Humanities Press, http://www.livingbooksaboutlife.org

Blas, Zach. n.d. 'Facial Weaponization Suite 2012-2014'. *Zach Blas* (website), accessed October 15, 2022, https://zachblas.info/works/facial-weaponization-suite/

Blaser, Mario and Marisol de la Cadena. 2018. 'Pluriverse: Proposals for A World of Many Worlds'. In *A World of Many Worlds*. Eds. Mario Blaser and Marisol de la Cadena. Durham, NC: Duke University Press.

Boggs, Abigail, Eli Meyerhoff, Nick Mitchell and Zach Schwartz-Weinstein. 2019. 'Abolitionist University Studies: An Invitation'. *abolitionjournal*, August 28, 1-29, https://abolition.university/wp-content/uploads/2019/08/Abolitionist-University-Studies_-An-Invitation-Release-1-version.pdf

Bookchin, Murray. 2014. *The Next Revolution: Popular Assemblies and The Promise of Direct Democracy*. London: Verso.

Borch-Jacobsen, Mikkel. 1993. 'Hypnosis in Psychoanalysis'. *The Emotional Tie: Psychoanalysis, Mimesis and Affect*. Stanford, California: Stanford University Press.

Bowie, Simon. 2022. 'What Is Computational Publishing?'. *COPIM* (blog), July 7, https://copim.pubpub.org/pub/computational-publishing/release/1

Buolamwini, Joy. 2023. *Unmasking AI: My Mission to Protect What Is Human in a World of Machines*. New York: Random House.

Bradley, Jean-Claude. 2007. 'Open Notebook Science Using Blogs and Wikis'. *Nature Precedings*, June 12, n. pag., https://www.nature.com/articles/npre.2007.39.1

Braidotti, Rosi. 2013a. 'Posthuman Humanities'. *European Educational Research Journal*, Volume 12, Number 1, 1-19, https://journals.sagepub.com/doi/pdf/10.2304/eerj.2013.12.1.1

Braidotti, Rosi. 2013b. *The Posthuman*. London: Polity.

Braidotti, Rosi. 2019. 'A Theoretical Framework for The Critical Posthumanities'. *Theory, Culture and Society*, Volume 36, Issue 6, 31-61.

Brembs, Björn. 2022. 'Elsevier Now Officially A "Predatory" Publisher'. *björn.brembs.blog*, December 11, http://bjoern.brembs.net/2019/12/elsevier-now-officially-a-predatory-publisher/

Bria, Francesca. 2023. 'Algorithms are Hiring and Firing Us Now – But Tougher EU Laws Could Protect Workers'. *The Guardian*,

October 12, https://www.theguardian.com/commentisfree/2023/oct/12/algorithms-eu-law-workers-ai-data

Bridle, James. 2022. *Ways of Being: Animals, Plants, Machines: The Search for a Planetary Intelligence*. London: Penguin.

Bridle, James. 2023. 'The Stupidity Of AI'. *The Guardian*, March 16, https://www.theguardian.com/technology/2023/mar/16/the-stupidity-of-ai-artificial-intelligence-dall-e-chatgpt

Brill. 2023. 'Joint Press Release: Brill and De Gruyter to Create Leading Academic Publisher in the Humanities'. *Brill* (website), October 12, https://brill.com/fileasset/downloads_static/static_investorrelations_brill_press_release_20231012.pdf

Broglio, Ron. 2022. *Animal Revolution*. Minneapolis: University of Minnesota Press.

Brown, Matthew and Rhian E. Jones. 2021. *Paint Your Town Red: How Preston Took Back Control and Your Town Can Too*. London: Repeater.

Brown, Wendy. 2001. *Politics Out of History*. London and Princeton, NJ: Princeton University Press.

Bruining, Dennis. 2013. 'A Somatechnics of Moralism: New Materialism or Material Foundationalism'. *Somatechnics*, Volume 3, Issue 1, 149-168.

Burdick, Anne, Johanna Drucker, Peter Lunenfeld, Todd Presner and Jeffrey Schnapp. 2012. *Digital_Humanities*. Cambridge, MA: MIT Press.

Burrows, Roger. 2012. 'Living with the H-Index? Metrics, Markets and Affect in The Contemporary Academy'. *The Sociological Review*, Volume 60, Issue 2, 355-372. (Quotations are taken from the revised pdf version, available here: http://research.gold.ac.uk/6560/2/Living_with_the_h-index_revised.pdf)

Butler, Leigh-Ann, Lisa Matthias, Marc-André Simard, Philippe Mongeon and Stefanie Haustein. 2023. 'The Oligopoly's Shift to Open Access. How the Big Five Academic Publishers Profit from Article Processing Charges'. *Quantitative Science Studies*, November 3, 778-799, https://direct.mit.edu/qss/article/doi/10.1162/qss_a_00272/118070/The-Oligopoly-s-Shift-to-Open-Access-How-the-Big

Cage, John. 1968. 'Experimental Music: Doctrine'. In *Silence: Lectures and Writings*. London: Calder and Boyars.

Calasso, Roberto. 2015. *The Art of The Publisher*. New York: Farrar, Straus and Giroux.

Cambridge University Press. n.d.-a. 'OA Book Pilot: Flip It Open'. *Cambridge Core: Cambridge University Press* (website), accessed August 5, 2022, https://www.cambridge.org/core/services/open-research/open-access/oa-book-pilot-flip-it-open

Cambridge University Press. n.d.-b. 'Gold Open Access Books'. *Cambridge Core: Cambridge University Press* (website), accessed March 4, 2023, https://www.cambridge.org/core/services/open-access-policies/open-access-books/gold-open-access-books

Cambridge University Press. n.d.-c. 'Flip It Open'. *Cambridge Core: Cambridge University Press* (website), accessed June 18, 2024, https://www.cambridge.org/core/open-research/open-access/flip-it-open

Campaign for the Arts & University of Warwick. 2024. *The State of the Arts, Campaign for the Arts & Centre for Cultural and Media Policy Studies, University of Warwick*, July, https://www.campaignforthearts.org/wp-content/uploads/2024/07/The-State-of-the-Arts.pdf

Carlson, Colin J., Gregory F. Albery, Cory Merow, Christopher H. Trisos, Casey M. Zipfel, Evan A. Eskew, Kevin J. Olival, Noam Ross and Shweta Bansal. 2022. 'Climate Change Increases Cross-species Viral Transmission Risk'. *Nature* 607, April 21, 555-562.

Cascone, Kim. 2000. 'The Aesthetics of Failure: "Post-Digital" Tendencies in Contemporary Computer Music'. *Computer Music Journal*, Volume 24, Number 4 (Winter), 12-18.

Cavalcante Silva, Guilherme. 2023. 'The South as A Laboratory (Again)? Dealing With Calls For "Alternatives" In the North'. *Canadian Association of Latin American and Caribbean Studies (CALACS) Conference 2022*, February 13, https://www.4sonline.org/the-south-as-a-laboratory-again-dealing-with-calls-for-alternatives-in-the-north/

Cegłowski, Maciej. 2019. 'The New Wilderness'. *Idlewords* (blog), June 6, https://idlewords.com/2019/06/the_new_wilderness.htm

Celis Bueno, Claudio and raúl rodríguez freire. Eds. 2022. Antropoficciones, *Culture Machine*, Volume 21, https://culturemachine.net/archives/vol-21-antropoficciones/

Celis Bueno, Claudio, Pei-Sze Chow and Ada Popowicz. 2024. 'Not 'What" But "Where is Creativity?": Towards a Relational-Materialist Approach to Generative AI'. *AI & Society*, March 22, n. pag., https://link.springer.com/article/10.1007/s00146-024-01921-3

Chan, Leslie. 2019. 'Platform Capitalism and The Governance of Knowledge Infrastructure'. *Digital Initiative Symposium*, University of San Diego, April 29-30, https://zenodo.org/record/2656601#.XNCUS-FRiTa,%20consultado%206%20de%20mayo%20de%202019

Chan, Leslie, Barbara Kirsop and Subbiah Arunachalam. 2011. 'Towards Open and Equitable Access to Research and Knowledge for Development'. *PLoS Medicine*, Volume 8(3), e1001016, n. pag., https://doi.org/10.1371/journal.pmed.1001016

Chan, Leslie, Budd Hall, Florence Piron, Rajesh Tandon and Lorna Williams. 2020. 'Open Science Beyond Open Access: For and With Communities. A Step Towards the Decolonization of Knowledge, (Version 1)'. *Canadian Commission for UNESCO's IdeaLab, Ottawa, Canada*, July, 1-18, https://zenodo.org/record/3946773#.X4Ahnhi7njA

Chadwick, Rachelle. 2023a. 'What Does It Mean to Do Generous Research?'. *LSE Impact Blog*, December 13, https://blogs.lse.ac.uk/impactofsocialsciences/2023/12/13/what-does-it-mean-to-do-generous-research/

Chadwick, Rachelle. 2023b. 'The Question of Feminist Critique'. *Feminist Theory*, August 6, 1-20.

Christensen, Martin-Brehm, Christian Hallum, Alex Maitland, Quentin Parrinello and Chiara Putaturo. 2023. *Survival of The Richest: How We Must Tax the Super-Rich Now to Fight Inequality*. Oxfam Annual Inequality Report, January 16, https://www.oxfam.org/en/research/survival-richest

Chun, Wendy Hui Kyong, Richard Grusin, Patrick Jagoda and Rita Raley. 2016. 'The Dark Side of Digital Humanities'. In *Debates in The Digital Humanities 2016*. Eds. Matthew K. Gold and Lauren F. Klein. Minneapolis: University of Minnesota Press, https://dhdebates.gc.cuny.edu/read/untitled/section/ca35736b-0020-4ac6-9ce7-88c6e9ff1bba#ch38

Cisneros, Teresa and Andrea Francke. 2020. 'Afterword: Nobody Wants to Deal with This Shit Internally'. In *Decolonizing the Curriculum, the Museum, And the Mind*. Ed. Marquard Smith. Vilnius: Vilnius Academy of Arts Press.

Ciston, Sarah and Mark C. Marino. 2021. 'How to Fork a Book: The Radical Transformation of Publishing'. *MarkCMarino* (blog), August 19, https://markcmarino.medium.com/how-to-fork-a-book-the-radical-transformation-of-publishing-3e1f4a39a66c

Clemente Vega, Paula. 2020. 'Community-led Open Publication Infrastructures for Monographs: An Open Insights Interview with Janneke Adema and Gary Hall'. *Open Insights* (blog), January 13, https://www.openlibhums.org/news/356/

CLES. n.d. 'What Is an Anchor Institution?'. *CLES: The National Organisation for Local Economies* (website), accessed March 10, 2023, https://cles.org.uk/what-is-community-wealth-building/what-is-an-anchor-institution/

cOAlition S. 2019. 'Rationale For the Revisions Made to The Plan S Principles and Implementation Guidance'. *Plan S* (website), May 31, https://www.coalition-s.org/rationale-for-the-revisions/

cOAlition S. 2021. 'cOAlition S Statement on Open Access for Academic Books'. *Plan S* (website), September 2, https://www.coalition-s.org/coalition-s-statement-on-open-access-for-academic-books/

cOAlition S. 2022. 'DIAMAS Receives Grant to Develop Diamond Open Access Publishing in Europe'. *Plan S* (website), September 20, https://www.coalition-s.org/diamas-receives-grant-to-develop-diamond-open-access-publishing-in-europe/.

cOAlition S. 2023a. 'cOAlition S Confirms the End of Its Financial Support for Open Access Publishing Under Transformative Arrangements After 2024'. *Plan S* (website), January 26, https://www.coalition-s.org/

coalition-s-confirms-the-end-of-its-financial-support-for-open-access-publishing-under-transformative-arrangements-after-2024/

cOAlition S. 2023b. 'Developing a Globally Fair Pricing Model for Open Access Academic Publishing', *Plan S* (website), February 6, https://www.coalition-s.org/developing-a-globally-fair-pricing-model-for-open-access-academic-publishing/

cOAlition S. 2024. 'Transformative Journals: Analysis From the 2023 Reports'. *Plan S* (website), June 28, https://www.coalition-s.org/blog/transformative-journals-analysis-from-the-2023-reports/

cOAlition S, n.d.-a. 'Plan S Rights Retention Strategy'. *Plan S* (website), accessed January 17, 2023, https://www.coalition-s.org/rights-retention-strategy/

cOAlition S. n.d.-b. 'Principles and Implementation'. *Plan S* (website), accessed March 4, 2023, https://www.coalition-s.org/addendum-to-the-coalition-s-guidance-on-the-implementation-of-plan-s/principles-and-implementation/

Coleman, Gabriella. 2014. *Hacker, Hoaxer, Whistleblower, Spy: The Many Faces of Anonymous*. London: Verso.

Collective Intelligence Project. n.d. 'About'. *AI For Institutions*, accessed December 21, 2023, https://www.ai4institutions.com/about

Colomina, Beatriz and Mark Wigley. 2017. *Are We Human? Notes On an Archaeology of Design*. Zurich: Lars Müller Publishers.

Colomina, Beatriz. 2018. 'The 24/7 Bed'. In *Work, Body, Leisure: Dutch Pavilion, Biennale Architettura 2018*. Ed. Marina Otero Verzier. Rotterdam: Het Nieuwe Instituut and Hatje Cantz Verlag GmbH, https://work-body-leisure.hetnieuweinstituut.nl/247-bed

Conner, Trey and Richard Doyle. Eds. 2010. *Wyrd To the Wiki: Lacunae Toward Wiki Ontologies*. London: Open Humanities Press, http://wyrd2thewiki.pbworks.com/w/page/5763581/FrontPage

Connor, Steven, David Trotter and James Purdon. Eds. n.d. Technographies. Open Humanities Press (website), accessed

January 29, 2024, http://www.openhumanitiespress.org/books/series/technographies/

Constant, 2019. *Authors of the Future: Re-Imagining Copyleft*. September 27, https://cryptpad.fr/file/#/2/file/dOo48lcR8gYDWfy8BVFyTRcA/

Constant. 2023. 'CC4r * Collective Conditions for Re-Use: Copyleft Attitude with A Difference – Version 1.0', *Constant* (website), March 16, 2023, https://constantvzw.org/wefts/cc4r.en.html

Cooperatives Europe. n.d. 'What is a Cooperative?'. *Cooperatives Europe* (website), accessed July 28, 2024, https://coopseurope.coop/what-cooperative/

COPIM. 2021. 'COPIM Response to New UKRI Open Access Policy'. *COPIM* (website), August 11, https://copim.pubpub.org/pub/copim-response-to-new-ukri-open-access-policy/release/2

COPIM. 2021. 'COPIM Statement on The Corporate Acquisition of OA Infrastructure'. *COPIM* (website), December 15, https://copim.pubpub.org/pub/copim-statement-corporate-acquisition-oa-infra/release/1

COPIM. 2022. 'Mutant Assembly'. *Experimental Publishing Compendium: Version 2.0*. Curated by Janneke Adema, Julien McHardy and Simon Bowie. Accessed December 12, 2023, https://compendium.copim.ac.uk/books/154

Cramer, Florian. 2012. 'Post-Digital Writing'. *Electronic Book Review*, December 12, n. pag., https://electronicbookreview.com/essay/post-digital-writing/

Crawford. Kate. 2021. *Atlas of AI: Power, Politics, and the Planetary Costs of Artificial Intelligence*. New Haven and London: Yale University Press.

Crawford. Kate. 2024. 'Generative AI's Environmental Costs are Soaring – and Mostly Secret'. *Nature*, February 20, n. pag., https://www.nature.com/articles/d41586-024-00478-x

Crouch, Colin. 2011. *The Strange Non-Death of Neoliberalism*. London: Polity.

Cubitt, Sean. 2014. 'How to Connect Everyone with Everything'. *Sean's Blog*, August 13, http://seancubitt.blogspot.co.uk/2014/08/how-to-connect-everyone-with-everything.html

DAIR. n.d. *Distributed AI Research Institute* (website), accessed May 5, 2024, https://www.dair-institute.org/

Dames, Nicholas. 2016. 'The New Fiction of Solitude'. *The Atlantic*, April, 92-101, http://www.theatlantic.com/magazine/archive/2016/04/the-new-fiction-of-solitude/471474/

Danowski, Déborah and Eduardo Viveiros de Castro. 2017. *The Ends of the World*. London: Polity.

Dark Side of the Digital. 2013. *Dark Side of the Digital: A Center for 21st Century Studies Conference*, University of Wisconsin-Milwaukee, May 2-4, accessed February 26, 2023, http://www.c21uwm.com/digitaldarkside/

Davidson, Miri. 2024. 'Decolonisation of the Far Right'. *e-Flux Notes*, May 24, 1-3, https://www.e-flux.com/notes/610730/decolonialism-of-the-far-right

de Rosa, Miriam and Wanda Strauven. 2020. 'Screenic (Re)orientations: Desktop, Tabletop, Tablet, Booklet, Touchscreen, Etc.'. In *Screen Space Reconfigured*. Eds. Susanne Saether and Synne Tollerud Bull. Amsterdam: Amsterdam University Press.

de Sousa Santos, Boaventura. 2016. 'Epistemologies of The South and The Future'. *From the European South*, 1, July 25, 17-29, http://europeansouth.postcolonialitalia.it/journal/2016-1/3.2016-1.Santos.pdf

de Sousa Santos, Boaventura. 2018. *The End of The Cognitive Empire: The Coming of Age of Epistemologies of The South*. Durham, NC: Duke University Press.

de Valk, Marloes. 2021. 'A Pluriverse of Local Worlds: A Review of Computing Within Limits – Related Terminology and Practices'. *Limits '21, Seventh Workshop on Computing within Limits June 14-15 2021*, June, https://computingwithinlimits.org/2021/papers/limits21-devalk.pdf

Debatty, Regine. 2018. 'Treebour: Do We Pay Trees Fairly for The Immaterial Labour They Perform for Us?'. *We Make Money Not Art* (website), August 6, https://we-make-money-not-art.com/

treebour-do-we-pay-trees-fairly-for-the-immaterial-labour-they-perform-for-us/

Deleuze, Gilles. 1997. *Essays Critical and Clinical*. Minneapolis: University of Minnesota Press.

Dempsey, Lorcan. 2016. 'Library Collections in The Life of The User: Two Directions'. *Liber Quarterly: The Journal of the Association of European Research Libraries*, Volume 26, Number 4, 338–359, https://liberquarterly.eu/article/view/10870

Denne, Brian. 2022. 'Flip It Open Jumps from Pilot to Programme'. *Cambridge Core Blog*. October 24, https://www.cambridge.org/core/blog/2022/10/24/openresearch-flip-it-open-jumps-from-pilot-to-programme/

Department For Education. 2020. 'Plan Your Relationships, Sex and Health Curriculum'. *GOV.UK* (website), September 24, https://www.gov.uk/guidance/plan-your-relationships-sex-and-health-curriculum

Derrida Jacques. 1974/1990. *Glas*. Lincoln: University of Nebraska Press.

Derrida, Jacques. 1981. *Dissemination*. London: Athlone Press.

Derrida, Jacques. 1988. *Limited Inc*. Evanston, IL: Northwestern University Press.

Derrida, Jacques. 1994. *Specters of Marx: The State of The Debt, The Work of Mourning, and The New International*. London: Routledge.

Derrida, Jacques. 1995. 'Passages – From Traumatism to Promise'. In *Points ... Interviews, 1974-1994*. Ed. Elizabeth Weber. Stanford, CA: Stanford University Press.

Derrida, Jacques. 2005. *Rogues: Two Essays on Reason*. Stanford, CA: Stanford University Press.

Derrida, Jacques. 2007. *Learning to Live Finally*. New York: Melville House.

Disler, Caroline. 2011. 'Benjamin's "Afterlife": A Productive (?) Mistranslation in Memoriam Daniel Simeoni'. *TTR: Traduction, terminologie, redaction*, Volume 24, Issue 1, 183-221, https://id.erudit.org/iderudit/1013259ar

Donnachie, Karen ann and Andy Simionato. 2019. *The Library of Nonhuman Books* (website). Computer Vision Art Gallery ICCV 2019, Seoul, Korea, https://computervisionart.com/pieces2019/the-library-of-nonhuman-books/

Doringer, Bogomir. 2018. 'Archiving Faceless'. In *Faceless: Re-inventing Privacy Through Subversive Media Strategies*. Eds. Bogomir Doringer, Brigitte Felderer and Matthias Tarasiewicz. Berlin: De Gruyter.

Drucker, Johanna. 2015. 'We Were Humanists Before We Were Digital'. Lecture given at Bucknell University, March 31.

Egginton, William. 2016. *The Man Who Invented Fiction: How Cervantes Ushered in The Modern World*. London: Bloomsbury.

Ellsworth, Elizabeth and Jamie Kruse. Eds. 2012. *Making The Geological Now: Responses to Material Conditions of Contemporary Life*. New York: punctum, http://geologicnow.com

Else, Holly. 2015. '"Evolving Manuscripts": The Future of Scientific Communication?'. *Times Higher Education*, May 14, https://www.timeshighereducation.com/news/evolving-manuscripts-the-future-of-scientific-communication/2020200.article

Embassy of the North Sea. n.d. *Embassy of The North Sea*, accessed January 31, 2023, https://www.embassyofthenorthsea.com/

Emery, Christina, Mithu Lucraft, Agata Morka and Ros Pyne. 2017. *The OA Effect: How Does Open Access Affect the Usage of Scholarly Books*, Springer Nature, November, https://media.springernature.com/full/springer-cms/rest/v1/content/15176744/data/v3

Eribon, Didier. 2013. *Returning to Reims*. Los Angeles: Semiotext(e).

Errejón, Íññigo and Chantal Mouffe. 2016. *Podemos: In the Name of The People*. London: Lawrence & Wishart.

Escobar, Arturo. 2020. *Pluriversal Politics: The Real and The Possible*. Durham, NC: Duke University Press.

Esposito, Roberto. 2012. *The Third Person: Politics of Life and Philosophy of the Impersonal*. London: Polity.

Esposito, Roberto. 2013. 'Community, Immunity, Biopolitics'. *Angelaki*, Volume 18, Number 3, 83-90.

European Parliament. 2020/2023. 'What is Artificial Intelligence and How is it Used?'. *European Parliament* (website), published September 4, 2020, last updated July 20, 2023, https://www.europarl.europa.eu/topics/en/article/20200827STO85804/what-is-artificial-intelligence-and-how-is-it-used

Fathallah, Judith May. 2021. '"Getting By" On 4chan: Feminine Self-Presentation and Capital-Claiming in Antifeminist Web Space'. *First Monday*, Volume 26, Number 6-7, n. pag., https://firstmonday.org/ojs/index.php/fm/article/view/10449

Fiormonte, Domenico, Sukanta Chaudhuri and Paola Ricaurte. Eds. 2022. *Global Debates in The Digital Humanities*. Minneapolis: University of Minnesota Press.

Fitzpatrick, Kathleen. 2009. *Planned Obsolescence: Publishing, Technology, And the Future of The Academy*. Media Commons Press, http://mediacommons.futureofthebook.org/mcpress/plannedobsolescence

Fitzpatrick, Kathleen. 2011. *Planned Obsolescence: Publishing, Technology, And the Future of The Academy*. New York: New York University Press.

Fitzpatrick, Kathleen. 2018. *Generous Thinking: The University and the Public Good*. *Humanities Commons* (website), https://generousthinking.hcommons.org/

Fitzpatrick, Kathleen. 2019. *Generous Thinking: A Radical Approach to Saving the University*. Baltimore: Johns Hopkins University Press.

Flores, Leonardo. 2021. 'Third-Generation Electronic Literature'. In *Electronic Literature as Digital Humanities: Contexts, Forms, and Practices*. Eds. Dene Grigar and James O'Sullivan. New York: Bloomsbury Academic.

Flusser, Vilém. 2011a. *Does Writing Have a Future?*. Minneapolis: University of Minnesota Press.

Flusser, Vilém. 2011b. *Into the Universe of Technical Images*. Minneapolis: University of Minnesota Press.

Foucault, Michel. 1984. 'What Is an Author?'. In *The Foucault Reader*. Ed. Paul Rabinow. Harmondsworth: Penguin.

Foucault, Michel. 1997. 'The Masked Philosopher'. *Ethics: Subjectivity and Truth: The Essential Works of Michel Foucault, 1954-1984*, Volume I. New York: New Press.

Foucault, Michel. 2008. *The Birth of Biopolitics: Lectures at The Collège De France, 1978-79*. London: Palgrave Macmillan.

Franzen, Jonathan. 2018. 'Jonathan Franzen's 10 Rules for Novelists'. *Literary Hub*, November 15, https://lithub.com/jonathan-franzens-10-rules-for-novelists/

Fukuyama, Francis. 2022. *Liberalism and Its Discontents*. London: Profile.

Furtherfield. n.d. 'The Treaty of Finsbury Park 2025'. *Furtherfield* (website), accessed January 31, 2023, https://www.furtherfield.org/the-treaty-of-finsbury-park-2025/

Garton Ash, Timothy. 2020. 'The Future of Liberalism'. *Prospect*, December 9, n. pag., https://www.prospectmagazine.co.uk/politics/40827/the-future-of-liberalism

Ghosh, Amitav. 2016. *The Great Derangement: Climate Change and The Unthinkable*. Chicago: University of Chicago Press.

Gill, Rosalind. 2010. 'Breaking the Silence: The Hidden Injuries of Neo-liberal Academia'. In *Secrecy and Silence in The Research Process: Feminist Reflections*. Eds. Róisín Ryan-Flood and Rosalind Gill. London: Routledge.

Giraldo, Isis. 2016. 'Coloniality at Work: Decolonial Critique and The Postfeminist Regime'. *Feminist Theory*, Volume 17, Issue 2, 157-173.

Goldberg, David Theo. 2014. *The Afterlife of The Humanities*. Irvine: University of California Humanities Research Institute, https://issuu.com/uchri/docs/afterlife

Goldsmith, Kenneth. 2003. *Day*. Great Barrington, MA: The Figures.

Goldsmith, Kenneth. 2011. *Uncreative Writing: Managing Language in The Digital Age*. New York: Columbia University Press.

Golumbia, David. 2022. 'ChatGPT Should Not Exist'. *Medium*, December 14, n. pag., https://davidgolumbia.medium.com/chatgpt-should-not-exist-aab0867abace

Gordon, John, Anna Blackett, Richard Fordham, Maria Garraffa, Stephanie Howard Wilsher, Eleanor Leist, Aisling Ponzo, Dan Smith, Allie Welsh and Georgios Xydopoulo. 2023. *Libraries for Living, and for Living Better: The Value and Impact of Public Libraries in the East of England*. Norwich: UEA Publishing Project.

Gorenflo, Neal. 2015. 'How Platform Coops Can Beat Death Stars Like Uber to Create a Real Sharing Economy'. *Shareable*, November 3, n. pag., http://www.shareable.net/blog/how-platform-coops-can-beat-death-stars-like-uber-to-create-a-real-sharing-economy

Goriunova, Olga. 2019. 'The Digital Subject: People as Data as Persons'. *Theory, Culture and Society*, Volume 36, Issue 6, 125-145.

Gottlieb, Sarah. 2020. 'A Conversation with Bob Stein from The Institute for The Future of The Book'. In *The Form of The Book Book*. Eds. Sara De Bondt and Fraser Muggeride. London: Occasional Papers.

Graham, Mark, Rob Kitchin, Shannon Mattern and Joe Shaw. Eds. 2019. *How to Run a City Like Amazon and Other Fables*. London: Meatspace.

Grant, Bob. 2007. 'Elsevier Ditches Arms Trade'. *The Scientist*, June 4, https://www.the-scientist.com/?articles.view/articleNo/25150/title/Elsevier-ditches-arms-trade/

Graeber, David. 2023. *Pirate Enlightenment: or the Real Libertalia*. New York: Farrar, Straus and Giroux.

Greenspan, Brian. 2019. 'The Scandal of Digital Humanities'. In *Debates in The Digital Humanities 2019*. Eds. Matthew K. Gold and Lauren F. Klein. Minneapolis: University of Minnesota Press.

Grosser, Ben. 2021. *Software for Less* (exhibition). Arebyte Gallery, London, August 20–October 23.

Grove, Jack. 2022. 'Journal Prestige Still Driving Reputation'. *Times Higher Education*, August 4, https://www.timeshighereducation.com/news/academic-reputation-still-driven-journal-prestige-survey

Grusin, Richard. 2014. 'The Dark Side of Digital Humanities: Dispatches from Two Recent MLA Conventions'. In 'In the Shadows of The Digital Humanities'. Eds. Elizabeth Weed and

Ellen Rooney. *differences: A Journal of Feminist Cultural Studies*, Volume 25, Number 1, 79-92.

Haifa Giraud, Eva and Sarah-Nicole Aghassi-Isfahani. 2020. 'Post-Truths, Common Worlds, And Critical Politics: Critiquing Bruno Latour's Renewed Critique of Critique'. *Cultural Politics*, Volume 16, Issue 1, March 1, 1-13.

Hall, Gary. 2002a. *Culture in Bits: The Monstrous Future of Theory*. London and New York: Continuum.

Hall, Gary. 2002b. 'Para-site'. In *The Cyborg Experiments: The Extensions of the Body in the Media Age*. Ed. Joanna Zylinska. London and New York: Continuum.

Hall, Gary. 2006. 'Cultural Studies and Deconstruction'. In *New Cultural Studies: Adventures in Theory*. Eds. Gary Hall and Clare Birchall. Edinburgh: Edinburgh University Press.

Hall, Gary. 2008. *Digitize This Book!: The Politics of New Media, or Why We Need Open Access Now*. Minneapolis and London: University of Minnesota Press.

Hall, Gary. 2010. 'Fluid Notes on Liquid Books'. In *Putting Knowledge to Work and Letting Information Play: The Center for Digital Discourse and Culture*. Eds. Timothy W. Luke and Jeremy W. Hunsinger. Center for Digital Discourse and Culture (CDDC) @ Virginia Tech, https://scholar.lib.vt.edu/vtpubs/books/putting_knowledge_to_work.pdf

Hall, Gary. 2011. 'Force of Binding: On Liquid, Living Books (Version 2.0: Mark Amerika Mix)'. *remixthebook.com* (website), June 8, https://issuu.com/remixthebook/docs/gary_hall_remixthebook_contributionvfinal

Hall, Gary. 2016a. *Pirate Philosophy*. Cambridge, MA: MIT Press.

Hall, Gary. 2016b. *The Uberfication of the University*. Minneapolis: University of Minnesota Press.

Hall, Gary. 2017. *The Inhumanist Manifesto: Extended Play*. Boulder: The Techne Lab, University of Colorado, http://art.colorado.edu/research/Hall_Inhumanist-Manifesto.pdf

Hall, Gary. 2020. 'Postdigital Politics'. In *Aesthetics of The Commons*. Eds. Cornelia Sollfrank, Shuhsa Niederberger and Felix Stalder. Zurich: DIAPHANES.

Hall, Gary. 2021a. *A Stubborn Fury: How Writing Works in Elitist Britain*. London: Open Humanities Press.

Hall, Gary. 2021b. 'Pluriversal Socialism – The Very Idea'. *Media Theory*, Volume 5, Number 1, 1-30, http://journalcontent.mediatheoryjournal.org/index.php/mt/article/view/126

Hall, Gary. 2022a. 'Defund Culture'. *Radical Philosophy*, 212, Spring, 62-68, https://www.radicalphilosophy.com/commentary/defund-culture

Hall, Gary. 2022b. 'Review of Bitstreams: The Future of Digital Literary Heritage'. *Modern Philology*, Volume 120, Issue 2, E62-E68.

Hall, Gary. 2023. 'How to Be a Pirate: An Interview with Alexandra Elbakyan and Gary Hall by Holger Briel'. In *The Piracy Years: Internet File Sharing in A Global Context*. Eds. Michael High, Markus Heidingsfelder and Holger Briel. Liverpool: Liverpool University Press.

Hall, Gary. 2024. 'Culture and the University as White, Male, Liberal Humanist, Public Space'. *New Formations*, special issue on 'Public Knowledge: The Academy and Beyond', Volume 2023, Number 110 & 111, 60-77.

Hall, Gary and Simon Morgan Wortham. Eds. 2007. *Experimenting: Essays with Samuel Weber*. New York: Fordham University Press.

Hall, Gary, Kamila Kuc and Joanna Zylinska. 2015. 'A Guide to Open and Hybrid Publishing (Or How to Create an Image-Based Open Access Book In 10 Easy Steps)'. *ESpace: Open Content Platform*, https://espace.okfn.org/items/show/262

Halpern, Orit and Robert Mitchell. 2023. *The Smartness Mandate*. Cambridge, MA: MIT Press.

Hategan, Vlad. n.d. 'Dead NFTs: The Evolving Landscape of the NFT Market'. *dappGambl*, n. pag., accessed September 28, 2023, https://dappgambl.com/nfts/dead-nfts/

Haraway, Donna. 1988. 'Situated Knowledges: The Science Question in Feminism and The Privilege of Partial Perspective'. *Feminist Studies*, Volume 14, Number 3 (Autumn), 575-599.

Haraway, Donna J. 1991. 'A Cyborg Manifesto: Science, Technology, And Socialist-Feminism in The Late Twentieth Century'. *Simians, Cyborgs and Women: The Reinvention of Nature*. New York: Routledge.

Haraway, Donna. 2007. *When Species Meet*. Minneapolis: University of Minnesota Press.

Haraway, Donna J. 2016. *Staying With the Trouble: Making Kin in the Chthulucene*. Durham, NC: Duke University Press.

Hardt, Michael and Antonio Negri. 2000. *Empire*. Cambridge, MA and London: Harvard University Press.

Hardt, Michael and Antonio Negri. 2004. *Multitude: War and Democracy in the Age of Empire*. Harmondsworth: Penguin.

Hardt, Michael and Antonio Negri. 2009. *Commonwealth*. Cambridge, MA and London: Harvard University Press.

Hardt, Michael and Antonio Negri. 2017. *Assembly*. Oxford: Oxford University Press.

Harman, Graham. 2007. 'The Importance of Bruno Latour for Philosophy'. *Cultural Studies Review*, Volume 13, Number 1 (March), 31-49.

Harman, Graham. 2009. *Prince of Networks: Bruno Latour and Metaphysics*. Melbourne: re.press.

Harvey, Adam. 2018. 'The Privacy Gift Shop: Camouflage and Commerce'. In *Faceless: Re-inventing Privacy Through Subversive Media Strategies*. Eds. Bogomir Doringer, Brigitte Felderer and Matthias Tarasiewicz. Berlin: De Gruyter.

Harvey, Adam. 2021. 'What Is a Face?'. In *Fake AI*. Ed. Frederike Kaltheuner. Manchester: Meatspace Press, https://fakeaibook.com/Chapter-11-What-is-a-face

Harvey, Adam. n.d. 'CV Dazzle'. *Adam Harvey* (website), accessed March 6, 2023, https://ahprojects.com/cvdazzle

Hayles, N. Katherine. 2002. *Writing Machines*. Cambridge, MA: MIT Press.

Hayles, N. Katherine. 2012. *How We Think: Digital Media and Contemporary Technogenesis*. Chicago: University of Chicago Press.

Heidegger, Martin. 1971. 'Building, Dwelling, Thinking'. *Poetry, Language, Thought*. New York: Harper Colophon Books.

Hemmings, Clare. 2011. *Why Stories Matter: The Political Grammar of Feminist Theory*. Durham, NC: Duke University Press.

Hendrix, Justin and Johnathan Flowers. 2022. 'The Whiteness of Mastodon'. *Tech Policy Press*, November 23, https://techpolicy.press/the-whiteness-of-mastodon/

Hewitt, Andrew and Mel Jordan. 2020. 'On Trying to Be Collective'. *Art & The Public Sphere*, Volume 9, Numbers 1 & 2, 63-84.

Hill, Kashmir. 2019. 'Goodbye Big Five: Life Without the Tech Giants'. *Gizmodo* (blog), January 22, https://gizmodo.com/life-without-the-tech-giants-1830258056

Hollis, Richard. 2020. 'Ways of Seeing Books'. In *The Form of The Book Book*. Eds. Sara De Bondt and Fraser Muggeride. London: Occasional Papers.

Howse, Martin. 2013. *Diff in June*. North Carolina: lulu.com, http://constantvzw.org/w/?u=https://pzwiki.wdka.nl/mediadesign/Interfacing_the_law

Jameson, Fredric. 1987. 'Reading Without Interpretation: Postmodernism and The Video-Text'. In *The Linguistics of Writing: Arguments Between Language and Literature*. Eds. Nigel Fabb, Derek Attridge, Alan Durant and Colin McCabe. Manchester: Manchester University Press.

Jaque, Andrés / Office for Political Innovation. n.d. 'Reggio School'. *Office for Political Innovation*, accessed January 19, 2023, https://officeforpoliticalinnovation.com/work/colegio-reggio-explora/

Jarvis, Jeff. 2023. *The Gutenberg Parenthesis: The Age of Print and Its Lessons for the Age of the Internet*. London: Bloomsbury.

Jarreau, Paige and Samantha Yammine. 2017. 'Scientist Selfies – Instagramming to Change Public Perceptions of Scientists'. *LSE Impact Blog*, August 21, https://blogs.lse.ac.uk/impactofsocia sciences/2017/08/21/scientist-selfies-instagramming-to-change-public-perceptions-of-scientists/

Jeffreys-Jones, Rhodri. 2017. *We Know All About You: The Story of Surveillance in Britain and America*. Oxford: Oxford University Press.

Jiang, Harry H., Lauren Brown, Jessica Cheng, Mehtab Khan, Abhishek Gupta, Deja Workman, Alex Hanna, Johnathan Flowers and Timnit Gebru. 2023. 'AI Art and Its Impact on Artists'. In *AAAI/ACM Conference on AI, Ethics, and Society (AIES '23), August 08-10, Montréal, QC, Canada*. Association for Computing Machinery (ACM), https://dl.acm.org/doi/fullHtml/10.1145/3600211.3604681

Johnson, Boris. 2021. *The Andrew Marr Show*. BBC One, October 3.

Johnson, Boris. 2022. 'Spring Conference 2022: Speech by Boris Johnson, Prime Minister'. *Conservatives* (website), March 19, https://www.conservatives.com/news/2022/spring-conference-2022--address-from-prime-minister-boris-johnson

Johnson, Khari. 2023. 'Iran Says Face Recognition Will ID Women Breaking Hijab Laws'. *Wired*, January 18, https://www.wired.com/story/iran-says-face-recognition-will-id-women-breaking-hijab-laws/

Jones, John. 1962. *On Aristotle and Greek Tragedy*. London: Chatto & Windus.

Jones, Nathan. 2022. *Glitch Poetics*. London: Open Humanities Press.

Josipovici, Gabriel. 2010. *What Ever Happened to Modernism*. New Haven: Yale University Press, electronic edition, n. pag.

Joy, Eileen A. 2017. 'Here Be Monsters: A Punctum Publishing Primer'. *punctum books* (blog), May 7, https://punctumbooks.com/blog/here-be-monsters-a-punctum-publishing-primer/

Joy, Eileen A. Fradenburg and Vincent W.J. van Gerven Oei. 2022. 'Veritas and Copyright: The Public Library in Peril'. *punctum books* (blog), September 26, https://punctumbooks.pubpub.org/

pub/veritas-and-copyright-the-public-library-in-peril/release/3

Kafka, Peter. 2021. 'Substack Writers Are Mad at Substack. The Problem is Money and Who's Making It'. *Vox* (website), March 19, https://www.vox.com/recode/22338802/substack-pro-newsletter-controversy-jude-doyle

Kierkegaard, Søren. 1959. 'The Ancient Tragical Motif as Reflected in The Modern'. *Either/Or*, Volume 1. New York: Doubleday.

Kirschenbaum, Matthew. 2014. 'What Is "Digital Humanities", And Why Are They Saying Such Terrible Things About It?'. In 'In the Shadows of The Digital Humanities'. Eds. Elizabeth Weed and Ellen Rooney. *differences: A Journal of Feminist Cultural Studies*, Volume 25, Number 1, 46-63.

Kirschenbaum, Matthew. 2021. *Bitstreams: The Future of Digital Literary Heritage*. Philadelphia: University of Pennsylvania Press.

Klein, Naomi. 2020. 'Screen New Deal: Under Cover of Mass Death, Andrew Cuomo Calls in The Billionaires to Build a High-Tech Dystopia'. *The Intercept*, May 8, https://theintercept.com/2020/05/08/andrew-cuomo-eric-schmidt-coronavirus-tech-shock-doctrine/

Klimašauskas, Valentinas and João Laia. 2020. *Máscaras (Masks)*. Exhibition at Galeria Municipal do Porto, Porto, Portugal, June 2–August 16, https://www.galeriamunicipaldoporto.pt/en/historico/2020/mascaras-masks-2020/

Koh, Adeline and Roopika Risam. 2013. 'Open Thread: The Digital Humanities as A Historical "Refuge" From Race/Class/Gender/Sexuality/Disability?'. *Postcolonial Digital Humanities* (blog), May 10, http://dhpoco.org/blog/2013/05/10/open-thread-the-digital-humanities-as-a-historical-refuge-from-raceclassgendersexualitydisability/

Koller, Guido *et al*. Eds. 2016. Living Books About History. *infoclio.ch: The Swiss Portal for The Historical Sciences*, https://www.livingbooksabouthistory.ch/en/

Kowaltowski, Alicia, Marcus Oliveira and Ariel Silber Hernan Chaimovich. 2021. 'The Push for Open Access Is Making

Science Less Inclusive'. *Times Higher Education*, August 31, https://www.timeshighereducation.com/opinion/push-open-access-making-science-less-inclusive

Kuc, Kamila and Joanna Zylinska. Eds. 2016. *Photomediations: A Reader*. London: Open Humanities Press.

Latour, Bruno. 1988. *The Pasteurization of France*. Cambridge, MA: Harvard University Press.

Latour, Bruno. 1993. *We Have Never Been Modern*. Cambridge, MA: Harvard University Press.

Latour, Bruno. 1999. *Pandora's Hope: Essays on The Reality of Science Studies*. Cambridge, MA: Harvard University Press.

Lapowsky, Issie. 2023. 'Why Timnit Gebru Wants AI Giants to Think Small'. *Fast Company*, September 19, https://www.fastcompany.com/90952740/why-timnit-gebru-wants-ai-giants-to-think-small

Leith, Sam. 2021. 'Circling Back'. *The Observer: Saturday*, November 6, https://www.theguardian.com/books/2021/nov/06/the-every-is-about-an-all-powerful-monopoly-that-seeks-to-eliminate-competition-why-dave-eggers-wont-sell-his-new-hardback-on-us-amazon

Leszczynski, Agnieszka and Rob Kitchin. 2019. 'The Seduction of UberCity'. In *How to Run a City Like Amazon and Other Fables*. Eds. Mark Graham, Rob Kitchin, Shannon Mattern and Joe Shaw. London: Meatspace.

Liang, Weixin, Mert Yuksekgonul, Yining Mao, Eric Wu and James Zou. 2023. 'GPT Detectors Are Biased Against Non-native English Writers'. *arXiv*, April 6, https://arxiv.org/abs/2304.02819

Lin, Shu Yang. 2023. 'Conversational AI for Non-Human Representation in Decision-Making'. *AI for Institutions* (website), October 15, https://www.ai4institutions.com/project-cards/blog-post-title-one-atyj7-p9zde-e4sa5-4lz4j-amdck-wt4wt

Liu, Alan. 2014. 'Theses on The Epistemology of The Digital: Advice for The Cambridge Centre for Digital Knowledge'. *Alan Liu* (blog), http://liu.english.ucsb.edu/theses-on-the-epistemology-of-the-digital-page/

Liu, Jing. 2020. 'Privacy Fears as China Continues to Collect Students' Location Data'. *Times Higher Education*, December 24, https://www.timeshighereducation.com/news/privacy-fears-china-keeps-tracking-student-locations

Lorey, Isabell. 2022. 'Martial Masculinity and Authoritarian Populism'. *Verso* (blog), April 7, https://www.versobooks.com/blogs/5318-martial-masculinity-and-authoritarian-populism

Lorusso, Silvio. 2016a. 'The Post-Digital Publishing Archive: An Inventory of Speculative Strategies'. *Journal of Electronic Publishing*, Volume 9, Number 2 (Fall), n. pag., https://quod.lib.umich.edu/j/jep/3336451.0019.209?view=text;rgn=main

Louis, Édouard. 2017. *The End of Eddy*. London: Vintage.

Ludovico, Alessandro. 2012. *Post-Digital Print: The Mutation of Publishing Since 1894*. Onomatopee 77.

Lyotard, Jean-François. 1979/1986. *The Postmodern Condition: A Report on Knowledge*. Manchester: Manchester University Press.

Magnani, Francesca. 2021. 'A Year in Masks'. *Hyperallergic*, March 22, https://hyperallergic.com/630814/a-year-in-masks-francesca-magnani/?utm_campaign=daily&utm_content=20210323&utm_medium=email&utm_source=newsletter

Mahfouz, Sabrina. 2019. 'Introduction'. In *Smashing It: Working Class Artists on Life, Art & Making It Happen*. Ed. Sabrina Mahfouz. London: The Westbourne Press.

Malraux, André. 1953/1974. 'Museum Without Walls'. In *Voices of Silence*. St Albans: Paladin.

Manchester University Press. n.d. 'Open Access Books'. *Manchester University Press* (website), accessed March 4, 2023, https://manchesteruniversitypress.co.uk/openmonographs/

Marczewska, Kaja. 2018. *This Is Not a Copy: Writing at The Iterative Turn*. London: Bloomsbury Academic.

Marder, Michael, with artworks by Anaïs Tonder. 2016. *The Chernobyl Herbarium: Fragments of An Exploded Consciousness*. London: Open Humanities Press.

Marginson, Simon. 2021. 'Decolonisation Does Not Threaten Science or Academic Freedom'. *Times Higher Education*,

September 30, https://www.timeshighereducation.com/opinion/decolonisation-does-not-threaten-science-or-academic-freedom

Marwick, Alice E. 2013. *Status Update: Celebrity, Publicity and Branding in The Social Media Age.* New Haven and London: Yale University Press.

Masterman, Ellie. 2020. '"Communists of Knowledge"? A Case for The Implementation of "Radical Open Access" In the Humanities and Social Sciences'. MA Publishing Media, Oxford Brookes University, September 22, http://dx.doi.org/10.17613/t5n3-x550

McElroy, Erin, Meredith Whittaker and Nicole E. Weber. 2021. 'Prison Tech Comes Home'. *Public Books*, August 18, https://www.publicbooks.org/prison-tech-comes-home/

McGill, Lou and Tim Gray. 2015. *Open Media Classes at Coventry University.* Jisc, July, http://repository.jisc.ac.uk/6069/1/JR0041_OPEN_EDUCATION_REPORT_V3.pdf

McHardy, Julien. 2014. 'Why Books Matter: There Is Value in What Cannot Be Evaluated'. *LSE Impact Blog*, September 30, http://blogs.lse.ac.uk/impactofsocialsciences/2014/09/30/why-books-matter/

McLuhan, Marshall. 1962. *The Gutenberg Galaxy: The Making of Typographic Man.* Toronto: University of Toronto Press.

McLuhan, Marshall. 1964/1994. *Understanding Media: The Extensions of Man.* Cambridge, MA: MIT Press.

McLuhan, Marshall and Quentin Fiore. 1967/2008. *The Medium Is the Massage.* London: Penguin.

McQuillan, Dan. 2023. 'AI As Algorithmic Thatcherism'. *danmcquillan.org* (bog), December 21, https://danmcquillan.org/category/blog.html

Melbourne Connect. 2022. 'Can a Building Have a Heart?'. *Melbourne Design Week: Design the World You Want, 17-27 March, 2022* (website), accessed June 25, 2024, https://2022.designweek.melbourne/program/can-a-building-have-a-heart/

mediastudies.press. n.d. 'About mediastudies.press'. *mediastudies. press* (website), accessed January 31, 2022, https://www.mediastudies.press/about

Méndez Cota, Gabriela. Ed. 2011. *Another Technoscience Is Possible: Agricultural Lessons for The Posthumanities.* London: Open Humanities Press, http://www.livingbooksaboutlife.org/books/Another_Technoscience_is_Possible

Méndez Cota, Gabriela, Ana Cecilia Terrazas Valdés, Marco Antonio Alcalá Flores, Alejandro Ahumada and Diego Alejandro Corrales Caro. Eds. 2016. *Eco-catástrofe y deconstrucción*. London: Open Humanities Press, http://liquidbooks.pbworks.com/w/page/110608507/Volumen%20 10%3A%20Naturaleza%2C%20deconstrucción%2C%20 traducción

Méndez Cota, Gabriela, Luz Elvira Torres and Ángela Arziniaga. 2018. *En busca del qualite perdido (In Search Of The Lost Quelite)*, https://web.archive.org/web/20180807002404/http://enbuscadelqueliteperdido.com/

Michaux, Henri. 1994. *Darkness Moves: An Henri Michaux Anthology, 1927-1984.* Berkeley: University of California Press.

Mignolo, Walter. 2002. 'The Geopolitics of Knowledge and The Colonial Difference'. *The South Atlantic Quarterly*, Volume 101, Issue 1, Winter, 57-96.

Milbank, John and Adrian Pabst. 2017. 'The Meta-Crisis of Liberalism'. In *The Philosophical Salon: Speculations, Reflections, Interventions.* Eds. Michael Marder and Patricia Viera. London: Open Humanities Press.

Milmo, Dan. 2023. 'AI Risk Must Be Treated as Seriously as Climate Crisis, Says Google DeepMind Chief'. *The Guardian*, October 24, https://www.theguardian.com/technology/2023/oct/24/ai-risk-climate-crisis-google-deepmind-chief-demis-hassabis-regulation

Minelle, Bethany. 2022. 'Banksy Urges Shoplifters to "Help Themselves" to Guess Clothing After Copyright Row'. *Sky News*, November 19, https://news.sky.com/story/banksy-urges-shoplifters-to-help-themselves-to-guess-clothing-after-copyright-row-12750932

Mintz, Steven. 2023. 'Rethinking the Future of Humanities'. *Inside Higher Education*, February 10, https://www.insidehighered.com/blogs/higher-ed-gamma/rethinking-future-humanities

Monbiot, George. 2022. 'Ask Yourself This Before You Vote: Can Anyone Truly Say the Tories Have Made Britain Better?'. *The Guardian*, May 5, https://www.theguardian.com/commentisfree/2022/may/05/vote-tories-britain-better-ham-country

Montesquieu, Baron de. 1899/1748. *The Spirit of Laws, Volume 1*. New York: The Colonial Press.

The Monthly Supplement of The Penny Magazine for The Diffusion of Useful Knowledge, December 31, 1833, to January 31, 1834, Volume III. London: Charles Knight.

Moore, Samuel. 2017. 'A Genealogy of Open Access: Negotiations Between Openness and Access to Research'. *Revue française des sciences de l'Information et de la Communication*, Volume 11, Issue 2, n. pag.

Moore, Samuel. 2018. 'Open Letter in Support of Open Access'. Posting to the Radical Open Access mailing list, December 1.

Moore, Samuel. 2019. 'Governing the Scholarly Commons: The Radical Open Access Collective'. *Samuel Moore – Publishing, Technology, Commons* (blog), July 8, https://www.samuelmoore.org/2019/07/08/governing-the-scholarly-commons-the-radical-open-access-collective/

Moore, Samuel. 2023. 'The Curious Internal Logic of Open Access Policymaking'. *Samuel Moore – Publishing, Technology, Commons* (blog) January 12, https://www.samuelmoore.org/2023/01/12/the-curious-internal-logic-of-open-access-policymaking/

Moore, Samuel and Janneke Adema. 2019. 'ROAC Governance -- Feedback Sought!'. Posting to the Radical Open Access mailing list, July 8.

Moran, Joe. 2018. *First You Write a Sentence: The Elements of Reading, Writing ... and Life*. Harmondsworth: Penguin.

Moreiras, Alberto. 2020. *Against Abstraction: Notes from An Ex-Latin Americanist*. Austin: University of Texas Press.

Morozov, Evgeny. 2011. *The Net Delusion: The Dark Side of Internet Freedom*. Cambridge, MA: Perseus Books.

Morozov, Evgeny. 2016. 'Public Transport by Uber, And Airbnb Social Housing? Not A Smart Solution'. *The Observer*, September 11, https://www.theguardian.com/commentisfree/2016/sep/10/only-public-sector-finds-smart-technology-sexy

Morrison, Heather and Anis Rahman. 2020. 'Knowledge and Equity: Analysis of Three Models'. *IAMCR 2020*, June 19, http://hdl.handle.net/10393/40664

Morton, Timothy. 2013. *Realist Magic*. London: Open Humanities Press.

Morton, Timothy. 2017. *Humankind: Solidarity with Nonhuman People*. New York: Verso.

Morton, Timothy. 2020. *Magia realista*. London: Open Humanities Press.

Mouffe, Chantal. 2000. *The Democratic Paradox*. London: Verso.

Mouffe, Chantal. 2005. *On the Political*. Abingdon: Routledge.

Mouffe, Chantal. 2013. *Agonistics: Thinking the World Politically*. London: Verso.

Mouffe, Chantal. 2022. *Towards A Green Democratic Revolution: Left Populism and The Power of Affects*. London: Verso.

Munster, Anna. 2016. 'Techno-Animalities – The Case of The Monkey Selfie'. Talk given at Goldsmiths College, University of London, June 16.

Musk, Elon. 2021. 'At Least 50% Of My Tweets Were Made on A Porcelain Throne'. *Twitter*, November 22, https://twitter.com/elonmusk/status/1462652210739884035

Najibi, Alex. 2020. 'Racial Discrimination in Face Recognition Technology'. *Harvard University: The Graduate School of Arts and Humanities* (blog), October 24, https://sitn.hms.harvard.edu/flash/2020/racial-discrimination-in-face-recognition-technology/#:~:text=Face%20recognition%20algorithms%20boast%20high,and%2018%2D30%20years%20old

Nancy, Jean-Luc. 1991. *The Inoperative Community*. Minneapolis: University of Minnesota Press.

National Audit Office. 2023. *Value for Money: COVID-19 Business Grant Schemes*. March 23, https://www.nao.org.uk/reports/covid-19-business-grant-schemes/?utm_source=Twitter&utm_medium=social&utm_campaign=Orlo

National Aeronautics and Space Administration. 2023. 'Request for Information: NASA Public Access Plan for Increasing Access to the Results of NASA-Supported Research'. *Federal Register: The Daily Journal of the United States Government*, May 18, https://www.federalregister.gov/documents/2023/05/18/2023-10643/request-for-information-nasa-public-access-plan-for-increasing-access-to-the-results-of

Naughton, John and Shoshana Zuboff. 2019. '"The Goal Is to Automate Us": Welcome to The Age of Surveillance Capitalism'. *The Observer*, January 20, https://www.theguardian.com/technology/2019/jan/20/shoshana-zuboff-age-of-surveillance-capitalism-google-facebook

Negarestani, Reza. 2014. 'The Labor of the Inhuman, Part I: Human'. *e-Flux Journal*, Issue 52, February, 1-12, https://www.e-flux.com/journal/53/59893/the-labor-of-the-inhuman-part-ii-the-inhuman/

Nelson, Alondra. 2022. 'Ensuring Free, Immediate, And Equitable Access to Federally Funded Research'. *Office Of Science and Technology Policy* (website), August 25, https://www.whitehouse.gov/wp-content/uploads/2022/08/08-2022-OSTP-Public-Access-Memo.pdf

Newfield, Christopher. 2003. *Ivy and Industry: Business and The Making of The American University, 1880-1980*. Durham, NC: Duke University Press.

Newfield, Christopher. 2016. *The Great Mistake: How We Wrecked Public Universities and How We Can Fix Them*. Baltimore: Johns Hopkins University Press.

Neylon, Cameron, Alkim Ozaygen, Lucy Montgomery, Chun-Kai (Karl) Huang, Ros Pyne, Mithu Lucraft, Christina Emery. 2021. 'More Readers in More Places: The Benefits of Open Access for

Scholarly Books'. *Insights*, Volume 3, December 21, 1-14, https://insights.uksg.org/articles/10.1629/uksg.558

Nixon, Rob. 2013. *Slow Violence and The Environmentalism of The Poor.* Cambridge, MA: Harvard University Press.

Nocek, Adam. 2023. 'On the Ecological Complexity of Algorithmic Media'. Talk given at King's College London, March 14.

North American Reggio Emilia Alliance. n.d. 'The Environment as The Third Teacher'. *Reggio Emilia* (website), accessed January 18, 2023, https://reggioemilia2015.weebly.com/environment-as-a-third-teacher.html

Ntombela, Nontobeko. 2018. 'Untranslatable Histories in Tracey Rose's *Hard Black on Cotton*'. In *The Stronger We Become: The South African Pavilion*. Eds. Nkule Mabaso and Nomusa Makhubu. Newcastle: Natal Collective Pty Ltd.

OAPEN. n.d. 'Browsing by Collection'. *OAPEN: Open Access Publishing in European Networks*, accessed July 12, 2024, https://library.oapen.org/browse?type=collection

Ochieng Okoth, Kevin. 2021. 'Decolonisation and Its Discontents: Rethinking the Cycle of National Liberation'. *Salvage*, September 22, n. pag., https://salvage.zone/decolonisation-and-its-discontents-rethinking-the-cycle-of-national-liberation/

Octopus. n.d. 'Frequently Asked Questions', *Octopus* (website), accessed February 4, 2023, https://www.octopus.ac/faq

Olah, Nathalie. 2019. *Steal as Much as You Can: How to Win the Culture Wars in an Age of Austerity*. London: Repeater.

Olin Wright, Erik. 2019. *How to Be an Anti-capitalist in the 21st Century*. London: Verso.

Open Book Collective. n.d. 'What We Stand For'. *Open Book Collective* (website), accessed July 12, 2024, https://www.openbookcollective.org/cms/fixed_page/values/

Open Humanities Press. n.d. 'About OHP Labs'. *Open Humanities Press* (website), accessed July 12, 2024, http://www.openhumanitiespress.org/labs/about-ohp-labs/

Opening the Future. n.d. 'Opening the Future: A New Model for Open Access Books'. *Opening the Future* (website), accessed March 5, 2023, https://www.openingthefuture.net/

Orwell, George. 1940. *Inside the Whale and Other Essays*. London: Victor Gollancz.

Parikka, Jussi and Tony Sampson. Eds. 2009. *The Spam Book: On Viruses, Porn and Other Anomalies from The Dark Side of Digital Culture*. New York: Hampton Press.

Parsons & Charlesworth. 2014. *Catalog for The Post-Human – Open Society Foundations (Futures)*. Parsons & Charlesworth (website), accessed July 12, 2024, https://www.parsonscharlesworth.com/catalog-for-the-post-human-2014/

Parsons & Charlesworth. 2020. *Catalog for The Post-Human*, Volume 1, Fall/Winter, https://www.parsonscharlesworth.com/catalog-for-the-post-human-pdf/

Parsons & Charlesworth. 2021. *Catalog for The Post-Human – Venice Architecture Biennale 2021 (Exhibitions, Featured, Futures)*: https://www.parsonscharlesworth.com/catalog-for-the-post-human-venice-architecture-biennale-2021/

Parsons & Charlesworth. n.d. *Catalog for The Post-Human*. Venice Biennale Press Release, accessed July 12, 2024, https://www.dropbox.com/s/w17sj0a1z6gsa68/P%26C%20VENICE%20BIENNALE%20PRESS%20RELEASE__5_26.pdf?dl=0

Pasquinelli, Matteo. 2023. *The Eye of the Master: A Social History of Artificial Intelligence*. London: Verso.

PFA Charity, in partnership with Signify Group and supported by Kick It Out. 2020. *AI Research Study: Online Abuse and Project Restart*, Professional Footballers Association, October 21, https://www.thepfa.com/news/2020/10/21/pfa-charity-ai-research-study

Pooley, Jeff. 2024. 'Large Language Publishing'. *Upstream* (blog), January 2, https://upstream.force11.org/large-language-publishing/

Pound, Ezra. 1968. *The Literary Essays of Ezra Pound*. New York: New Directions.

Poynder, Richard. 2020. *Open Access: 'Information Wants To Be Free'?*, December 2, https://richardpoynder.co.uk/Information_Wants_to_be_Free.pdf

Preciado, Paul B. 2020. 'Learning From the Virus'. *Artforum*, May/June, n. pag, https://www.artforum.com/print/202005/paul-b-preciado-82823?fbclid=IwAR3Mkv95d2HuiTD6xRPdVyj4HuB2tLCyOnSYJJMnMGisXprkNlrWdGVzfq4&dm_i=56G9,7AG1,1263Q7,SA9K,1

Prideaux, Sue. 2018. *I Am Dynamite!: A Life Of Friedrich Nietzsche*. London: Faber & Faber.

Radical Open Access Collective. n.d. 'About the Collective'. *Radical Open Access* (website), accessed July 12, 2024, http://radicaloa.disruptivemedia.org.uk/about/

Ratti, Carlo, with Matthew Claudel. 2015. *Open Source Architecture*. London: Thames & Hudson.

Rayner, Samantha J. and Rebecca Lyons. Eds. 2017. *The Academic Book of the Future BOOC (Books as Open Online Content)*. London: UCL Press, https://www.uclpress.co.uk/products/84084

Redhead, Claire. 2023. 'OASPA response to NASA RFI 2023'. *Open Access Scholarly Publishing Association*, August 17, https://oaspa.org/oaspa-response-to-nasa-rfi-2023/

Research Community. 2018. 'Reaction of Researchers to Plan S (Version 2)'. *Zenodo*, November 12, http://doi.org/10.5281/zenodo.1484544

Reily, Markus. 2023. 'The Future of Reading: How AI is Changing Ebooks'. *Good e-Reader*, August 11, https://goodereader.com/blog/e-book-news/the-future-of-reading-how-ai-is-changing-ebooks

Risam, Roopika. 2019. *New Digital Worlds: Postcolonial Digital Humanities in Theory, Praxis and Pedagogy*. Evanston, IL: Northwestern University Press.

Risam, Roopika and Kelly Baker Josephs. Eds. 2021. *The Digital Black Atlantic*. Minneapolis: University of Minnesota Press.

Rivera Garza, Cristina. 2020. *The Restless Dead: Necrowriting and Disappropriation*. Tennessee: Vanderbilt University Press.

Roberts, Maggie. 2020. *Becoming Octopus Meditations* (website), accessed January 31, 2023, https://imagemusictext.com/maggie-roberts-becoming-octopus/

Rogoff, Irit. 2003. 'From Criticism to Critique to Criticality' *Transversal* (blog), January, https://transversal.at/transversal/0806/rogoff1/en

Ronell, Avital. 1991. *The Telephone Book: Technology, Schizophrenia, Electric Speech*. Lincoln: University of Nebraska Press.

Rose, Jonathan. 2001. *The Intellectual Life of The British Working Classes*. New Haven and London: Yale University Press.

Rourke, Lee and Tom McCarthy. 2009. '"I Suppose You Could View What I Do as a Kind of Grand Anti-Humanist Manifesto"'. *The Guardian*, September 18, https://www.theguardian.com/books/2010/sep/18/tom-mccarthy-lee-rourke-conversation

Rumsey, Sally. 2022. 'Reviewing the Rights Retention Strategy – A Pathway to Wider Open Access?'. *LSE Impact Blog*, October 26, https://blogs.lse.ac.uk/impactofsocialsciences/2022/10/26/reviewing-the-rights-retention-strategy-a-pathway-to-wider-open-access/

Schneider, Florian. 2006. 'Collaboration: The Dark Side of The Multitude'. In *Sarai Reader 06: Turbulence*. Eds. Monica Narula, Shuddhabrata Sengupta, Ravi Sundaram, Jeebesh Bagchi and Geert Lovink. Delhi: The Sarai Programme, Centre for the Study of Developing Societies, http://fls.kein.org/view/174

Schneier, Bruce. 2023. 'A Robot the Size of the World'. *Schneier on Security* (blog), December 15, https://www.schneier.com/blog/archives/2023/12/a-robot-the-size-of-the-world.html

ScholarLed. 2019. 'The Enclosure of Scholarly Infrastructures, Open Access Books & The Necessity of Community'. *ScholarLed* (blog), June 5, https://blog.scholarled.org/open-research-library/

Schumpeter, Joseph. 1947. *Capitalism, Socialism, Democracy*. New York: Harper & Brothers.

Scott, Jordan and Stephen Collis. 2013. *Decomp*. Toronto: Coach House Books, https://chbooks.com/Books/D/Decomp

Works Cited

Shaviro, Steven. 2003. *Connected: Or What It Means to Live in The Network Society*. Minneapolis: University of Minnesota Press.

Shaviro, Steven. 2014. *The Universe of Things: On Speculative Realism*. Minneapolis: University of Minnesota Press.

Shields, David. 2011. *Reality Hunger*. London: Penguin.

Sigoma (Special Interest Group of Municipal Authorities). 2023. 'One in Ten SIGOMA Councils Facing Section 114 Notice'. *Sigoma* (website), August 29, https://www.sigoma.gov.uk/news/2023/one-in-ten-sigoma-councils-facing-section-114-notice

Simondon, Gilbert. 2016. *On the Mode of Existence of Technical Objects*. Minneapolis: University of Minnesota Press.

Simpson, Leanne Betasamosake. 2014. 'Land as Pedagogy: Nishnaabeg Intelligence and Rebellious Transformation'. *Decolonization: Indigeneity, Education & Society*, Volume 3, Number 3, 1-25, https://jps.library.utoronto.ca/index.php/des/article/view/22170/17985

Sivertsen, Gunnar and Lin Zhang. 2022. 'Article Processing Charges (APCs) and the New Enclosure of Research'. *LSE Impact Blog*, August 11, https://blogs.lse.ac.uk/impactofsocialsciences/2022/08/11/article-processing-charges-apcs-and-the-new-enclosure-of-research/

Smith, Ali. 2022. '"The Novel Can't Just Leave the War Out": Ali Smith on Fiction in Times of Crisis'. *The Guardian*, March 26, https://www.theguardian.com/books/2022/mar/26/the-novel-cant-just-leave-the-war-out-ali-smith-on-fiction-in-times-of-crisis

Smith, Peter J. 2021. 'Bard Gets Lost in A Riot of Scenery'. *Times Higher Education*, December 9.

Smith, Aaron and Monica Anderson. 2018. 'Social Media Use in 2018: Appendix A: Detailed Table'. *Pew Research Centre* (website), March 1, https://www.pewresearch.org/internet/2018/03/01/social-media-use-2018-appendix-a-detailed-table/

Smits, Robert-Jan and Rachael Pells. 2022. *Plan S For Shock: Science. Shock. Solution. Speed.* London: Ubiquity Press, https://www.ubiquitypress.com/site/books/m/10.5334/bcq/

Soares, Ana Luisa, Francisco Castro Rego, E. Gregory McPherson, James R. Simpson, Paula J. Peper and Qingfu Xiao. 2011. 'Benefits and Costs of Street Trees in Lisbon, Portugal'. *Urban Forestry & Urban Greening*, Volume 10, Issue 2, 69-78, https://www.fs.usda.gov/psw/publications/mcpherson/psw_2011_mcpherson(soares)002.pdf

Sohn, Samantha, Philipa Rees, Bethany Wildridge, Nicola J. Kalk and Ben Carter. 2019. 'Prevalence of Problematic Smartphone Usage and Associated Mental Health Outcomes Amongst Children and Young People: A Systematic Review, Meta-analysis and GRADE of the Evidence'. *BMC Psychiatry*, Volume 19, Issue 1, 1-10, https://bmcpsychiatry.biomedcentral.com/articles/10.1186/s12888-019-2350-x#citeas

Sohn, Sei Yon, Lauren Krasnoff, Philippa Rees, Nicola J. Kalk, and Ben Carter. 2021. 'The Association Between Smartphone Addiction and Sleep: A UK Cross-Sectional Study of Young Adults'. *Frontiers In Psychiatry*, March 2, 1-10, https://www.frontiersin.org/articles/10.3389/fpsyt.2021.629407/full

Soon, Winnie and Geoff Cox. 2020. *Aesthetic Programming: A Handbook of Software Studies*. London: Open Humanities Press, http://www.openhumanitiespress.org/books/titles/aesthetic-programming/

Stacey, Jackie. 2022. 'Personal Value, Impersonal Subjects'. Talk given at the Centre for Postdigital Cultures, Coventry University, March 7, https://www.youtube.com/watch?v=9r9yyXn2ai8&t=4s

Stalder, Felix. 2014. *Digital Solidarity*. Lüneburg: Post-Media Lab Books.

Stavrides, Stavros. 2022. 'Reclaiming Public Space as Commons: Learning from Latin American Movements'. *INVI Magazine*, 37, Number 106, n. pag., https://doi.org/10.5354/0718-8358.2022.67215

Stengers, Isabelle. 2005. 'Introductory Notes on An Ecology of Practices'. *Cultural Studies Review*, Volume 11, No.1, 183-196.

Stengers, Isabelle. 2011. 'Comparison as A Matter of Concern'. *Common Knowledge*, Volume 17, Issue 1, 48-63.

Stengers, Isabelle. 2018. 'The Challenge of Ontological Politics'. In *A World of Many Worlds*. Eds. Mario Blaser and Marisol de la Cadena. Durham, NC: Duke University Press.

Stiegler, Bernard. 2002. 'The Discrete Image'. In Jacques Derrida and Bernard Stiegler, *Echographies of Television: Filmed Interviews*. London: Polity.

Stiegler, Bernard. 2009. *Technics and Time, 2: Disorientation*. Stanford, CA: Stanford University Press.

Stone, Christopher. 1972. 'Should Trees Have Standing? – Toward Legal Rights for Natural Objects'. *Southern California Law Review*, Volume 45, Number 2, 450-501, https://iseethics.files.wordpress.com/2013/02/stone-christopher-d-should-trees-have-standing.pdf

Strauss, Valerie. 2020. 'Cuomo Questions Why School Buildings Still Exist – And Says New York Will Work with Bill Gates to "Reimagine Education"'. *Washington Post*, May 6, https://www.washingtonpost.com/education/2020/05/06/cuomo-questions-why-school-buildings-still-exist-says-new-york-will-work-with-bill-gates-reimagine-education/

Suber, Peter and Heather Joseph. 2023. 'Commentary on Op-ed Released in Vol 22, Iss 01'. *JSPG: Journal of Science Policy & Governance*, March 28, n. pag., https://www.sciencepolicyjournal.org/news/commentary-on-op-ed-released-in-vol-22-iss-01

Tabbi, Joseph. 2020. 'Something There Badly Not Wrong: The Life and Death of Literary Form in Databases'. *Electronic Book Review*, August 5, n. pag., https://electronicbookreview.com/essay/something-there-badly-not-wrong-the-life-and-death-of-literary-form-in-databases/?utm_source=mailpoet&utm_medium=email&utm_campaign=ebr-august-2020

Táíwò, Olúfémi O. 2022. *Elite Capture: How the Powerful Took Over Identity Politics (And Everything Else)*. London: Pluto.

Thiong'o', Ngũgĩ wa. 1981. *Decolonising the Mind: The Politics of Language in African Literature*. Harare: Zimbawe Publishing House.

Thoburn, Nicolas. 2011. 'To Conquer the Anonymous: Authorship and Myth in The Wu Ming Foundation'. *Cultural Critique*, Number 78 (Spring), 119-150.

Timmis, Matthew A., Herre Bijl, Kieran Turner, Itay Basevitch, Matthew J. D. Taylor and Kjell N. van Paridon. 2017. 'The Impact of Mobile Phone Use on Where We Look and How We Walk When Negotiating Floor Based Obstacles'. *PLoS One*, June 30, 1-20, http://journals.plos.org/plosone/article?id=10.1371/journal.pone.0179802

Todd, Zoe. 2016. 'An Indigenous Feminist's Take on The Ontological Turn: "Ontology" Is Just Another Word for Colonialism'. *Journal of Historical Sociology*, Volume 29, Number 1, March, 4-22.

Toshkov, Dimiter. 2018. 'The "Global South" Is A Terrible Term. Don't Use It!'. *Research Design Matters* (blog), November 6, http://re-design.dimiter.eu/?p=969

Towler, Breton. 2022. 'E-readers vs Books: Which are Better for the Environment?'. *Commercialwaste*, May 21, n. pag., https://commercialwaste.trade/e-readers-vs-books-better-environment/

Traynor, Cath and Laura Foster. n.d. 'Principles and Practice in Open Science: Addressing Power and Inequality Through Situated Openness'. *Open and Collaborative Science in Development Network* (website), accessed July 12, 2024, https://ocsdnet.org/principles-and-practice-in-open-science-addressing-power-and-inequality-through-situated-openness/

Tsing, Anna Lowenhaupt. 2012. 'On Nonscalability: The Living World Is Not Amenable to Precision-Nested Scales'. *Common Knowledge*, Volume 18, Issue 3 (Fall), 505-524.

Tsing, Anna Lowenhaupt. 2015. *The Mushroom at The End of The World: On the Possibility of Life in Capitalist Ruins*. Princeton, NJ: Princeton University Press.

TUC. 2021. 'Seven Ways Platform Workers Are Fighting Back'. *TUC*, November 5, https://www.tuc.org.uk/sites/default/files/2021-11/Platform%20essays%20with%20polling%20data.pdf

Tuck, Eve and K. Wayne Yang. 2012. 'Decolonization Is Not a Metaphor'. *Decolonization: Indigeneity, Education & Society*, Volume 1, Number 1, 1-40.

Tuhiwai Smith, Linda. 1999. *Decolonizing Methodologies: Research and Indigenous Peoples*. London: Zed Books.

Twain, Mark. 1903. 'Letter to Helen Keller from Mark Twain (St. Patrick's Day, 1903)'. *American Foundation for the Blind*, accessed November 16, 2023, https://www.afb.org/about-afb/history/helen-keller/letters/mark-twain-samuel-l-clemens/letter-miss-keller-mark-twain-st

UCU. 2022. *UK Higher Education: A Workforce in Crisis*. University and College Union, March, https://www.ucu.org.uk/media/12532/UK-higher-education---a-workforce-in-crisis/pdf/UK_HE_Report_24_Mar22.pdf

UCU. n.d. *Higher Education Joint Unions' Claim 2022/23*. University and College Union, accessed February 3, 2023, https://www.ucu.org.uk/media/12528/HE-unions-claim-2022-23/pdf/TUJNCHESclaim202223FINAL.pdf

UKRI. 2021. 'UKRI Announces New Open Access Policy'. *UK Research and Innovation* (website), August 6, https://www.ukri.org/news/ukri-announces-new-open-access-policy/

UKRI. 2022/2024. 'Shaping Our Open Access Policy'. *UK Research and Innovation* (website), July 28, https://www.ukri.org/what-we-do/supporting-healthy-research-and-innovation-culture/open-research/open-access-policies-review/; last updated June 28, 2024, https://www.ukri.org/what-we-do/supporting-healthy-research-and-innovation-culture/open-research/open-access-policies-review/implementing-our-open-access-policy/

UKRI. 2023. 'Update on UKRI Open Access Policy and Fund for Books'. *UK Research and Innovation* (website), November 15, https://www.ukri.org/news/update-on-ukri-open-access-policy-and-fund-for-books/

uncertain commons. 2013. *Speculate This!*. Durham, NC: Duke University Press.

Universities UK. 2013. *Massive Open Online Courses: Higher Education's Digital Moment?*. Universities UK, May, http://www.universitiesuk.ac.uk/policy-and-analysis/reports/Pages/massive-open-online-courses.aspx

Van Mourik Broekman, Pauline, Gary Hall, Ted Byfield, Shaun Hides and Simon Worthington. 2014. *Open Education: A Study in Disruption*. London: Rowman & Littlefield International.

Velie, Elaine. 2023. 'What's in Store for NFTs in 2023?'. *Hyperallergic*, January 3, https://hyperallergic.com/784662/whats-in-store-for-nfts-in-2023/?utm_medium=email&utm_campaign=D010423&utm_content=D010423+CID_e8031877179d58e6c43c40b2076259e6&utm_source=hn&utm_term=whats+in+store+for+the+once-buzzy+art+medium

Waidner, Isabel. 2021. *Sterling Karat Gold*. London: Peninsula Press.

Walton, Robert, Zaher Joukhadar and Lindsay Bick. 2020. 'Interview: Imagining A Building with Heart'. *Robert Walton* (website), May 29, 2020, accessed July 15, 2024, https://robertwalton.net/interview-imagining-a-building-with-heart/

Walton, Robert. n.d. 'The Heart'. *Robert Walton* (website), accessed September 25, 2022, http://robertwalton.net/project/the-heart/

Wark, McKenzie. 2013. 'The Engine Room of Literature: On Franco Moretti'. *Los Angeles Review of Books*, June 5, https://lareviewofbooks.org/article/the-engine-room-of-literature-on-franco-moretti/#!

Wark, McKenzie. 2015. *Molecular Red: Theory for The Anthropocene*. London: Verso.

Wark, McKenzie. 2017a. 'Alexander R. Galloway – An Interview with McKenzie Wark'. *b20: the online community of the boundary 2 editorial collective*, April 7, n. pag., https://www.boundary2.org/2017/04/alexander-r-galloway-an-interview-with-mckenzie-wark/

Wark, McKenzie. 2017b. 'Eduardo Viveiros de Castro: In and Against the Human'. *Verso* (blog), June 12, https://www.versobooks.com/en-gb/blogs/news/3265-eduardo-viveiros-de-castro-in-and-against-the-human

Works Cited

Wark, McKenzie. 2017c. *General Intellects: Twenty-One Thinkers for The Twenty-First Century*. London: Verso.

Wark, McKenzie. 2017d. 'On The Obsolescence of The Bourgeois Novel in The Anthropocene'. *Verso* (blog), August 16, https://www.versobooks.com/blogs/3356-on-the-obsolescence-of-the-bourgeois-novel-in-the-anthropocene

Wark, McKenzie, 2020. *Sensoria: Thinkers for The Twenty-first Century*. London: Verso.

Weber, Samuel. 1978. 'It'. *Glyph* 4, 1-31.

Weber, Samuel. 2000. 'The Future of The Humanities: Experimenting'. *Culture Machine*, 2, n. pag., https://culturemachine.net/the-university-culture-machine/the-future-of-the-humanities/

Weinberg, Justin. 2023. 'Wiley Removes Goodin as Editor of the *Journal of Political Philosophy*'. *Daily Nous: News For & About the Philosophy Profession*, April 27, https://dailynous.com/2023/04/27/wiley-removes-goodin-as-editor-of-the-journal-of-political-philosophy/

Weinmayr, Eva. 2020. *Noun to Verb: An Investigation into The Micro-Politics of Publishing Through Artistic Practice*. Thesis submitted for the degree of Doctor of Philosophy in Artistic Practice at HDK-Valand – Academy of Art and Design, Faculty of Fine, Applied and Performing Arts, University of Gothenburg, http://wiki.evaweinmayr.com/index.php/5_Reflection,_theorization_of_projects, electronic edition, n. pag.

Weinmayr, Eva and Femke Snelting. 2022. 'Ecologies of Dissemination: Decolonial Knowledge Practice, Feminist Methodology and Open Access'. Proposal for a two-year research project to be run in cooperation with the Centre for Postdigital Cultures, Coventry University (UK) and Constant (Belgium).

Weizman, Eyal. 2016. 'Are They Human?'. *Superhumanity*, October, 1-11, https://www.e-flux.com/architecture/superhumanity/68645/are-they-human/

Wilde, Oscar. 1891. 'The Soul of Man Under Socialism'. *libcom.org*, September 8, 2005, n. pag., https://libcom.org/article/soul-man-under-socialism-oscar-wilde

Williams, Gareth. 2016. 'The Subalternist Turn in Latin American Postcolonial Studies, or, Thinking in The Wake of What Went Down Yesterday (November 8, 2016)'. *Política Común*, Volume 10, n. pag., http://dx.doi.org/10.3998/pc.12322227.0010.016

The World Counts. n.d.-a. 'Environmental Impact of Paper'. *The World Counts* (website), accessed October 3, 2023, https://www.theworldcounts.com/challenges/consumption/other-products/environmental-impact-of-paper

The World Counts. n.d.-b. 'Paper Waste Facts'. *The World Counts* (website), accessed October 3, 2023, https://www.theworldcounts.com/stories/paper-waste-facts

Yoose, Becky and Nick Shockey. 2023. *Navigating Risk in Vendor Data Privacy Practices: An Analysis of Elsevier's ScienceDirect*. SPARC, November 7, https://zenodo.org/records/10078610

Yusoff, Kathryn. 2019. *A Billion Black Anthropocenes or None*. Minneapolis: University of Minnesota Press.

Zhang, Michael. 2021. 'Canon Uses AI Cameras That Only Let Smiling Workers Inside Offices'. *PetaPixel*, June 17, n. pag., https://petapixel.com/2021/06/17/canon-uses-ai-cameras-that-only-let-smiling-workers-inside-offices/

Zuboff, Shoshana. 2019. *The Age of Surveillance Capitalism: The Fight for A Human Future at The New Frontier of Power*. New York: Public Affairs.

Zylinska, Joanna. 2015. 'Photomediations: An Introduction'. In *Photomediations: An Open Book*. Eds. Joanna Zylinska et al., https://photomediationsopenbook.net/data/index.html#ch2

Zylinska, Joanna. 2018. *The Ends of Man: A Feminist Counterapocalypse*. Minneapolis: University of Minnesota Press.

Zylinska, Joanna. 2020. *AI Art: Machine Visions and Warped Dreams*. London: Open Humanities Press.

Zylinska, Joanna *et al.* Eds. 2010. *Technology And Cultural Form: A Liquid Theory Reader*. London: Open Humanities Press, http://

liquidbooks.pbworks.com/w/page/21175721/Technology%20and%20Cultural%20Form%3A%20A%20Liquid%20Reader

Zylinska, Joanna, Kamila Kuc, Jonathan Shaw, Ross Varney and Michael Wamposzyc. 2015a. 'Creative Jam Cards'. In *Photomediations: An Open Book*. Eds. Joanna Zylinska, Kamila Kuc, Jonathan Shaw, Ross Varney and Michael Wamposzyc. London: Open Humanities Press, http://photomediations.disruptivemedia.org.uk/creative-jam-cards/

Zylinska, Joanna, Kamila Kuc, Jonathan Shaw, Ross Varney and Michael Wamposzyc. 2015b. 'Photomediations Flatpack Exhibition'. In *Photomediations: An Open Book*. Eds. Zylinska *et al.*, https://www.europeana-space.eu/open-hybrid-publishing-pilot/photomediations-exhibition/

Zylinska, Joanna, Kamila Kuc, Jonathan Shaw, Ross Varney and Michael Wamposzyc. 2015c. 'Remix Generator'. In *Photomediations: An Open Book*. Eds. Zylinska *et al.*, http://photomediations.disruptivemedia.org.uk/remix-generator/

www.ingramcontent.com/pod-product-compliance
Lightning Source LLC
Chambersburg PA
CBHW061249230426
43663CB00022B/2950